THE

EVERYTHING®

GUIDE TO
LAS VEGAS

Hotels, casinos, restaurants, major family attractions, and more

Jason Rich

Adams Media Corporation
Holbrook, Massachusetts

An Everything® Series Book.
Everything® is a registered trademark of Adams Media Corporation.

Published by Adams Media Corporation
260 Center Street, Holbrook, MA 02343. U.S.A.
www.adamsmedia.com

ISBN: 1-58062-438-3

Printed in the United States of America.

J I H G F E D C B

Library of Congress Cataloging-in-Publication data
available upon request from the publisher.

This publication is designed to provide accurate and authoritative information with regard to the subject matter covered. It is sold with the understanding that the publisher is not engaged in rendering legal, accounting, or other professional advice. If legal advice or other expert assistance is required, the services of a competent professional person should be sought.
— From a *Declaration of Principles* jointly adopted by a Committee of the American Bar Association and a Committee of Publishers and Associations

Illustrations by Barry Littmann

This book is available at quantity discounts for bulk purchases.
For information, call 800-872-5627.

Contents

Acknowledgments

First, thanks to my family and two closest and dearest friends, Mark Giordani and Ellen Bromfield (with whom I have traveled to Las Vegas many times), for their ongoing support and encouragement.

I'd also like to thank all of the casino, hotel, motel, resort, attraction, show, and restaurant owners and operators (especially their PR departments) for the assistance I received while gathering information for this book. This book is dedicated to all of the entertainers, hotel workers, architects, designers, visionaries, and support personnel who over the years have made Las Vegas the incredible business and leisure travel destination that it is today. As you'll soon come to realize, Las Vegas is like no other place in the world.

A special thanks goes out to Paul Speirs and the entire cast of *Imagine* (a show that was at the Luxor but has since moved to a resort in Reno, Nevada) for showing me parts of Las Vegas the typical "tourist" never gets to see. I wish everyone involved with *Imagine* the best of luck in their future endeavors.

Thanks also to Pamela Liflander, Bob Adams, and everyone at Adams Media Publishing for allowing me to work on this project.

Finally, I'd like to thank my two good friends, Andy Lawson and Nic Womble, members of the pop music group B-Factor (*www.BFactorMusic.com*), for helping to make several of my trips to Las Vegas much more entertaining. It was a blast traveling with Nic, a talented singer who could expertly impersonate Las Vegas's top Elvis impersonators, as well as with Andy who hasn't yet figured out the fine art of roulette. (Hey Andy, I'm glad you finally got to ride the roller coaster at New York–New York . . . I hear it was the only thing in Las Vegas you really wanted to do!)

If you're about to visit Las Vegas for the first time, whether it be for pleasure or business, my true hope is that this book will help make your trip one you'll never forget!

Introduction

Get ready to experience a tourist destination the likes of which you've probably never seen before. Along one stretch of roadway, Las Vegas Boulevard South (a.k.a. the Strip), you're going to find thirty or so extremely large hotels, resorts, and mega-resorts, all containing state-of-the-art casinos, shops, restaurants, and in some cases, world-class guest room accommodations. Some of these properties even have full-size theme parks (complete with roller coasters), while others offer things like animal exhibits plus theaters or arenas bigger than what you'd find in most cities.

What sets the Strip apart from any other long road lined with hotels is that almost every property is built around a different theme. You're going to see a giant pyramid next to a castle, which is down the street from a look-alike Empire State Building and Statue of Liberty. Drive (or walk) a bit farther down the Strip and you'll come across a tremendous circus big top and large-scale re-creations of the Eiffel Tower and dozens of other world famous landmarks.

The very first hotel and casino (offering legalized gambling) in Las Vegas opened on April 3, 1941. The El Rancho contained a mere 63 rooms. A year later, the 107-room Hotel Last Frontier opened in October 1942. From that point on, new hotels and casinos have been opening along Las Vegas Boulevard South and re-creating themselves practically nonstop.

In the late-1940s, Las Vegas Boulevard South was a two-lane highway that ran through Las Vegas. The most famous resort along the Strip at the time was the Flamingo Hotel, built by mobster Bugsy Seigel. In the 1950s, the Desert Inn, Sand's Hotel, Riviera, Tropicana, and Stardust were built.

As these larger hotels and casinos gained popularity, some of the world's most popular entertainers began performing in Las Vegas. In the casino's showrooms, singers and comedians performed nightly. In the late 1950s, these single-person acts expanded to become musical stage spectaculars, featuring sexy showgirls and other specialty acts.

Over the years, dozens of hotels and casinos have come and gone. Today, the Strip is dominated by mega-resorts, which cater not just to gamblers, but to business travelers (convention goers), vacationers, families, honeymooners, wedding couples, and other thrill seekers. Instead of basic hotels, containing a few hundred rooms, what's being built along the Strip these days are mega-resorts, containing thousands of guest rooms. Construction costs for each of these new properties are often in the billions of dollars.

These mega-resorts offer all of the amenities and features you'd expect from a top resort located anywhere in the world, from state-of-the-art spas to swimming pools, upscale shops, world famous restaurants, and theaters. Of course, these properties also contain large casinos offering slot machines, video poker machines, keno lounges, race and sports books, and popular table games (like blackjack, poker, craps, and roulette).

A never-ending lineup of large-scale shows and productions takes place in the theaters and arenas of mega-resorts. Many properties have headline shows year-round, while others feature limited-engagement or special events, such as concerts with big-name artists or major sporting events. In recent years, in addition to offering original musical extravaganzas (like *EFX* at the MGM Grand) and master magicians and illusionists (like Siegfried and Roy or Lance Burton), the resorts are bringing in Broadway productions that are suitable for the entire family.

Combine these resort highlights with topnotch service and the various themes around which each of these properties is built, and you wind up with one of the most exciting, unique, and fun-filled destinations in the world.

And, no matter how you approach Las Vegas (by air, train, or car), especially if it's after sunset, you'll immediately see what makes the Strip one of the world's best-known places—the neon and flashing lights. The spotlight shining above the Luxor, for example, is so bright, it can be seen from space.

Although Las Vegas was built around legalized gambling and all of the resort properties contain casinos, these days they cater to nongamblers as well. Nevertheless, the companies operating these properties continue to do their best to lure people into their casinos to gamble.

At the end of Chapter 2, you'll find a form to help you plan your budget for a Las Vegas trip. Whether or not you're visiting Las Vegas to gamble, think about setting aside at least a few dollars to try your luck at the slots or a table game (like blackjack, craps, or roulette). Once you're in Las Vegas, you'll find the temptation to gamble hard to resist. Whatever you do, just make sure you stick to your budget, especially when it comes to gambling.

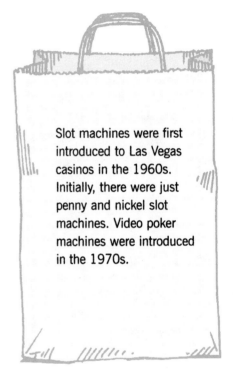

Slot machines were first introduced to Las Vegas casinos in the 1960s. Initially, there were just penny and nickel slot machines. Video poker machines were introduced in the 1970s.

In Spanish, "Las Vegas" translates to "The Meadows." The area was first identified by a Mexican scout named Rafael Rivera in 1830. Later, in 1855, the area was settled by Mormons. When the railroad came to Las Vegas (around 1904), saloons, shops, and hotels began to appear, and on May 15, 1905, Las Vegas was officially founded. By 1941, construction of the Hoover Dam as well as legalized gambling helped Las Vegas's population to grow dramatically.

The Las Vegas Strip has had several names over the years. It's been called Arrowhead Highway, Salt Lake Highway, Route 91, the Los Angeles Highway, and is currently known as Las Vegas Boulevard South.

If you'll be traveling to Las Vegas with children or young adults (under 21), keep in mind that minors are not permitted in any casino. If there's a casino in the lobby of your hotel, a designated walkway will be available for minors to get to and from the guest rooms. Minors are not even permitted to watch adults gamble.

With advance planning, it's easy to have an exciting and fun-filled trip to Las Vegas. As you begin planning your trip, it's always best to book your travel (airfare, hotel accommodations, etc.) as far in advance as possible in order to save money. Chapter 1, "Planning a Trip to Las Vegas," offers useful tips for saving money and planning the best trip possible.

Throughout this book, you'll read several times that Las Vegas is constantly evolving. Besides the flashy signs, lights, and miles upon miles of neon, one of the first things you'll see along the Strip is construction. Every few years, most of the hotels, resorts, and mega-resorts undergo renovations or expansion, while new properties are constantly being built. Thus, while the information in this book was accurate (and complete) at the time it was written, by the time you actually travel to Las Vegas, chances are there will be new things to see and do.

In addition to using this book as a resource while planning your trip, if you have access to the Internet, be sure to use it. Virtually all of the hotels, resorts, casinos, and attractions in Las Vegas have their own Web sites. Many travel services also have Web sites containing useful information for travelers to Las Vegas. Two extremely useful Web sites are *www.Vegas.com* and *www.las-vegas-guide.com*. Finally, if you're going to Las Vegas to gamble, be sure to pick up a copy of *The Everything Casino Gambling Book* by George Mandos (Adams Media).

Get ready to experience a trip to Las Vegas that you'll probably remember for a lifetime!

Jason R. Rich
E-mail: jr7777@aol.com
Web site: *www.jasonrich.com*

CHAPTER ONE

Planning a Trip to Las Vegas

So, you've decided to follow in the footsteps of hundreds of millions of other business travelers, honeymooners, and families—you're planning a trip to Las Vegas, Nevada. Well, you're in for an experience that you'll remember for a lifetime. This book will help you plan out your trip (whether it's for business or pleasure) and save money.

Your first step in planning a Las Vegas trip is to determine the length of your trip and your overall budget. Next, you'll need to book your airfare, hotel accommodations, and possibly reserve a rental car.

This chapter will help you save money and time as you take care of these initial trip planning steps. Once you know when your trip will begin, where you'll be staying, and how many days you have to enjoy yourself, you can begin to plan your itinerary and choose which of Las Vegas's many resorts, casinos, shows, and attractions you want to experience first-hand. Although most of this book describes just about everything you'll find along the world famous Las Vegas Strip, it also outlines some of the smaller resorts, casinos, and attractions located in Las Vegas, including the downtown area.

If you'll be traveling with other people, including family members (and children), it's an excellent idea to have everyone help select which attractions and activities you want to check out. If everyone gets to share his or her own input in the itinerary planning, you're more likely to have a relaxing and enjoyable experience.

This book makes the assumption that the majority of your time in the Las Vegas area will be spent visiting the many resorts, casinos, theme parks, shows, restaurants, shops, and attractions located on the Strip. There's plenty to do there, but it's ultimately up to you to determine how you want to spend your trip time.

Other travel books suggest specific three-, four-, five-, and seven-day itineraries; however, these itineraries don't take into account people's individual interests. For example, if you're a fan of theme parks and roller coasters, you might prefer to spend two full days riding all of the roller coasters and other rides at the various resorts. However, if you prefer to play keno or blackjack, choosing which casino to spend your time in will probably be more of a priority. Perhaps you're traveling to Las Vegas to pamper yourself at one of the world-class spas the city is quickly becoming famous for, or maybe you prefer to spend time relaxing at your resort's or hotel's swimming pool or playing tennis or golf. If you enjoy exploring malls and unique shops, the shopping opportunities in Las Vegas are also well worth experiencing.

Based on the descriptions in this book, you should be able to plan an itinerary that is designed just for you and your traveling companions. As the title of this book suggests, you're about to read descriptions of just about *everything* you can see, do, and experience along the Las Vegas Strip and nearby, so grab a pen and paper and prepare to take notes as you plan the ultimate trip!

There's Always Something New in Las Vegas

Not only is Las Vegas one of the country's top tourist destinations, it's also one of the most popular cities for conventions. Las Vegas was also recently named one of the five most romantic cities in the United States by *Honeymoon Magazine*, so an even greater number of couples are coming to Las Vegas to get married, while others are coming to the world-class mega-resorts to spend their honeymoon. Las Vegas is also a choice destination for couples celebrating an anniversary or other special occasion. In addition, the city has begun attracting families with children.

Las Vegas has worked hard to attract all sorts of visitors, but it continues to be a city filled with casinos. Thus, if you're interested in playing slot machines, video poker machines, table games (blackjack, craps, roulette, etc.), or keno, or betting on virtually any sporting event in the world (by visiting a race and sports book), Las Vegas is the place for beginners to expert gamblers.

If you've never gambled, many casinos offer free gaming lessons to help you get started. There are also countless instruction videos and "how-to" books that teach the finer arts of gambling. As mentioned earlier, *The Everything Casino Gambling Book* by George Mandos is an excellent resource.

Las Vegas is an ever growing and changing city. While some of the resorts, hotels, and casinos you'll be reading about have been around for decades, many of the mega-resorts (such as the MGM Grand, the Bellagio, the Venetian, Luxor, Aladdin, New York–New York, and Paris Las Vegas were built a lot more recently (most within the last decade).

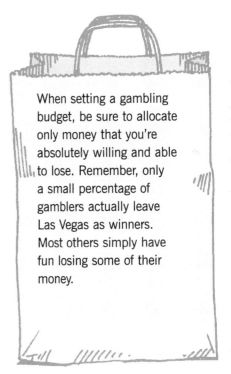

When setting a gambling budget, be sure to allocate only money that you're absolutely willing and able to lose. Remember, only a small percentage of gamblers actually leave Las Vegas as winners. Most others simply have fun losing some of their money.

As you look down the famous Las Vegas Strip, you'll also see a tremendous amount of construction taking place. New mega-resorts, hotels, casinos, theme parks, and other attractions are always being built, spurred on by tourism. Thus, don't be surprised if certain resorts or attractions are a bit different in real-life than the descriptions you're about to read. In Las Vegas, things are always changing!

Throughout this book, you'll be reading terms like hotel and casino, resort, and mega-resort, which are defined as follows:

- Hotel and casino—In Las Vegas, there are literally hundreds of traditional hotels and motels. The majority of these smaller properties have a built-in casino and maybe a few restaurants, but they're not meant to be full-service resorts, nor do they offer the amenities of resorts.
- Resort—A resort is a hotel (almost always with a built-in casino) that also offers other activities and amenities for guests, such as a spa, tennis courts, golf course, swimming pool(s), multiple restaurants, shows, lounges and bars, shops, and perhaps theme park rides and attractions (like roller coasters). Many of the resorts in Las Vegas are also built around a specific theme, which is reflected in the property's architecture, guest room accommodations, shops, and shows. For example, the Luxor has an ancient-Egypt theme, while Caesars Palace has an ancient-Rome theme.
- Mega-resort—These incredibly large properties often have 2,000 to 4,000 guest rooms and suites, and are meant to be vacation destinations unto themselves, offering everything a guest could want during a stay in Las Vegas, including world-class casinos, famous fine-dining restaurants, shows, shops, and plenty of activities.

Packing for and Planning the Perfect Las Vegas Trip

When flying, be sure to attach luggage tags with your name, address, and phone number on all of your suitcases and carryon bags. Also, place your address and phone number on the inside of the bag. In addition, it's an excellent idea to put some type of easily identifiable mark on your suitcases, in order to help ensure that someone won't acciden-

tally take your bag(s) at the baggage claim. Keep a list of your suitcases' contents with you, in case your bags get lost.

If you're planning on bringing a carryon bag onto the plane, you might consider including a change of clothes, or at least an extra T-shirt and pair of shorts. If your other bags get lost or you spill something on yourself during the flight, you'll have something to change into in a pinch. Most airlines are very strict about allowing each ticketed passenger to check only two suitcases, plus have two small carryon bags, so pack accordingly.

If your luggage gets damaged or lost by the airline, it's critical that claims be made in person, before leaving the airport. Should a problem arise, visit your airline's lost baggage counter located near the baggage claim area in the airport.

Some people have problems with excessive pressure in their ears when they fly. If you think you might have an ear problem, bring along chewing gum and consider purchasing earplugs that you can wear during the flight. Most pharmacies and drugstores, as well as many shops in airports, carry a product called EarPlanes (manufactured by Cirrus Air Technologies) for under $5 a pair. These are designed to help travelers who have a head cold or the flu or tend to suffer from earaches when flying. Special child-size EarPlanes are also available.

If you have a long flight to Las Vegas, consider bringing a book, magazines, a deck of cards, a portable tape player/CD player, hand-held video game system, or something else to do on the plane during the flight. You should also bring along some type of nonperishable snack. The food on airplanes isn't always too good, and if your flight experiences delays, you could wind up very hungry.

Before packing, try to determine what weather conditions are expected during your visit. The following Internet services offer up-to-date weather reports for the Las Vegas area:

- The Weather Channel—*www.weather.com*
- The National Weather Service—*tgsv7.nws.noaa.gov/weather/current/ KLAS.html*
- Yahoo! Weather—*weather.yahoo.com/forecast/Las_Vegas_NV _US_f.html*
- *Las Vegas Sun* newspaper—*www.lasvegassun.com*
- *Las Vegas Review-Journal* newspaper—*www.lvrj.com*

Write Out Your Proposed Itinerary in Advance

As you read this book, take notes about which activities interest you, what attractions you want to see, and where you think you might want to eat. Next, plan out your tentative itinerary, in writing, before you leave for Las Vegas. If you'll be traveling with family members, make your itinerary planning a group project, allowing everyone to have input. After you've decided how you want to break up your time, you'll be able to figure out a preliminary budget. Once you arrive in Las Vegas, be prepared to make minor changes to your schedule, and allow for flexibility throughout each day.

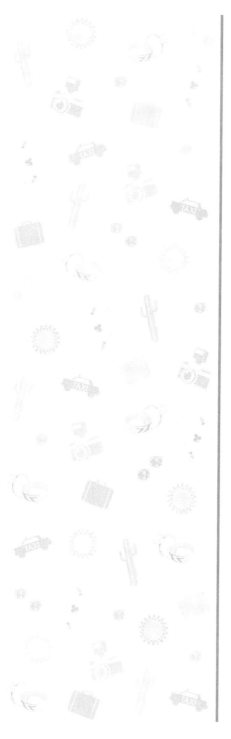

Average Temperatures in Las Vegas

MONTH	AVERAGE HIGH TEMPERATURE (°F)	AVERAGE LOW TEMPERATURE (°F)
January	56°	32°
February	62°	37°
March	68°	42°
April	78°	50°
May	88°	59°
June	98°	68°
July	104°	75°
August	102°	73°
September	94°	65°
October	81°	53°
November	66°	40°
December	57°	33°

Get Yourself Packed and Ready to Go: Choosing Your Luggage

Knowing what you want to bring with you to Las Vegas is the first step, but choosing your luggage and than actually packing your bags can be a challenging and somewhat confusing task. Chad Mellen, vice president of marketing for Tumi Luggage, Inc., offers his advice for purchasing or choosing your luggage and packing.

Tumi Luggage, Inc. manufactures a line of top-quality, high-end luggage in a wide range of styles. Unlike many other luggage manufacturers, Tumi's products are covered by a lifetime guarantee against defects in materials and workmanship. All of the company's products are made in the U.S.A., using ultra-strong Tru-Ballistic™ nylon or napa leather. In addition to providing superior workmanship, each bag is expertly designed with multiple (and often expandable) compartments and storage pockets.

If you don't yet own luggage that's suitable for airplane travel, the first step is to determine how you'll be using your luggage. The actual pieces of luggage a business traveler might purchase are very different from the luggage a family going on vacation would use. "A family that takes just one trip per year doesn't need to spend as much on their luggage as an individual or family that travels often," said Mellen. "No matter who you are, you should purchase good quality luggage. Luggage that will be checked at the airport, as opposed to being carried on an airplane, needs to be extremely durable. Some luggage is specifically designed to keep clothing, such as suits and dresses, wrinkle free, while other luggage pieces are designed to hold a lot of casual clothing."

When you go shopping for new luggage, Mellen suggests looking at the quality of the fabric or the leather. "Tumi luggage is manufactured using napa leather, which is a wonderfully soft, yet incredibly strong leather, or Tru-Ballistic nylon, which was originally developed for the military for use in bulletproof vests. The Tru-Ballistic nylon is pretty indestructible, and when you realize what your bags go through once you check them at the airport, you'll appreciate the strength of this material. The outer covering of bags tends to go through a lot of wear and tear. Some less expensive luggage materials simply can't hold up to repeat abuse, which means it'll have to be fixed or replaced much sooner. No matter what style or brand of luggage you purchase, choosing luggage manufactured with durable fabric is critical," added Mellen. "Likewise, if you're buying luggage with wheels, it's important to evaluate the quality of those wheels. Do they spin smoothly? Do they wobble? Tumi, for example, uses the same wheels used on in-line skates, so they have a minimum of friction. This is important when you're dragging 30 to 60 pounds of luggage behind you through the airport, which often requires walking over one-half-mile along crowded airport concourses."

Don't forget to examine the handle system on the luggage. Look for handles that are strong, comfortable, and durable. Tumi's luggage, for example, offers a steel core that is surrounded by three layers of padding and high quality leather. The handles are then secured to the bag using solid steel rings and screws.

Overall, luggage needs to be strong and lightweight. All of the stitching should be tight, with no loose threads visible. Another thing to look for when choosing luggage is to examine how well it's laid out. Mellen added, "Are the compartments where you'd want to put them? Do the compartments provide added efficiency? Also, is all of the space in the bag useable for packing? Can any of the pockets be

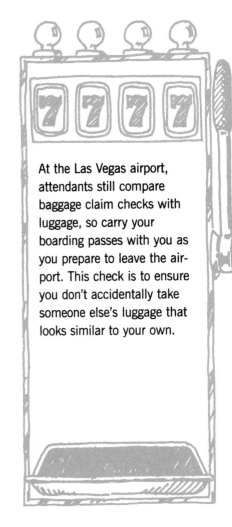

At the Las Vegas airport, attendants still compare baggage claim checks with luggage, so carry your boarding passes with you as you prepare to leave the airport. This check is to ensure you don't accidentally take someone else's luggage that looks similar to your own.

accessed from the outside? You should be able to open the bag and say to yourself, 'Wow, this bag was laid out well and will be able to hold all of the belongings I plan on traveling with.'"

These days, the materials and fabrics used to manufacture soft-body luggage are as durable, if not more durable, than hard-body luggage. In addition, thanks to expandable compartments, most soft-body luggage is much lighter weight and can often hold more than same-size hard-body luggage or suitcases. Ballistic nylon, used to manufacture many soft-body pieces of luggage, is water-resistant, usually puncture proof, and much easier to carry and store.

When shopping for luggage, Mellen suggests visiting a specialty luggage store or a major department store that carries a lot of luggage styles, from different manufacturers. "You want to purchase luggage from a retailer that will fix or replace your luggage if it gets damaged or has a manufacturer's defect. If you don't buy from a reputable dealer, they probably won't try to help you get your luggage fixed or replaced, no matter who it was manufactured by. The most important thing to do is test-drive the luggage at the retailer before you buy it. If it's on wheels, fill up a sample bag and walk around the store with it to see how it feels," said Mellen. A final thing to look at when purchasing luggage is the manufacturer's warranty.

Since many pieces of luggage look alike, and most bags come in standard solid colors, like black, it's a good idea to make your bag look a bit different when you check it at the airport. To make your bags stand out, so that the wrong person doesn't accidentally pick it up off the baggage claim conveyor belt, tie a bright colored ribbon around the handle. Also, make sure you have a well attached luggage tag on each bag that lists your full name, address, and phone number (some people choose to use a work address and phone number for security reasons). In addition to having this information on a luggage tag on the outside of the bag, it's also an excellent idea to include this information inside the bag, so if your bag gets lost, and the luggage tag falls off, the person who finds it can still contact you.

Mellen suggests travelers should avoid using the paper luggage tags supplied by the airlines. These tags fall off bags too easily. "Many luggage companies, including Tumi, will monogram your luggage. This is another way to make your bags more easily identifiable," he explained. "If you're traveling to Las Vegas from outside of the U.S. or you're trav-

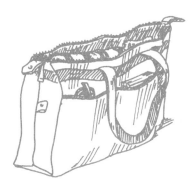

eling overseas, make a photocopy of your passport and place it inside your luggage, near the top."

Once your bag is packed, it's always a good idea to use the locks that come with the suitcase or bag, not so much to prevent theft, but more to insure that the bag won't accidentally open while in transit. "Once a bag is checked at the airline, there really isn't anything a traveler can do to protect their bags from receiving physical abuse. The only thing a traveler can do is buy the best made luggage they can find or afford. Incidents of baggage theft are minimal, but travelers should never pack jewelry, computer equipment, cameras, or other valuables in the luggage that will be checked at the airport. These items should be carried onto the plane in a carryon bag," said Mellen.

For families going on vacation together, the best pieces of luggage to purchase are large, soft-body suitcases that are on wheels. Mellen recommends families use large packing cases on wheels. Tumi's style #2246 Wheel-A-Way Suiter Packing Case, for example, measures 22" x 29" x 12", and will hold plenty of clothing. Using two of these bags, a family of four could easily pack a week or more worth of clothing. Another excellent piece of luggage for families to consider is a large duffel bag on wheels (such as Tumi's style #2252 or #2253, which measure 30" x 14.5" x 13" and 35" x 16" x 13," respectively). These types of bags aren't great for fancy suits or dresses, but they can hold a tremendous amount of casual clothing (and other items) and they're easy to carry or roll around an airport with. Each traveler can also pack a carryon bag, which should have both a handle and a shoulder strap for convenience.

Travelers planning to take along several formal outfits (dresses, gowns, sport jackets, tuxedos, or suits) should consider packing those garments in a garment bag, since the suitcases with special suit compartments are only designed to hold one or two formal garments. Overpacking formal attire will cause them to wrinkle.

Luggage may not be an item that you'll use often, but consider it an investment that you want to last for many years. Thus, by spending a bit more to purchase quality suitcases, your chances of having the luggage fall apart while you're on a trip are minimized. Finally, be sure to look for luggage that offers features that add convenience and ease of mobility, such as wheels, handles, shoulder straps, compartments, etc.

What about Pets?

With the exception of seeing-eye dogs, animals and pets are not allowed in virtually all of the Las Vegas resorts or hotels along the Strip. A few hotels and motels located near the Strip, however, do permit pets. Your best bet is to leave your pet(s) at home with a friend or family member, or at a licensed kennel or boarding facility.

The following are a few kennels or boarding facilities in the Las Vegas area. For additional resources, check the Las Vegas Yellow Pages or contact the hotel where you'll be staying.

- AAA Pink Poodle Parlor— (702) 870-7196
- Canine College— (702) 269-3017
- Critter Care Grooming— (702) 395-2581
- Desert Breeze Pet Grooming & Boarding— (702) 645-6986
- Nellis Hap-E-Dog Inn— (702) 452-1963

Dozens of different manufacturers offer luggage in a wide range of colors and styles, and at a variety of price points. Keep in mind, quality varies greatly between manufacturers, and while two bags from different manufacturers might look similar, their overall quality level and price might be very different, which is why examining each bag before you purchase it is important.

Other popular luggage manufacturers include:

- Atlantic
- American Tourister
- Andiamo
- Biggs & Riley
- Dakota Metro
- Hartmann
- Kipling
- Samsonite
- Travelpro

Packing Tips from the Pros

- Never check any items that you absolutely must have when you get off the plane, such as prescription medications.
- If you're planning to pack fancy clothes that can't get wrinkled, use a garment bag or a suitcase with a special compartment designed for suits and dresses.
- Some experts suggest rolling casual clothes and placing them in your luggage. This takes up less space, and works best with jeans and casual pants, socks, casual shirts, sweaters, and sweatshirts, and other casual clothing items.
- Place cosmetics, shampoos, perfume bottles, toothpaste, and anything else that could leak in sealable plastic bags.
- While packing your luggage, make a list of each bag's contents and leave the list at home. If your bag gets lost or stolen, having a list of missing items will help you get reimbursed by the airline or insurance company.
- Keep your bags with you at all times until they are safely checked with the airline at a designated baggage check-in location.

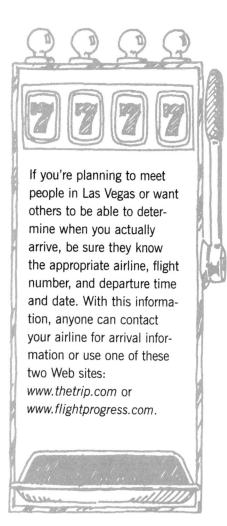

If you're planning to meet people in Las Vegas or want others to be able to determine when you actually arrive, be sure they know the appropriate airline, flight number, and departure time and date. With this information, anyone can contact your airline for arrival information or use one of these two Web sites: www.thetrip.com or www.flightprogress.com.

Getting to and from Las Vegas

People come to Las Vegas from all over the world using every popular mode of transportation, including by plane, car, and train. This section describes some of your travel options.

Airline Reservations

All of the airlines listed in this section (and possibly a few others) offer competitive rates and travel packages to Las Vegas, so be sure to shop around for the best airfares and flights.

As a general rule, you want to book your flight as far in advance as possible. Many airlines offer their best prices if you book and pay for your tickets 21 days in advance. You can, however, also obtain good fares if you make your reservations (and pay for your airline tickets) 14 days or 7 days early. When making travel plans, try to have the most flexible schedule possible, and, if your schedule permits, you'll almost always get a better airfare if your stay includes a Saturday night.

Keep in mind that with "discounted" or "special" airfares, the tickets are usually not refundable, and there will be a fee to change your travel date(s). The change fee is usually $50 to $100, plus the price difference in the airfare itself. To avoid this change fee, most airlines will allow you to fly standby; however, this does not guarantee you a seat on a specific flight. This is especially troublesome for families; if the flight is crowded, your chances of all getting on the same flight are slim, especially during peak travel periods.

If you want to use frequent flier miles to book your airline ticket(s) to Las Vegas, keep in mind that seats may be difficult to reserve during peak travel periods, so make your reservations early. The advantages of using a frequent flier ticket are that it's free, plus most airlines allow you to change your travel plans last minute, with no penalties or fees.

Always ask airline reservation representatives for the absolutely best airfares available. After a fare is quoted to you, ask again if it is the best deal. Next, ask if there are other flights to and from Las Vegas at about the same time that are less expensive. You often won't be quoted the absolute lowest prices the first time you ask. Also, check the travel section of your local newspaper for advertised special

Redeye flights (overnight) that leave Las Vegas around midnight and get you to your home city (on the East Coast) the following morning are almost always the cheapest return flights available. Although most people hate flying all night, you can sometimes save up to several hundred dollars when traveling to and from the West and East coasts via a redeye flight on any airline.

If you live in a city with more than one airport, or you live between two cities that both have airports, price your airline tickets going to and from the airports closest to you. Airlines often offer special deals and promotions from certain airports.

fares and promotions. You can make a reservation that will be held for 24 hours without having to pay for the ticket, so make an unpaid reservation and then shop around by calling additional airlines.

There are several alternatives available when it comes to securing the best airfares. You can surf the Internet and visit the various travel-related Web sites. You can use the special software that many airlines offer to their frequent fliers that allows you to shop multiple airlines via your computer, or you can call a travel agency and have them do the busywork for you. Travel agents have computer systems that allow them to search for flight availability on all airlines at once. Most travel agents will be happy to work with you over the telephone, so it's not necessary to take time out of your busy schedule to visit a travel agent's office. When choosing a travel agent, find someone who comes highly recommended by someone you trust. Travel agents can be extremely helpful and save you money, but some will purposely quote you higher airfares since they're receiving a commission from the airline based on the price of the tickets they sell. If you're a member of AAA or have an American Express card, both of these companies offer highly reputable travel agencies that offer their services either in-person or by telephone to members.

Of course, you can also call each airline directly and shop around yourself for the best airfares. Finally, you might want to look into package deals offered by the various airlines. Many packages include airfare, hotel, rental car, and perhaps meals or show tickets.

Using a Travel Agent or Service

Because Las Vegas is such a popular destination, travel agents and travel services can be helpful when it comes to planning a trip to Las Vegas. You can find a travel agent in the Yellow Pages, but it's always a better idea to use a travel agent who comes highly recommended by a friend, coworker, or relative. Nationwide travel agencies and services include:

- American Express Travel Services—(800) 937-3639
- AAA Travel Services—(800) 222-7448
- Yahoo! Travel—*travel.yahoo.com*
- Priceline.com—(800) PRICELINE / *www.priceline.com*
- America Online Travel (keyword: travel)
- Preview Travel—*www.previewtravel.com*

As you choose the actual times of your flights, if you plan on sleeping during the flight and book an early-morning or late-night flight, beware. When it comes to tourism, the Las Vegas airport is one of the busiest in the world, and with tourists and family travelers going to and from Las Vegas come cute babies and adorable young children who tend to spend the first few moments of a flight happy and cheerful, but can wind up screaming and crying on airplanes. Sure, kids are wonderful people, but if you're trying to sleep on a plane and you're surrounded by crying babies, you're not going to be a happy traveler.

McCarran International Airport

General Information: (702) 261-5211

www.mccarran.com

The closest airport to Las Vegas and the Las Vegas Strip is McCarran International Airport. The airport itself is divided into two terminals. Terminal 1 is used primarily for domestic flights and has four main gates (labeled A, B, C, and D). Terminal 2 is used primarily for international flights and domestic charter services.

The following airlines fly to and from this international airport. (Airlines subject to change.) Not all of these airlines will service your home city, so call the airline to inquire about flight availability.

- Air Canada (800) 776-3000 / *www.aircanada.ca/index.html*
- Alaska Airlines (800) 426-0333 / *www.alaskaair.com*
- Allegiant Air (877) 202-6444 / *www.allegiant-air.com*
- AmericaWest Airlines (800) 2-FLY-AWA / *www.americawest.com*
- American Airlines / American Eagle (800) 433-7300 / *www.aa.com*
- American Trans Air (800) I-FLY-ATA / *www.ata.com*
- COMAIR (800) I-FLY-ATA / *www.fly-comair.com*
- Continental (800) 525-0280 / *www.continental.com*
- Delta Airlines / Delta Express (800) 221-1212 / *www.delta-air.com*
- Frontier Airlines (800) 432-1359 / *www.flyfrontier.com*
- Hawaiian Air (800) 367-5320 / *www.hawaiianair.com*
- Japan Airlines (800) 525-3663 / *www.jal.co.jp/english/index_e.html*

For general information about McCarran International Airport, call (702) 261-5211. For parking information, call (702) 261-5121. For flight information (all airlines), call (702) 261-INFO. To have someone paged within the airport, call (702) 261-5733. The airport's lost and found can be reached by calling (702) 261-5134. Wheelchair service is available within the airport. It's best to call (702) 261-5475 or (702) 261-5622 in advance to arrange for this service.

- Midwest Express   (800) 452-2022 / *www.midwestexpress.com*
- National Airlines   (888) 757-5387 / *www.nationalairlines.com*
- Northwest Airlines   (800) 225-2525 / *www.nwa.com*
- Southwest   (800) I-FLY-SWA / *www.southwest.com*
- Sun Country Airlines   (800) 752-1218 / *www.suncountry.com*
- Sunrise Airlines   (800) I-FLY-ATA
- TWA   (800) 221-2000 / *www.twa.com*
- United   (800) 241-6522 / *www.ual.com*
- United Express   (800) 453-9417 / *www.ual.com*
- US Airways Trip Packages   (800) 455-0123 / *www.usairways.com*
- US Airways   (800) 428-4322 / *www.usairways.com*

A handful of other airlines also operate charter flights to and from McCarran International Airport and other major U.S. cities and foreign countries.

Services available at McCarran International Airport include ticket counters for all of these airlines, shops, restaurants, full service banks, ATM machines, a chapel, lockers and baggage check room, a smoking lounge, many information desks, foreign currency exchanges, taxi and shuttle bus ground transportation desks, access to many rental car companies (Hertz, Avis, Budget, National, and many others), parking, a post office, newsstands, and airline clubs (membership required).

Getting from the Airport to the Strip

Once you arrive at McCarran International Airport, the Las Vegas Strip is just a short drive away by rental car, limousine, or taxi. Shuttle buses are also available that will take you directly to your hotel. From baggage claim, follow the appropriate signs to your desired ground transportation.

It is not necessary to preschedule a taxi from the airport to your hotel, since taxis will be waiting in the designated area (on the west side of baggage claim). However, you can call in advance for taxi service (the following taxi companies operate in the Las Vegas area). Airport personnel are available on the taxi curb to assist passengers.

The average price for one to five passengers to travel by taxi from the airport to a Las Vegas area hotel or resort should be as follows (tips and airport fee not included):

- South Strip $8.50 to $12
- Central Strip $10 to $14
- North Strip $11 to $15
- Downtown $15 to $19

Las Vegas Area Taxi Companies

- ABC Union Cab Co. (702) 736-8444
- Ace Cab Co. (702) 736-8383
- A-North Las Vegas Cab (702) 643-1041
- Checker Cab Co. (702) 873-CABS
- Courtesy Limo (702) 367-1000
- Deluxe Taxicab Service (702) 568-7700
- Lucky Cab Company (702) 466-7555
- On Demand Sedan (702) 876-2222
- Premier Limousine (702) 365-9999
- Star Cab Co. (702) 873-8012
- A Vegas Western Cab Co. (702) 736-6121
- Western Cab Co. (702) 382-7100
- Whittlesea Blue Cab (702) 334-6111

Limousine Services

Limousine and town car or sedan service should be scheduled in advance. Check with your hotel's concierge for discounts and recommendations. These services offer door-to-door service throughout the Las Vegas area. Airport trips are often on a flat-fee basis, while other trips are charged by the hour. Major credit cards are typically accepted. The hourly fee for a limo is usually $29 to $45 an hour for an eight-passenger vehicle. A flat-rate fare from the airport should run $30 to $35 (plus tip). Limo services operating in the Las Vegas area include:

- 24 Hour Limo (702) 384-9998
- A.K.A. (702) 257-7433
- AKA Luxury Limo Service (702) 257-7433
- Ambassador Limousines (702) 362-6200
- Anytime Limo Service (702) 641-8300
- A-Star Limousine (702) 275-4323

Getting to the airport in your home city, consider using public transportation to save money. It'll almost always be cheaper than spending around $15 per 24-hour period to park your own car at the airport. If you're taking a car to the airport and you're not in a hurry, look into the availability of discounted long-term parking lots located a short distance from virtually every major airport. The cheapest option is to have a friend or family member drop you off at the airport and pick you up when you return. Another option is to use a door-to-door shuttle bus service.

- Bell Trans (702) 739-7990
- Fox Limousine (702) 597-0400
- Highroller Limousine (702) 868-5600
- A Hook Up Entertainment (702) 649-4328
- A-Humvee 4x4 Limo (702) 275-4323
- A Limousine Service (702) 739-6265
- Lucky Limousine (702) 733-7300
- LVL (702) 736-1419
- On Demand Sedan & Limo Service (702) 876-2222
- Premier Luxury Coach (702) 365-9999
- Presidential Limousine (702) 731-5577
- Rent-A-Limo (702) 791-5466
- Silver Star Limousine (702) 251-8105
- Western Limousine Service (702) 382-7100

Airport Shuttle Services

The following shuttle bus services are available to and from the airport and the Las Vegas Strip (and surrounding areas). All prices and hours of operation are subject to change. These shuttles can be met directly outside the airport's baggage claim area.

Bell Trans Shuttle Bus
Strip Hotels—$3.75
Downtown Hotels—$5
Off-Strip Hotels—$5
Hours—7:45 A.M. to midnight

C.L.S.
Strip Hotels—$4
Downtown Hotels—$5
Hours—24 Hours

Gray Line/Coach USA/Express Shuttle
Strip Hotels—$4.40
Downtown Hotels—$5.50
Off-Strip Hotels—$6.60
Hours—7:00 A.M. to 1:30 A.M.

Las Vegas Limousine

Strip Hotels—$4
Downtown Hotels—$5
Off-Strip Hotels—$7 to $21
Hours—7:00 A.M. to 2:00 A.M.

Star Transit

Strip Hotels—$4
Downtown Hotels—$5
Off-Strip Hotels—$10 to $18
Hours—7:00 A.M. to 1:00 A.M.

Getting to Las Vegas by Train

Amtrak service to Las Vegas is available from most major U.S. cities. For travel schedules, rates, and other information, call (800) USA-RAIL.

Amtrak offers travel discounts to all students as well as to AAA members who present their membership card when purchasing a train ticket. Amtrak train tickets can be purchased from many travel agents, by visiting any Amtrak ticket office, or by calling Amtrak directly and using a major credit card.

Getting to Las Vegas by Bus

For information, schedules, and rates for Greyhound Bus service to and from Las Vegas, call (800) 231-2222.

Renting a Car

As you can see from the following extensive list of rental car companies with branches in Las Vegas, there are many places to call when you need a rental car. Keep in mind, however, that the minimum age to rent a car from virtually all of these rental car companies is 25, and often, a major credit card is needed (even if you ultimately plan to pay for the rental with cash, traveler's check, or a regular check). A valid driver's license is also required. You must present the actual license when you rent a car. Photocopies or fax copies of your license aren't accepted.

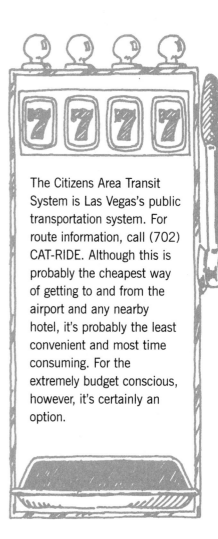

The Citizens Area Transit System is Las Vegas's public transportation system. For route information, call (702) CAT-RIDE. Although this is probably the cheapest way of getting to and from the airport and any nearby hotel, it's probably the least convenient and most time consuming. For the extremely budget conscious, however, it's certainly an option.

Most of the rental car companies will accept a U.S. driver's license, or a license issued by a Canadian province or a country that participated in the 1949 Geneva Convention on Road Traffic or the 1943 Convention on the Regulation of Inter-American Automobile Traffic, or has a reciprocal agreement with the United States. If you have a driver's license issued outside of the U.S., check with the rental car company when you make your reservation to ensure it will be accepted.

Several of these car rental companies have locations at the airport. Others offer complimentary shuttle service from the airport to the car rental office. Several of these rental car companies also have rental desks at the various Las Vegas resorts and hotels. Contact the concierge at your hotel for details if you're interested in renting a car after you arrive at your hotel. The following rental car companies have locations in the Las Vegas area:

- Airport Rent-A-Car* (800) 785-8578
- Aladdin Rent-A-Car (702) 891-0807
- Alamo (800) 354-2322
- Allstate* (800) 634-6186
- Avis* (800) 331-1212
- Budget* (800) 527-0700
- Dollar* (800) 800-4000
- Enterprise (800) RENT-A-CAR
- E-Z Rent-A-Car (888) 755-4555
- Hertz Gold Club Reservations (800) CAR-GOLD
- Hertz* (800) 654-3131
- National* (800) 227-7368
- Payless Car Rental (800) PAY-LESS
- Practical Rent-A-Car (877) 401-7368
- PriceLess (800) TOO-SAVE
- Rent-A-Wreck (800) 227-0292
- Savon Rent-A-Car (702) 432-6627
- Sunbelt Car Rental (877) 808-6117
- Thrifty (800) 367-2277
- X-Press Rent A Car (702) 795-4007 / (702) 736-2663

*These rental car companies have counters or offices at McCarran International Airport.

If you want to enjoy the luxury and novelty of a renting a flashy or exotic vehicle (such as a Jaguar, Hummer, BMW, Bentley, Porsche, Mercedes, Viper, Rolls Royce, Ferrari, Lamborghini, Range Rover, or Aston Martin), call Rent-A-Vette at (702) 736-2592 or (800) 372-1981. Rentals are available by the day, week, or month. You can also contact Dream Car Rentals at (702) 731-6452 or Resort Rent-A-Car at (802) 795-3800 to rent an exotic sports car.

Luxury Car Rental (702-736-CARS) is located along the Strip and offers a wide range of exotic vehicles, including Lamborghinis, Ferraris, Bentleys, Mercedes, Vipers, Prowlers, and motorcycles. Open 8:00 A.M. to 5:00 P.M., this company will rent to customers who are 18 or older and possess a valid driver's license. A cash deposit is often required. Luxury Car Rentals offers the newest fleet of exotic cars in Las Vegas. Daily rentals are based on a 24-hour period.

Rental Car Tips

Just as when making airline reservations, there are several tricks to use when reserving a rental car that will help ensure you get the lowest rate possible. For starts, reserve your rental car as far in advance as possible (seven days in advance, minimum), and if you can, try to get the weekly rate instead of the daily rate offered by the car rental company. Most rental car companies will apply their weekly rates to five- to seven-day rentals.

Especially in tourist areas like Las Vegas, rental car companies are always running special promotions, so be sure to ask about them, and look in your local newspaper and in your favorite magazines for their ads. In addition, many of the rental car companies provide a discount to AAA members, so after getting the company's best rate, ask for a AAA member discount. The Entertainment Book also has discount coupons and special offers that apply to many of the popular rental car companies.

If you're a member of any airline's frequent flier program, you can often receive a rental car discount from promotional partners of that airline. Check your monthly frequent flier statement for information about special rental car offers.

Some popular credit cards also have special promotional deals with the major rental car companies, so call the customer service phone

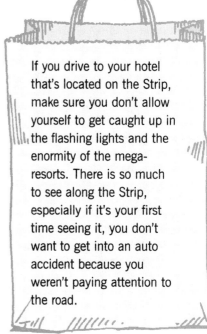

If you drive to your hotel that's located on the Strip, make sure you don't allow yourself to get caught up in the flashing lights and the enormity of the mega-resorts. There is so much to see along the Strip, especially if it's your first time seeing it, you don't want to get into an auto accident because you weren't paying attention to the road.

One of the best things about Las Vegas is that travel agents, airlines, the major resorts, and other organizations often have special package deals and other promotions that make getting to and from Las Vegas (during certain nonpeak periods) relatively inexpensive. Be sure to investigate any available packages and promotions before booking your travel arrangements. In addition to contacting a travel agent, call the travel office operated by your credit card company (if applicable), or the travel center of any organization, such as AAA, that you may belong to. Chapter 2 provides additional details on money-saving strategies.

number listed on your credit cards and inquire about what deals they offer for renting a car. While you're on the phone, also ask if your credit card automatically provides rental car insurance if you use that credit card to pay for the rental. American Express, Diner's Club, and virtually all Visa and MasterCards (issued as part of an airline's frequent flier program) automatically offer rental car insurance.

If you think you've found an awesome rental car rate, reserve the car, but shop around. Call three or four other companies and see if they'll beat the deal you've been offered. Many travelers believe that the best known rental car companies are always the most expensive, but this isn't always the case. You'll often be pleasantly surprised to discover that companies like Hertz, Avis, and National offer highly competitive rates once you take advantage of their special promotional deals, airline frequent flier discounts, and AAA member (or any auto club) discount.

When making a reservation, make sure unlimited mileage is included in the rental price. Some companies charge by the mile, in addition to the daily rental fee, so make sure you understand what's included in the price you're being quoted. Extremely low daily or weekly rental rates often do not include unlimited mileage, and once you travel more than the allowed miles, you're charged a hefty fee per mile.

No matter what hourly, daily, or weekly rate you're quoted, it will not include the insurance options offered or tax. If you choose to pay for all of the different types of insurance options offered, the quoted rate for the rental car often more than doubles. What most travelers don't know, however, is that they do not need all of the optional insurance, because their own insurance policies as well as the travel insurance provided free of charge by some credit card companies offer more than adequate protection.

Prior to renting a car, call the customer service number for your auto insurance company as well as your home owner's insurance company. Ask if rental car insurance is automatically offered under your existing policy. If it is, you probably don't need any of the insurance offered by the rental car companies. If you rely on your existing insurance, however, and you're forced to make a claim due to an accident in the rental car, your regular insurance rates could go up in the future. One benefit of purchasing the optional insurance from the rental car companies is that your existing policies won't be affected if a claim has to be made (assuming any damage or injury claims are under the limit of the insurance you purchase).

Understanding the Rental Car Insurance Options

The various rental car companies will offer several optional insurance plans that you can accept and pay for (per day) for the length of your rental agreement. The renter's financial responsibility for loss of or damage to the rental car varies by state. According to Hertz's literature, "the customer is responsible for loss of or damage to the car, up to its full value regardless of who is at fault, due to collision, rollover and, in many instances, a limited number of other causes as specified in the rental agreement. The customer is generally not responsible for damage to the car resulting from acts of nature and accidental fire, provided the car is used in accordance with all terms and conditions of the rental agreement."

Collision Damage Waiver (CDW) or Loss Damage Waiver (LDW)—CDW and LDW are not insurance, but according to Hertz's literature, "is an option available for an additional daily charge which, when offered and accepted, waives or reduces the customer's responsibility for loss of or damage to the rental car, provided the car is used in accordance with all terms and conditions of the rental agreement. CDW or LDW charges apply to each full day or partial rental day, CDW and/or LDW may not be available at some locations, and the charge varies by location and by car group/class."

Liability Insurance Supplement (LIS)—According to Hertz's literature, "LIS is an optional supplement which will increase the limits of liability protection to a combined total of $1,000,000 (one million U.S. dollars)."

Personal Accident Insurance (PAI)—According to Hertz's literature, PAI is an optional service offered by Hertz [and most rental car companies]. It covers your accidental death and medical expenses resulting from bodily injury. Total indemnity for any one accident is limited to $225,000 (U.S. dollars). Benefits are payable in addition to any other coverage for

which you are eligible. The renter is covered for the duration of the rental if they are in or out of the vehicle as follows:

- Loss of Life $175,000
- Medical up to $2,500
- Ambulance up to $250

When renting a Hertz car, passengers are only covered while entering, occupying, or leaving the Hertz vehicle as follows (most other rental car companies offer similar benefits, but be sure to inquire about them):

- Loss of Life $17,500
- Medical up to $2,500
- Ambulance up to $250

Personal Effects Coverage (PEC)—This is another optional service offered by the rental car companies. According to Hertz's literature, "PEC provides protection for loss of or damage to covered personal effects of the renter and their immediate family traveling with the renter and residing with the renter. Some exclusions apply. The maximum coverage per person is $600.00 (U.S. dollars) with a total of $1,800.00 (U.S. dollars)."

Combined PAI/PEC are available for a single fee of approximately $5 per day from Hertz, and are not sold separately. Once again, check with the rental car company you choose to obtain specific details about what insurance options are offered and the additional costs and benefits associated with them.

Special Services from Rental Car Companies

Most rental car companies will provide child safety seats, either free of charge or for a small daily fee, but these seats must be reserved in advance. This will save you the hassle of having to bring your own child safety seat(s) with you on your trip.

If you're a nonsmoker, be sure to ask for a nonsmoking vehicle when you make your reservation.

When you pick up your rental car in Las Vegas, computer-generated driving directions and maps are often provided, free of charge, from the airport to virtually any location in the Las Vegas area, including all of the popular hotels and attractions.

Before leaving home, be sure to get some cash to carry with you. Too much cash may be risky, however, so it's an excellent idea to carry traveler's checks and credit cards. Also, in case you lose your wallet while traveling, it's a good idea to hide one of your credit cards in your luggage or in your carryon, so it's separate from your wallet.

Many rental car companies now offer cellular phone rentals, however, the rates are extremely high. If you have a handheld or transportable cellular phone that you can bring with you to Las Vegas, you're better off paying the roaming charges than the high daily rental and per-minute service fees associated with renting a cellular phone.

When you pick up the rental car, ask about the rental car company's policy for additional drivers. Typically, when you rent a car, only the person whose name appears on the rental agreement is legally permitted to drive the car, unless additional paperwork is completed. Some rental car companies charge to add names to the rental contract, allowing for multiple drivers. The following are often exempt from additional driver charges (but check with the rental car company): the renter's employer or regular fellow employee when on company business, the renter's spouse, the renter's mate, life companion, significant other or live-in, and disabled renters who have completed a special form.

For a listing of special events happening throughout the year in the Las Vegas area, contact the Las Vegas Chamber of Commerce at (702) 735-1616 or visit *www.lasvegas25hours.com*

Final Questions to Ask and Additional Money Saving Tips When Renting a Car

- First, ask if you're required to return the car with a full tank of gas, or if you're paying for the gas in advance. If you're required to return the car with a full tank of gas and you fail to do so (which many people do), you'll be billed up to three times the going rate per gallon of gas needed to fill the tank. Before returning the car, find a low-priced gas station and fill the tank with basic unleaded gasoline. This will fulfill your obligation to return the car with a full tank of gas.
- If you pick up the car at 3:00 P.M., for example, you must return the car before 3:00 P.M. on the day your rental agreement ends, or you'll automatically be billed for additional hours at a high rate. When you pick up the car, ask what time the car must be returned by to ensure you won't be billed overtime hours, and ask what the overtime rate is.
- When returning your car, plan on arriving at the airport about 90 minutes prior to your flight time. You will most likely be returning your car several miles from the actual airport, and

If you're worried about getting lost, Hertz offers a new (optional) feature in some of their rental cars called NeverLost. The NeverLost unit identifies exactly where you are at any time and shows and tells you how to get wherever you want to go. You can drive with confidence without having to fumble with maps, hunt for street signs, or ask for directions. There's less wasted travel time and more peace of mind.

NeverLost uses the Global Positioning System (GPS)—with smart sensors to achieve the accuracy needed for true turn-by-turn guidance. It is the most advanced on-board system ever engineered by Magellan, a leader in satellite navigation technology.

you'll need to allow ample time to return the car, take the complimentary shuttle bus to your airline terminal, check in at the airline terminal, check your bags, and get to the actual gate. It's a common problem for travelers to miss their flight because they didn't allow enough time to return their rental car, so plan accordingly.

- As soon as you pick up your car, before leaving the rental car company's parking lot, make sure there is nothing obviously wrong with the vehicle. If there's a problem, report it immediately. Once you leave the rental car company's parking lot, if you notice a problem, call the rental car company and report it. Likewise, if you get stuck on the road, call the rental car company and report your situation. Free assistance, often including towing services, will be provided, and you'll often be given a replacement rental car.

- Finally, if you've had a long flight, you'll land in Las Vegas, pick up your rental car, and be driving in unfamiliar territory while you're tired. This provides an ideal condition to become involved in an auto accident, so before getting behind the wheel, make sure you're totally awake and alert and that you have detailed driving directions for reaching your destination. If you're too tired to be driving, take a taxi or shuttle bus to your hotel and pick up your rental car later in the day or the following day, but be sure to call the rental car company and mention your change of plans to avoid being charged.

Deciding to reserve a rental car is a matter of personal preference and convenience. No matter where you'll be going in the Las Vegas area, taxi service is available outside of every hotel, resort, casino, restaurant, and attraction along the Strip, and cab rides between locations on the Strip are always under $10 (each way). If you choose to rent a car, free parking is available at every hotel, resort, and casino, but for the added convenience of visitors, valet parking is also almost always available.

Unless you're planning to drive outside of the Strip area, most people traveling to Las Vegas rely on taxis, shuttle services, and limos. Renting a car, however, is a matter of personal preference and convenience.

CHAPTER TWO

Choosing Hotel or Resort Accommodations in Las Vegas

Wherever you go in Las Vegas, you're going to encounter casinos, slot machines, video poker machines, keno, and other opportunities to gamble—even at supermarkets and McDonald's. Even if you don't consider yourself a gambler, it's easy to get caught up in the glitz, glamour, and hype of Las Vegas, starting from the moment you step off the plane. To keep from overspending during your trip, allocate some money in your budget for gambling and then stick to that allocation, no matter what.

L as Vegas has more hotel rooms within the boundaries of the relatively small city than anywhere else in the world. Just one of the things that make hotel rooms in this city so unique is that many of them were created based on a special theme. So, if you're staying in the Luxor, for example, the guest rooms and public areas are decorated in an ancient-Egyptian motif. As you'll see from reading this book, when it comes to booking your hotel, you have many choices.

As you consider where you'd like to stay, keep in mind that there are inexpensive motels and hotels (such as the Residence Inn by Marriott, La Quinta Inn, Best Western, Budget Suites of America, Comfort Inn, Travelodge, Quality Inn, Econo Lodge, Motel 6, and Super 8) located near (but not directly on) the Strip.

There are also more expensive hotels (along the Strip and nearby) that offer casinos, shops, and restaurants on-property, plus other amenities, but aren't full-service resorts.

Finally, there are many full-service resorts and mega-resorts that offer all sorts of guest room accommodations (from basic rooms to multi-bedroom luxurious suites) and amenities, plus on-property attractions and activities (ranging from shows to tennis courts and/or golf courses, swimming pools, health clubs, spas, salons, theme park attractions, etc.).

Of course, as you start thinking about where you'd like to stay in Las Vegas, consider who you'll be traveling with, what your budget is, what accommodations you require, and what type of place you'd enjoy staying at. Also, be sure to take into account recommendations from friends, family members, coworkers, and travel agents, especially if you're planning your very first trip to Las Vegas.

Over the past decade, many Las Vegas resorts have shifted their focus from gambling and adult-oriented entertainment to family-oriented accommodations and entertainment (in addition to the gambling, of course). As a result, there are now resorts that cater to business travelers, honeymooners, adults traveling alone, convention goers, families with teenagers, families with young children, and senior citizens.

Along the Strip (and surrounding areas), you'll find some extremely inexpensive hotels and motels in addition to some of the most luxurious and upscale resorts in the world. You could easily spend anywhere from $30 to $5,000 (or more) per room, per night, based on where you stay and what type of room or suite you reserve.

Thus, when choosing where you'll ultimately stay during your trip to Las Vegas, consider the following:

- What type of accommodations do you need? How many beds? What size beds (twin, queen, or king)? How many bedrooms, bathrooms? Will you be requiring extra cots to be placed in the room? If so, how much does the hotel charge per night for extra cots?
- Would you enjoy staying at a hotel with a theme? Many of the hotels and resorts are built around a theme, which is carried out in the architecture, décor, and even in the amenities offered.
- Since most room rates are based on double occupancy, is there an extra charge for each child who stays in your room?
- What type of amenities do you need?
- What type of hotel services/amenities are you looking for? (Swimming pool, spa, health club, fine-dining restaurants, shows, tennis courts, golf courses, salon, wedding chapel, child-care facilities, in-room Jacuzzi, shopping, laundry facilities/dry cleaning, activities for the children, a full-service business center, casino, etc.)
- Is a complimentary shuttle bus offered to and from the airport? Is a shuttle bus offered to and from nearby attractions?
- How close is the hotel to locations along the Strip and other attractions you plan on visiting?
- Does the hotel offer complimentary parking (if you're renting a car)? If not, how much will parking fees increase your overall hotel bill?
- Does the hotel charge for local phone calls or for calling toll-free numbers? If so, how much? Is the hotel equipped with phone jacks for laptop computers, so you can access the Internet or check your e-mail?
- Is an in-room safe provided for your valuables?
- Will the hotel be able to guarantee you a nonsmoking room (if you request one when you make your reservation)?
- What is your nightly budget for a hotel room?

The world famous Strip is where you'll find most of the well known Las Vegas resorts and casinos. Just off the Strip are dozens of smaller, less

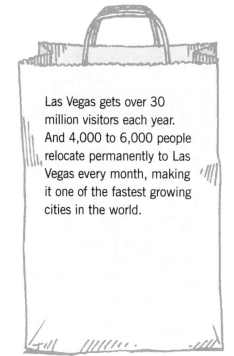

Las Vegas gets over 30 million visitors each year. And 4,000 to 6,000 people relocate permanently to Las Vegas every month, making it one of the fastest growing cities in the world.

expensive hotels and motels, plus a handful of other famous resorts and casinos, such as the Rio and Hard Rock Hotel and Casino. There's also the downtown Las Vegas area that over the years has gone from being a prime tourist destination to a much less popular neighborhood. In recent years, great efforts have been made to revitalize the downtown area; however, most people traveling to Las Vegas continue to stay somewhere on the Strip or near it. As a result, this book doesn't cover the downtown area in-depth other than in Chapter 4, which discusses the Golden Nugget and provides information about the downtown area and what's offered there.

The various hotels and resorts in Las Vegas can certainly be rated based on their quality, beauty, and amenities, but as you'll soon learn, daily room rates in Las Vegas vary dramatically and are based primarily on demand. While Las Vegas is one of America's most popular tourist destinations, the city also contains the most convention space in a single city. Thus, some of the biggest conventions held in the world take place in Las Vegas. During these conventions, especially the larger ones where tens of thousands of convention goers converge in Las Vegas, room rates go up dramatically.

As a result, a room that goes for $69 one night could cost $500 during a convention. Since the room rates fluctuate so much (based mainly on the season and demand for rooms), it's difficult to offer guidelines as to which hotel or resort to stay at based solely on your budget.

If, for example, you want to spend less than $100 a night for accommodations, there are a handful of resorts and hotels along the Strip that generally offer rooms in this price range. If you happen to be visiting Las Vegas during a slow period where the city isn't close to capacity, chances are your $100 budget per night will allow you to stay at one of the Strip's top resorts. On the other hand, if you're visiting the city during a peak period, when rooms are in short supply, you may be forced to stay at a hotel or motel located off of the Strip in order to stay within your budget.

Aside from simply calling the toll-free reservation numbers listed in this book to make a room reservation, there are other ways to book hotel accommodations, which may result in lower room rates:

- Take advantage of special promotions advertised in newspapers or magazines by a resort or hotel. Pay careful attention to the restrictions. Many special offers have blackout dates, require up to a 21-day advance purchase, a minimum number of nights stay, a Saturday night stay, or cannot be canceled or changed.

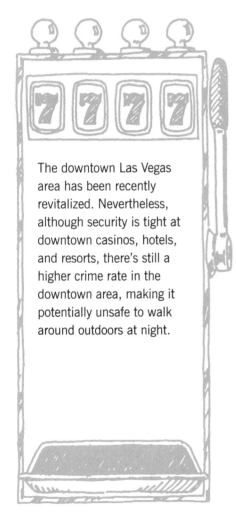

The downtown Las Vegas area has been recently revitalized. Nevertheless, although security is tight at downtown casinos, hotels, and resorts, there's still a higher crime rate in the downtown area, making it potentially unsafe to walk around outdoors at night.

- Take advantage of online specials. Virtually all of the Las Vegas hotels and resorts have their own Web sites. If you make your reservation online, you can often take advantage of specials that aren't advertised anywhere else. If you have access to the World Wide Web, always check the hotel or resort's Web site for specials before calling the toll-free reservations number.
- Take advantage of AAA (800-222-7448) discounts or other travel club promotions, such as the Entertainment Book (800-445-4137 / *www.entertainment-gold.com*).
- Take advantage of corporate discounts.
- Contact independent travel agents. Many travel agents are able to offer rates that aren't available to the general public.
- Take advantage of discount travel services, such as Priceline (800-PRICELINE / *www.Priceline.com*), a service that allows you to make an offer based on how much you'd pay for an otherwise unsold hotel room. Another similar service is Preview Travel (*www.previewtravel.com* or AOL keyword: *previewtravel*). More information on Priceline appears later in this chapter.
- Call your credit card company to see if any special travel discounts are offered to cardholders. For example, American Express offers American Express Travel Services, a full-service travel agency (800-AXP-3429) to its cardholders.
- Contact airlines about package deals that include airfare, hotel accommodations, and possibly a rental car, meals, or show tickets. Delta Airlines, American Airlines, AmericaWest, and US Airways are a few of the airlines that offer vacation packages.
- If you're attending a convention, contact the convention producers, sponsors, or coordinators. Chances are they've already negotiated special room rates for attendees.
- Contact Independent Las Vegas Hotel Reservation Services. These agencies keep in constant contact with all of the Las Vegas area hotels and resorts and know where rooms are available and for how much. Using one of these services, you can often find special discounted deals or room accommodations when virtually all of the hotels and resorts report they're sold out. These services include:

  - Reservations Plus (800) 805-9528
  - Room Finders USA (800) 473-7829

No matter which hotel, motel, resort, or mega-resort you select, be sure to allocate plenty of time to explore the other world-class properties located along (and near) the Strip. As you'll see, many of these properties offer attractions, shows, restaurants, shops, spas, and other activities you may want to experience first-hand. The majority of services and activities the various properties offer are open to guests and visitors alike.

Specialized themes offered by famous resorts and hotels along the Strip include:

- Bellagio—Inspired by an Italian village that overlooks Lake Como
- Caesars Palace—Ancient Rome
- Circus Circus—A circus big top
- Excalibur—A medieval castle circa King Arthur's era
- Hard Rock Hotel & Casino—Rock 'n' Roll
- Harrah's Las Vegas—Carnaval
- Luxor—Ancient Egypt
- MGM Grand—The Golden Age of Hollywood
- The Mirage—Polynesian village
- New York–New York—New York City
- Paris Las Vegas—The city of Paris, France
- Treasure Island—An 18th century pirate village

- Accommodations Express (800) 444-7666
- Vegas Bargains (888) 818-6269
- First Star Hotel Reservations (877) 404-3747
- Las Vegas Holidays (800) 926-6836
- Las Vegas Magic (800) 444-3090
- Las Vegas Convention Connection (800) 926-6836

On the Internet, point your Web browser to one of the following sites:

- *www.180096hotel.com*
- *www.lasvegashotel.com*
- *www.lasvegasreservations.com*
- *www.lasvegasholidays.com*
- *www.vegasrooms.com*
- *www.bookvegas.com*
- *www.Vegas.com*
- *www.las-vegas-guide.com*

Contact the Las Vegas Convention and Visitors Authority at (800) 332-5334.

Using Priceline.com to Find Great Deals

(800) PRICELINE / *www.Priceline.com*

Priceline.com is a new type of buying service where you can save money by naming your own price for the things you need, such as hotel rooms or airline tickets. If you want a hotel room in Las Vegas, for example, but you only want to pay $100 a night, Priceline.com will take your offer to its participating, name-brand hotels in Las Vegas to see if any will agree to your price. If the company is successful, you've got the room you want at the price you want to pay.

Thanks in part to the company's spokesperson (actor William Shatner, Captain James T. Kirk from Star Trek), Priceline.com has quickly become one of the most recognized brands on the Internet. Instead of spending hours calling around or surfing Web sites for the best hotel rates (or airfares), you can name the price you want to pay and Priceline.com will let you know if any of our name-brand or independent hotels accept your

Calculating Approximate Vacation Costs

Use this form to help calculate the approximate cost of your Las Vegas trip, in advance. Planning your itinerary in advance and setting budgetary spending limits will help you enjoy your trip without going into unexpected debt or spending outside of your budget.

TRANSPORTATION

Adult Airfare(s): $_____ per ticket x ____ (# of people) = $_____
Child Airfare(s): $_____ per ticket x ____ (# of children) = $_____
Rental Car: $_____ per day/week x ____ (# of days/weeks) = $_____
Taxi/Bus $_____ per trip x ____ (# of trips) = $_____
Hotel $_____ per night x ____ (# of nights) = $_____

ATTRACTION TICKETS

For Adults $_____ per person x ____ (# of days, if applicable) = $_____
For Children $_____ per child x ____ (# of days, if applicable) = $_____

SHOW TICKETS

For Adults $_____ per person x ____ (# of days, if applicable) = $_____
For Children $_____ per child x ____ (# of days, if applicable) = $_____
Gambling Budget $_____ per day x (# of days, if applicable) = $_____

NIGHTTIME ENTERTAINMENT

Budget (Adults) $_____ per person x ____ (# of nights) = $_____
Budget (Children) $_____ per person x ___ (# of nights) = $_____
Meal Budget $_____ per person x ____ (# of meals) x ____ (# of days) = $_____
Snack/Drink Budget $_____ per person x ____ (# of days) = $_____
Souvenir Budget $_____ per person = $_____
Child-Care/Babysitting Budget $_____ per child x ____ (# of days/nights) = $_____
Kennel Costs (or Pet Boarding) $_____ per pet x ____ (# of days) = $_____
Airport Parking (in your home city) $_____ per day x ____ (# of days) = $_____
Other _____ $_____ = $_____
Miscellaneous $_____ = $_____

APPROXIMATE VACATION EXPENSES TOTAL: = $_____

price. It only takes a few minutes to complete a hotel request, and the service is free of charge.

This service works primarily because hotels have empty rooms they'd like to fill. According to Priceline.com, "Every night, thousands of hotel rooms go unsold throughout the country. That's lost revenue for the hotels, and a great opportunity for Priceline.com customers! That's because Priceline.com lets you name the price you want to pay for these hotel rooms, whether you're traveling tomorrow or six months from now!"

When naming your price online for a hotel room, tell Priceline.com where and when you want to go, then select the hotel quality level (1 to 5 stars). Next, tell Priceline.com how much you want to pay, and guarantee your request with a major credit card. The company will then take your offer to all the participating hotels in the city or area you select. If your offer is accepted, your reservation will then immediately be booked at the price you want to pay.

While you cannot choose specific hotels in Las Vegas, you can choose what area of the city you'd like to stay (including what area of the Strip). Keep in mind, once you agree to a price you'd be willing to pay and Priceline.com finds hotel accommodations for you, you'll be obligated to pay in full for your reservation (using a major credit card), in advance, and you can't change or cancel that reservation.

Upon submitting a request online, Priceline.com will respond in less than one hour, whether or not your request is accepted. If the company finds a hotel to agree to your price, you'll be provided with complete details on where you'll be staying, including directions, phone numbers, and anything else you might need. If you're unsuccessful, Priceline.com will give you tips on how to try your request again. If no hotel agrees to your price, you pay nothing. To save additional money, Priceline.com has special offers you can choose to accept or decline. For example, if you apply for a specific credit card online when you make your room reservation bid, you could save an additional $25 to $50.

Before logging onto the Priceline.com Web site (*www.Priceline.com*), the company recommends following these four steps:

1. Shop around for the lowest available hotel rates before you name your price.

Besides staying at a hotel or resort, there are RV trailer parks, home exchange services (like HomeLink International, 305-294-7766), and very inexpensive hostels in the Las Vegas area.

2. If the lowest rate you find fits your budget in a hotel you want to stay in, it is recommended that you reserve those rooms, since rates and availability change constantly.
3. If not, let Priceline.com try to find available high quality hotel rooms for you, at the price you want to pay.
4. Remember, the more reasonable your price, the better your chance of getting hotel rooms through Priceline.com.

The Best Times to Visit Las Vegas

Las Vegas has truly become a year-round vacation, tourist, and convention destination. Thus, there is no longer any guaranteed "slow season." Typically holidays and weekends are the most crowded (and the most expensive).

Holiday weekends, such as New Years, Christmas, the weekend of Super Bowl, Valentine's Day, President's Day, the weekend of the NCAA Final Four (or any major sporting event), Memorial Day, and July 4th, are usually the most crowded. Not only will you probably pay a premium for hotel accommodations, but you'll need to reserve your rooms as far in advance as possible.

Choosing Your Accommodations

As mentioned earlier, Chapter 4 provides detailed information about all of the hotels, resorts, and casinos along the Las Vegas Strip, as well as detailed information about some of the more popular resorts located close to, but not on the Strip. In Chapter 4, you'll also find a listing of all hotels and motels in the Las Vegas area, plus a listing of hotels, resorts, and casinos located in the downtown Las Vegas area.

For each detailed hotel or resort description, the following information is offered:

- The hotel or resort's theme
- Room rate
- Number of rooms
- Casino size
- Dining options

The Las Vegas Strip is a three-and-a-half mile stretch of highway along which you'll find some of the world's most famous casinos, resorts, and hotels.

Room rates in Las Vegas may appear arbitrary, especially if you're staying for multiple nights in the same room at the same hotel or resort. For example, rates can fluctuate from $69 to $300 (or more) from night to night. When making a hotel reservation, always ask more than once if there are cheaper rooms available or if any special promotions are running. If you're a member of AAA or another club or association, be sure to mention this as well.

The RV Park Alternative

If staying at a hotel or resort is out of your budget or you prefer staying in the comfort of your own RV, here's a listing of RV parks located in the Las Vegas area. Contact them directly to make a reservation or inquire about their services or amenities.

- American Campgrounds, 3440 N. Las Vegas Boulevard (702) 643-1222
- Boulder Lakes Resort RV Resort, 6201 Boulder Highway (702) 435-1157
- Circusland RV Park, 2880 S. Las Vegas Boulevard (702) 794-3757
- Covered Wagon RV Park, 6635 Boulder Highway (702) 454-7090
- Desert Sands RV Park & Motel, 1940 N. Boulder Highway (702) 736-5879
- Good Sam—Hitchin' Post Camper Park, 3640 N. Las Vegas Boulevard (702) 644-1043
- Holiday Travel Trailer Park, 3890 S. Nellis Boulevard (702) 451-8005
- KOA Kampground—Las Vegas Resort, 4315 Boulder Highway (702) 451-5527
- King's Row Trailer Park Inc., 3660 Boulder Highway (702) 457-3606

- Lakeshore Trailer Village, 268 Lakeshore Road (702) 293-2540
- Lovell Canyon Ranch, 2840 Alpine Place (702) 258-8575
- Maycliff RV Mini Storage & RV Park, 4001 E. Sahara (702) 457-3553
- Nevada Palace VIP Travel Trailer Park, 5325 Boulder Highway (702) 451-0232
- Oasis Las Vegas RV Resort, 2711 Windmill Lane (702) 260-2020
- Riviera Travel Trailer Park, 2200 Palm Street (702) 457-8700
- Road Runner RV Park, 4711 Boulder Highway (702) 456-4711
- Sam's Town Hotel & Gambling Hall, 4040 S. Nellis Boulevard & 5225 Boulder Highway (702) 454-8055
- Showboat RV Park, 2800 Fremont Street (702) 383-9333
- Silverton Hotel Casino & RV Resort, 3333 Blue Diamond Road (702) 263-7777
- Sunrise Resort and RV Park, 4445 Boulder Highway (702) 458-7275
- Sunrise RV Park, 4575 Boulder Highway (702) 948-8000
- Western RV Park, 1023 Fremont Street (702) 384-1033

- Primary show and/or special attractions
- Reservations phone number
- Web site address
- Address
- An overall rating based on amenities and rates
- Information about guest room accommodations
- Information about the hotel or resort's fine-dining options
- Information about the hotel or resort's casual-dining options
- Information about the hotel or resort's lounges
- Detailed descriptions of the hotel or resort's special attractions and shows
- Detailed information about the hotel or resort's casino(s)
- Information about the shops and boutiques available on-property at each hotel or resort
- Information about planning a banquet, function, or convention at each hotel or resort

Understanding the Room Rates

Since room rates at the various Las Vegas hotels and resorts vary greatly, based on season and demand, the room rates listed in this book are provided as a general reference only. Under each hotel or resort's description, you'll see the heading "Room Rate" followed by dollar signs ($). Use the following key to better understand the average room rate for each hotel, motel, or resort.

Keep in mind, all of the Las Vegas hotels and resorts offer guest rooms and suites equipped to accommodate guests with specific needs or who have some form of physical disability. Be sure to discuss your needs, in advance, when making a reservation. Don't wait until you arrive in Las Vegas and you're ready to check in to request special accommodations.

$ = Under $50 per night
$$ = $51 to $100 per night
$$$ = $101 to $250 per night
$$$$ = $251 and up per night

In addition to choosing a room based on its price, many of the hotels and resorts cater to specific guests. Thus, this book offers a rating system to help you determine the overall rating for each hotel or resort based on its price, amenities, and overall quality. This chart will help you determine if any given hotel or resort is suitable for:

- Young children (up to five years old)
- Children (ages six to 15)
- Teenagers and young adults (ages 16 to 20)

- Adults (21 and up)
- Senior citizens

Within the chart will be one to three die for each age category (or the words "Not Suitable"—meaning the hotel isn't suitable for a specific age group).

= Fair value/interest level

= Good value/interest level

= Excellent value/interest level

Sample Overall Resort Rating Based on Amenities and Rates

Ages Up to 5	Ages 6–15	Ages 16–20	Ages 21 & Up	Senior Citizens

According to the previous sample chart, this property would not necessarily be suitable for families traveling with young children (hence it received only one star in this category). Based on the chart, the hotel probably offers a few amenities targeted to older children, such as an arcade, rides and attractions, or a babysitting service, but doesn't specifically cater to this age group (which is why it received two stars). Since the chart lists three stars for the remaining age groups, it probably offers topnotch amenities and services, plus luxurious accommodations (based on its price point), and is therefore recommended to families traveling with teens, adults traveling alone, and/or senior citizens.

Similar charts are offered throughout the book for the major shows and attractions offered at each hotel and casino. These charts are designed to help you plan your time in Las Vegas so everyone you're traveling with has the best time possible. After all, some shows and attractions in Las Vegas continue to be adult-oriented (and not suitable for children), while some of the theme park rides and attractions are designed specifically for younger children and teens, but won't necessarily be enjoyable to adults or seniors.

As soon as you arrive in Las Vegas, you'll quickly discover that each of the popular resorts and hotels is a city onto itself, offering shops, restaurants, attractions, shows, spas, health clubs, pools, etc. In terms of the dining options, many of the properties offer fine-dining as well as casual-dining options, in addition to an all-you-can-eat buffet (which is one of the things Las Vegas is famous for) and 24-hour in-room dining (room service).

Dining Guidelines

To help you choose the best places to eat, based on your budget, each restaurant is categorized based on the average price of the entrees. You'll find one to three dollar signs ($) next to each restaurant's name and description.

$ = Entrees are priced under $10 each

$$ = Entrees are priced under $20 each

$$$ = Entrees are priced over $20 each

At any full-service restaurant, you're expected to leave a tip for your server. The customary amount to leave is 15 percent of the total bill, however, you may choose to leave slightly more or less depending on the quality of service you receive. Many restaurants automatically add a gratuity to the bill for groups, so be sure to determine if a gratuity has already been added to your meal bill if you're dining with a group of people.

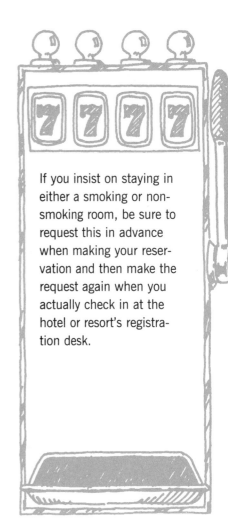

If you insist on staying in either a smoking or non-smoking room, be sure to request this in advance when making your reservation and then make the request again when you actually check in at the hotel or resort's registration desk.

Tipping Calculator		
MEAL PRICE	SUGGESTED TIP AMOUNT (15%)	SUGGESTED TIP AMOUNT (20%)
$5	$.75	$1
$10	$1.50	$2
$12	$1.80	$2.40
$14	$2.10	$2.80
$16	$2.40	$3.20
$18	$2.70	$3.60
$20	$3	$4
$25	$3.75	$5
$30	$4.50	$6
$35	$5.25	$7
$40	$6	$8
$45	$6.75	$9
$50	$7.50	$10
$55	$8.25	$11
$60	$9	$12
$65	$9.75	$13
$70	$10.50	$14
$75	$11.25	$15
$80	$12	$16
$85	$12.75	$17
$90	$13.50	$18
$95	$14.25	$19
$100	$15	$20
$125	$18.75	$25
$150	$22.50	$30

CHAPTER THREE

The Las Vegas Strip at a Glance

F inding out what to see and do in the Las Vegas area is as easy as reading this book and making a few quick telephone calls to make reservations, confirm schedules, or obtain more information. This chapter provides a summary of the main phone numbers for the major Las Vegas hotels and resorts. You'll also find a directory of the main shows and phone numbers for booking reservations.

For more details about any of the major hotels or resorts along the Strip or for details about shows, see Chapter 4.

If you're looking for activities and attractions located outside of a resort or hotel, be sure to read Chapter 6, entitled "More Attractions and Activities." There you'll learn about helicopter tours, golf courses, bowling alleys, museums, and many other exciting things to do while visiting Las Vegas.

The Resort Hotels and Casinos

You can use these phone numbers:

- to contact guests staying at any of the properties listed,
- to get transferred to the reservations desk,
- to make dining reservations at one of the on-property restaurants, or
- to be transferred to the property's box office to purchase show tickets.

This listing contains major hotels and resorts located along the Strip, directly off the Strip, and in the Las Vegas downtown area (around Fremont Street).

Aladdin	(702) 736-7114	Maxim	(702) 731-4300
Bally's	(702) 739-4111	MGM Grand	(702) 891-1111
Barbary Coast	(702) 737-7111	The Mirage	(702) 791-7111
Bellagio	(702) 693-7111	Monte Carlo	(702) 730-7777
Binion's Horseshoe	(702) 382-1600	New York–New York	(702) 740-6969
Boardwalk Casino (Holiday Inn)	(702) 735-2400	Orleans	(702) 365-7111
Boulder Station	(702) 432-7777	Palace Station	(702) 367-2411
Bourbon Street	(702) 737-7200	Paris Las Vegas	(702) 946-7000
Caesars Palace	(702) 731-7110	Primm Valley Resort	(702) 382-1212
Circus Circus	(702) 734-0410	Rio	(702) 252-7777
El Cortez	(702) 385-5200	Riviera	(702) 734-5110
Excalibur	(702) 597-7777	Sahara	(702) 737-2111
Fiesta	(702) 631-7000	Sam's Town	(702) 456-7777
Fitzgerald's	(702) 388-2400	San Remo	(702) 739-9000
Flamingo Hilton	(702) 733-3111	Showboat	(702) 385-9123
Four Queens	(702) 385-4011	Silver City	(702) 732-4152
Fremont	(702) 385-3232	Silverton	(702) 263-7777
Frontier	(702) 794-8200	Slots-A-Fun	(702) 734-0410
Gold Coast	(702) 367-7111	Stardust	(702) 732-6111
Golden Gate	(702) 385-1906	Stratosphere	(702) 380-7777
Golden Nugget	(702) 385-7111	Sunset Station	(702) 547-7777
Hard Rock	(702) 693-5000	Texas Station	(702) 631-1000
Harrah's	(702) 369-5000	Treasure Island	(702) 894-7111
Imperial Palace	(702) 731-3311	Tropicana	(702) 739-2222
Lady Luck	(702) 477-3000	Vacation Village	(702) 897-1700
Las Vegas Hilton	(702) 732-5111	Venetian	(702) 897-1700
Luxor	(702) 262-4000	Westward Ho	(702) 731-2900
Main Street Station	(702) 387-1896	Wild Wild West	(702) 740-0000
Mandalay Bay	(702) 632-7777		

The Las Vegas Shows

The following is a list of the major shows in the Las Vegas area. This list does not include special events or limited engagements. For information about specific events, such as concerts, sporting events, or limited engagements, contact the appropriate resort, theater, arena, or venue directly.

SHOW NAME	BOX OFFICE	VENUE
"O" (Cirque du Soleil)	(702) 693-7790	Bellagio
American Superstars	(702) 380-7711	Stratosphere
An Evening at La Cage	(702) 794-9433	Riviera
The Best of the Follies Bergere	(702) 739-2411	Tropicana
Bill Acosta Master Vocal Impressionist	(702) 262-4400	Luxor
Blue Man Group Live	(702) 262-4400	Luxor
Broadway Cabaret	(800) 822-7366	Hotel San Remo
C2K	(702) 414-1000	Venetian
Caesars Magical Empire	(702) 731-7333	Caesars Palace
Catch a Rising Star (comedy club)	(800) 929-1111	MGM Grand
Chicago: The Musical	(702) 632-7580	Mandalay Bay
Comedy Club	(800) 634-6753	Riviera
Comedy Fun House	(800) 634-6045	Four Queens Hotel
Comedy Loft	(800) 854-7666	Casino Royale
The Comedy Stop	(800) 634-4000	Tropicana
Crazy Girls	(702) 794-9433	Riviera

SHOW NAME	BOX OFFICE	VENUE
David Cassidy at the Copa	(702) 252-7776	Rio
Dr. Naughty X-Rated Hypnotist	(800) 634-6956	Bourbon Street
The Dream King	(702) 730-3194	Boardwalk
EFX	(702) 891-7777	MGM Grand
Forever Plaid	(702) 733-3333	Flamingo Hilton
The Great Radio City Spectacular	(702) 733-3333	Flamingo Hilton
Hawaiian Hot Luau	(800) 634-6441	Imperial Palace
Hip-Nosis	(702) 737-1343	Flamingo O'Shea's
The Illusionary Magic of Rick Thomas	(702) 739-2411	Tropicana
Improv at Harrah's	(702) 369-5111	Harrah's
Jubilee!	(702) 967-4567	Bally's
Master Magician Lance Burton	(702) 730-7160	Monte Carlo
Legends in Concert	(702) 794-3261	Imperial Palace
Marriage Can Be Murder 2	(800) 826-2800	Showboat
Michael Flatley's Lord of the Dance	(702) 740-6815	New York–New York
Midnight Fantasy	(702) 262-4400	Luxor
Mysteré (Cirque du Soleil)	(702) 894-7722	Treasure Island
Notre Dame De Paris	(702) 946-4567	Paris Las Vegas
Riviera Comedy Club	(702) 794-9433	Riviera
Siegfried & Roy	(702) 792-7777	The Mirage
Spellbound	(702) 369-5111	Harrah's
Splash!	(702) 794-9433	Riviera
Steve Wyrick, World Class Magician	(800) 523-9582	Lady Luck
Titanic: The Exhibition	(702) 252-7776	Rio
Tournament of Kings	(702) 597-7600	Excalibur
Viva Las Vegas	(702) 380-7711	Stratosphere
Wayne Newton	(800) 824-6033	Stardust
World's Greatest Circus Acts	(800) 634-3450	Circus Circus

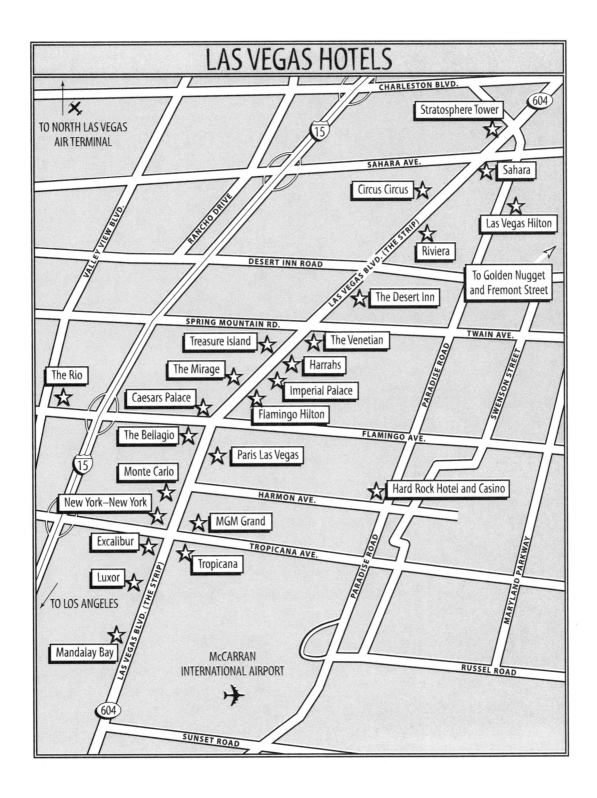

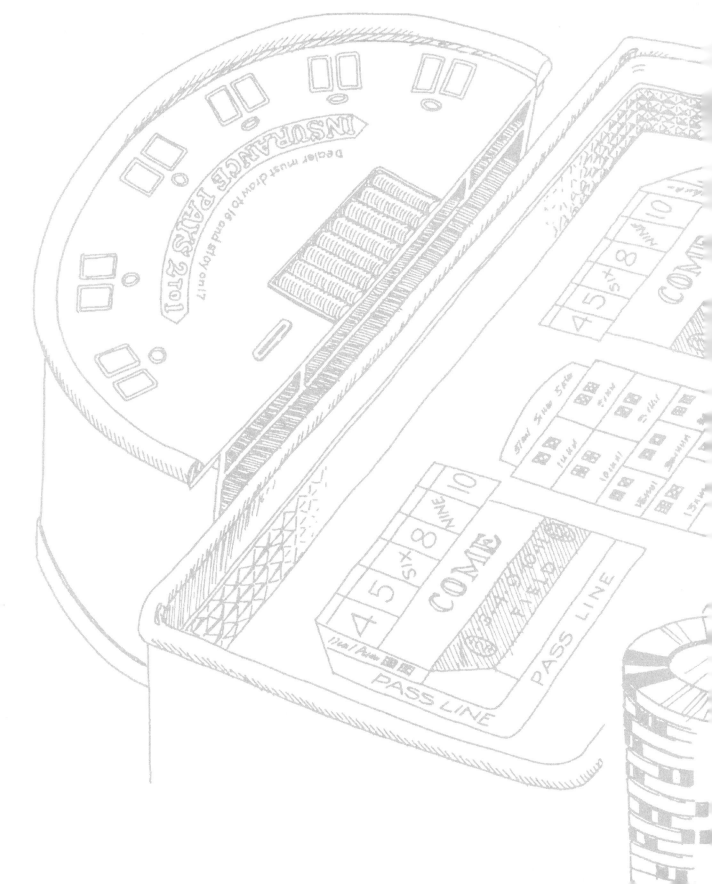

CHAPTER FOUR

The Big Hotels and Casinos

The Bellagio

Theme:	The Italian village of Bellagio, which overlooks Lake Como
Room Rate:	$$$$ ($251+)
Number of Rooms:	3,005 guest rooms, including approximately 400 suites
Casino:	116,000 square feet—making it one of the nicest, most upscale casinos along the Strip, and featuring thousands of slot and video poker machines, all of the popular table games, a keno lounge, and a race and sports book
Dining:	Ten fine-dining restaurants, and a handful of casual restaurants and lounges, most catering to an upscale crowd
Primary Show:	*Cirque du Soleil 'O'*
Special Attractions:	The Conservatory and Botanical Gardens, the Bellagio Gallery of Fine Art, Via Bellagio Shopping Promenade, the Bellagio Spa
Reservations:	(888) 987-3456
Web Site:	*www.bellagiolasvegas.com*
Address:	3600 Las Vegas Boulevard South Las Vegas, NV 89177

Overall Resort Rating Based on Amenities and Rates

Ages Up to 5	Ages 6–15	Ages 16–20	Ages 21 & Up	Senior Citizens
Not Suitable	⚀	⚀ ⚁	⚀ ⚁ ⚂	⚀ ⚁ ⚂

Located near the center of the Strip, the Bellagio is one of the most expensive resorts in Las Vegas but worth every penny if you can afford to indulge yourself in the finest of everything, from accommodations to entertainment and dining. Without being overly pretentious, Bellagio offers luxury, beauty, and attention to detail, whether you're looking at the overall architecture, the room accommodations, the restaurants, shops, or attractions. According to the resort's management, "Bellagio is a study in informal elegance."

Bellagio is the perfect place for adults, honeymooners, and anyone looking for a romantic getaway. The amenities also make it ideal for business travelers who enjoy luxuries found primarily in the world's most expensive and prestigious hotels and resorts. The only drawback to this resort is that it's so beautiful and has become so popular, the property itself has become a tourist attraction. At any given time, day or night, the resort's main lobby, casino, shops, and garden areas are typically packed with tourists not necessarily staying at Bellagio. To limit crowds, many areas of the resort are open to guests only.

Guest Room Accommodations

Everything about the Bellagio is extremely elegant and impressive, so it should come as no surprise that each deluxe guest room offers an excellent view of the resort's lake, surrounding mountains, or the Las Vegas skyline. Each spacious room is also equipped with virtually every amenity a guest could want. Rooms are decorated with European-style furnishings and art.

An armoire in each room houses a remote-controlled cable television, stereo, electronic in-room safe, and a lighted wardrobe section that can accommodate full-length gowns. There's also a writing desk (equipped with a two-line telephone and computer/fax accessible data ports), and a small table with two chairs. Guests are offered a choice of one king-size or two queen-size beds, all triple-sheeted.

The larger and more elaborate guest suites offer even more luxurious surroundings. Additional amenities include a marble foyer, separate living room, and bedroom(s), an entertainment center (containing a remote controlled cable television, VCR, and stereo), powder room, wet bar (with refrigerator and ice maker), private fax machine, separate climate control in the bedroom, two master bathrooms (one with a steam shower and the other equipped with a whirlpool tub), a second cable television set, a telephone in the bedroom, robes, slippers, and an assortment of spa products.

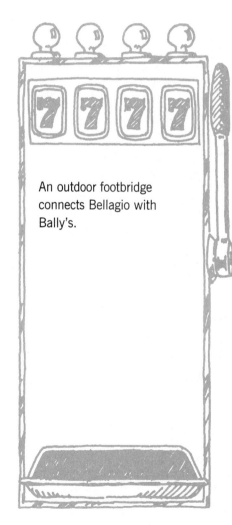

An outdoor footbridge connects Bellagio with Bally's.

Fine Dining

Careful attention to detail has obviously been paid to every restaurant and menu item served within these fine-dining eating establishments. Award-winning chefs have been brought in and offer a wide range of cuisine types in order to cater to each guest's diverse tastes. Whether you're planning a romantic dinner for two, a business dinner for a small group, or an outing with friends, when you dine at one of Bellagio's restaurants, you can be certain the food and service will be topnotch and the atmosphere will be elegant, if not extravagant.

Le Cirque ($$$)

Reservations: Required, call (702) 693-8100

Open seven nights a week, between 5:30 P.M. and 11:30 P.M., this restaurant serves contemporary French cuisine in an elegant setting that overlooks the resort's lake. A la carte main courses range in price from $28 to $39, while five- and seven-course meals are available for $90 and $120 per person, respectively. The dress code is formal (a jacket and tie is required for men). This restaurant is rather small (it seats 80 people), so reservations are an absolute must.

Osteria Del Circo ($$ / $$$)

Reservations: Recommended, call (702) 693-8150

Open every day for lunch (11:30 A.M. to 2:30 P.M.) and dinner (5:30 P.M. to 11:00 P.M.), this restaurant serves home-style Tuscan food inspired by Egidiana Maccioni. Lunch entrees are priced between $16 and $22, while dinner entrees average $19 to $26. The wine list offered at Osteria Del Circo includes more than four hundred selections. The dining room has seating for 175 guests, plus two private dining rooms are available. The restaurant is located along the lake, next to Le Cirque. The dress code is described by the management as "casual elegance."

Picasso ($$$)

Reservations: Recommended, call (702) 693-7223

Picasso overlooks Bellagio's lake and is open every evening for dinner (except Wednesday), between 6:00 and 10:00 P.M. (11:00 P.M. on Friday and

For information about all-inclusive vacations to Bellagio, visit Mirage Resorts' Vacations Web site at *www. mirageresortsvacations.com*. Fly on any of these airline partners: Southwest Airlines, US Airways, Delta Air Lines, United Airlines, AirTran Airways, Alaska Airlines, TWA, AmericaWest, and Continental Airlines. A variety of discount packages are available. Prices vary based on time of year, duration of your stay, etc.

$ = entrees under $10; $$ = under $20; $$$ = over $20

Saturday nights). It features elegant French cuisine seasonally prepared with a hint of Spanish influence, accompanied by a large selection of American and European wines. Dinner costs $65 to $75 per person. The dress code is casual elegance.

Aqua ($$ / $$$)

Reservations: Recommended, call (702) 693-7223

Michael Mina and Charles Condy's world-renowned San Francisco–based seafood restaurant now has a second location, adjacent to the Bellagio Gallery of Fine Art. Open daily for dinner, between 5:30 P.M. and 11:00 P.M., the menu offers a selection of contemporary seafood dishes prepared with French influenced cooking techniques using California and Mediterranean products. Main courses range in price from $28 to $34, while a five-course tasting costs $70 per person. (A vegetarian five-course meal is $55 per person.) The dress is casual elegance.

Olives ($$ / $$$)

Reservations: Recommended, call (702) 693-7223

Modeled after the Olives restaurant in Boston, Chef Todd English offers a casual Mediterranean cafe atmosphere located in the heart of the Via Bellagio shopping area, between the Giorgio Armani and Hermés boutiques. From a lively open kitchen, lunch and dinner are served from 11:00 A.M. to midnight Sunday through Thursday, and from 11:00 A.M. to 1:00 A.M. Friday and Saturday. Olives describes its style of food as "interpretive Mediterranean," with lunch main courses priced $9 to $17, and dinner main courses $19 to $27. The dress code is casual. Food is served in the main dining area as well as on an outside patio.

Prime Steakhouse ($$ / $$$)

Reservations: Recommended, call (702) 693-7223

If you're in the mood for a hearty steak, chops, or seafood dinner, Prime Steakhouse offers everything you'd find on the menu of a 1930s chophouse, complete with an extensive wine list. Dinner is served nightly

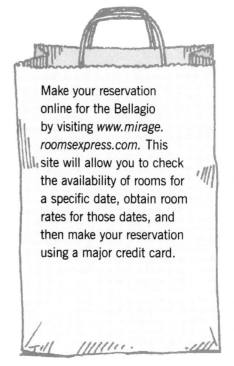

Make your reservation online for the Bellagio by visiting *www.mirage. roomsexpress.com*. This site will allow you to check the availability of rooms for a specific date, obtain room rates for those dates, and then make your reservation using a major credit card.

$ = entrees under $10; $$ = under $20; $$$ = over $20

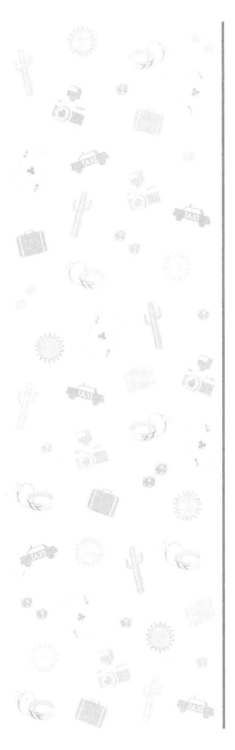

between 5:30 and 11:00 P.M. Main entrees are priced between $18 and $54. Men are asked to wear jackets at this lakeside restaurant.

Jasmine ($$ / $$$)

Reservations: Recommended, call (702) 693-7223

The décor of this restaurant features subtle European influences, but the food selection is contemporary Chinese and traditional Hong Kong Cantonese. Dinner is served nightly from 5:30 to 11:00 P.M. Main courses range in price from $16 to $29. The restaurant itself is located alongside the resort's lake, which offers a stunning view of the fountains.

Shintaro ($$ / $$$)

Reservations: Recommended, call (702) 693-7223

Authentically prepared Teppanyaki, sushi, and multicourse California-inspired tasting menus are the highlights of this lakefront restaurant. The bar offers a selection of Japanese beers and sakes, plus a large selection of American and French wines. Shintaro is open nightly, from 5:30 to 11:00 P.M. Entrees range in price from $16 to $30. The Kaiseki menu is priced at $95 per person. The dress code is casual elegance.

Noodles ($$)

Reservations: Not required

The chefs here offer traditional noodle dishes from Thailand, Japan, China, and Vietnam, as well as authentic Hong Kong–style barbecue dishes. Traditional Chinese *dim sum* is also served daily. Noodles is a casual restaurant open daily for lunch and dinner from 11:00 A.M. to 3:00 A.M.

Sam's American ($$ / $$$)

Reservations: Recommended, call (702) 693-7223

Seasonal American cuisine is served at this elegant restaurant, with dinner entrees from $19 to $25, and a five-course tasting menu at $48 per person. The wine list is extensive and the dress code is casual. Dinner is

$ = entrees under $10; $$ = under $20; $$$ = over $20

served Sunday through Thursday from 5:30 to 11:00 P.M., and on Friday and Saturday nights from 5:30 P.M. to midnight. Sam's American is located near the entrance of the Via Bellagio shopping promenade.

Casual Dining

The Bellagio also offers the following casual-dining options for light meals and snacks throughout the day and evening:

- Cafe Bellagio
- The Breads of La Brea Bakery
- The Buffet at Bellagio
- Cafe Gelato Ice Cream & Sweets
- The Pool Cafe
- Palio Espresso Bar

Lounges

- Fontana Bar—Located in the heart of Bellagio's casino, live entertainment (between 2:00 P.M. and 4:00 A.M.), and full bar service are available.
- Allegro Bar—This full-service bar is located within Bellagio's casino and offers everything from Bordeaux to cognacs. Open 24 hours a day, live entertainment is presented every afternoon and evening.
- Petrossian Bar—Offering afternoon tea (between 2:00 and 5:00 P.M.) along with the finest champagnes, plus caviar and smoked salmon, this bar is an elegant place to meet and enjoy a drink with friends or loved ones. The bar is located in the lobby and is open 24 hours. Food is served from 11:00 A.M. to 11:00 P.M.
- Baccarat Bar—Located next to the Baccarat Salon, this bar offers a selection of cocktails, including martinis, fruit-blended wine drinks, and Italian Bellinis. Live piano music is presented every afternoon and evening. The bar is open 24 hours a day.
- Pool Bar—Open 8:00 A.M. to 5:00 P.M., enjoy a drink poolside.

$ = entrees under $10; $$ = under $20; $$$ = over $20

Special Attractions

Bellagio offers an array of interesting shows, exhibits, shops, and activities, designed primarily for adult guests.

Cirque du Soleil 'O'

Ticket Price: $100 each

Show Times: 7:30 and 10:30 P.M. (Friday through Tuesday)

Tickets: (888) 488-7111

Of all the shows and attractions in Las Vegas, only a handful can boast being sold out every night. With the opening of Bellagio, the popular French circus troupe Cirque du Soleil created their most ambitious show ever. On October 19, 1998, the show called 'O' premiered and introduced audiences to an entirely original form of live entertainment.

The show's name was inspired by the concept of infinity, the circle of life, and the elegance of its purest form. 'O', phonetically speaking, is the French word for water (spelled *eau*). While this show incorporates all of the elements that have made Cirque du Soleil a worldwide phenomenon—costumes, live music, special effects, and incredible circus talent—'O' adds a new component to Cirque du Soleil's unusual form of entertainment: water.

With an international cast of over seventy-five, the performance takes place in the air, on a traditional stage, and under water. This 90-minute production is truly original, breathtaking, imaginative, and absolutely entertaining! If you can see just one show while visiting Las Vegas, this is the one adults should see!

'O' marks Cirque du Soleil's first venture into aquatic theater. Acrobats, trapeze artists, clowns, high-wire performers, and others are intertwined with synchronized swimming and other water-based acts like high diving. The state-of-the-art theater includes a 1.5-million-gallon pool. For much of the show, the pool acts as the stage.

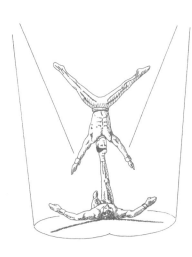

This show is probably the most expensive production in Las Vegas, and as a result, ticket prices are steep—$100 each. If you're planning to stay at any of the Mirage resorts, tickets can be purchased up to ninety days in advance by calling (888) 488-7111. (Nonguests can purchase tickets up to twenty-eight days in advance.) This is definitely the hottest selling show in

Las Vegas, so ordering your tickets as far in advance as possible is an absolute must.

Two performances are held Friday through Tuesday nights at 7:30 P.M. and 10:30 P.M. There are no performances Wednesday or Thursday nights. If you can't purchase tickets well in advance, unclaimed tickets go on sale shortly before each performance; however, people start lining up to buy these tickets several hours before show time.

Anyone who appreciates ballet and synchronized swimming will truly love 'O', which is very different than Cirque du Soleil Mysteré (presented at Treasure Island), or any of the troupe's touring performances. 'O' definitely appeals to an adult crowd, since some of the show may be too sophisticated for children and teens to truly appreciate and enjoy.

Cirque du Soleil 'O'

Ages Up to 5	Ages 6–15	Ages 16–20	Ages 21 & Up	Senior Citizens
Not Suitable	⚀	⚀ ⚁	⚀ ⚁ ⚂	⚀ ⚁ ⚂

For more information about Cirque du Soleil, visit their official Web site at *www.cirquedusoleil.com.*

The Bellagio Gallery of Fine Art

Hours: 8:00 A.M. to 11:00 P.M. (daily)

Admission: $12 per person ($6 for Nevada residents)

Only a handful of art museums throughout the world offer extensive collections that include works from artists like Matisse, Miró, Monet, Picasso, Renoir, and van Gogh. But that's what you will find at the Bellagio Gallery of Fine Art, which is located in the convention corridor across from the pool area. Housing one of the greatest art collections in America, the gallery is open daily between 8:00 A.M. and 11:00 P.M. A taped audio tour explaining each painting and piece of artwork on display is included in the admission price. All net revenues from admission receipts are donated to charity.

Understandably, this gallery has become an extremely popular attraction, so tickets should be purchased in advance. Tickets can be purchased up to seven days in advance by calling (888) 488-7111 or (702) 693-7722.

The Conservatory and Botanical Gardens

Hours:	24 hours (daily)
Admission:	Free

While travelers from around the world visit Bellagio to see the artwork on display at the Bellagio Gallery of Fine Art, located across the resort's front lobby is one of the prettiest attractions in all of Las Vegas—The Conservatory and Botanical Gardens. This is a free attraction that is virtually always crowded, yet well worth shuffling through the crowds to see first-hand. Hotel guests and visitors alike can stroll through this area and enjoy the colors and fragrances of thousands of flowering plants, arranged to create living art. The floral displays change regularly with the seasons.

The Fountains of Bellagio

Hours:	Ongoing during afternoons and evenings
Admission:	Free

A stunning dancing water show is presented every afternoon and evening on the lake in front of Bellagio. This free show features over one thousand shooting fountains, synchronized with colored lights and music. The show is presented Monday through Friday every 30 minutes from 3:00 to 8:00 P.M. and every 15 minutes from 8:00 P.M. to midnight. On Saturdays, Sundays, and holidays, the show is presented every 30 minutes from noon to 8:00 P.M. and every 15 minutes from 8:00 P.M. to midnight.

This show is reminiscent of the dancing waters show at Disneyland, and is suitable for all ages. The accompanying music ranges from Copland, Strauss, and Pavarotti to Sinatra and famous Broadway tunes. The show is more impressive after dark.

Pool and Courtyards

The swimming pool area at Bellagio is divided into six courtyard settings. Six swimming pools, plus spas and private cabanas (available for a fee) are available to guests. The landscaping around the pool area, like everything else at Bellagio, conveys pure elegance and beauty.

Spa and Salon

Appointments: (702) 693-7472

Hours: 6:00 A.M. to 8:00 P.M. (daily)

Laurent D, a well known stylist from Hollywood, California, brings his exclusive West Hollywood salon, Privé, to Bellagio. Between the full-service salon services offered at Privé and the adjacent Spa Bellagio, guests can expect to be pampered as they experience any of the available treatments, services, and amenities. Massages, hydrotherapy, facials, body treatments, and Vichy showers are available at the spa, while the exercise room offers a full line of Cybex workout equipment.

Separate men's and women's facilities include steam rooms, saunas, whirlpools and lounge areas (where fruit juices and fresh fruit are available). The spa is open to hotel guests only. There is a $25 daily fee to use these facilities. Of course, additional services, such as massages, cost extra.

Casino

Catering to the discriminating gambler, the casino at Bellagio offers a wide range of table games, including blackjack, Big Six, craps, Let It Ride, roulette, Pai Gow, Caribbean Stud poker, and baccarat. There's also a poker room, keno lounge, and a race and sports book, plus thousands of slot and video poker machines. At the table games, the minimum bets tend to be higher than at most of the other casinos.

Shopping

The Las Vegas area features several upscale malls and shopping areas, such as the Forum Shops at Caesars Palace. Within many of the resorts along the Strip, you'll also find a few fine shops and exclusive boutiques. At Bellagio, however, you'll find a collection of upscale shops the likes of which you won't find anywhere else on the Strip. Whether you have a wallet full of cash to spend or you want to spend several hours browsing, the shopping experience at Bellagio is memorable.

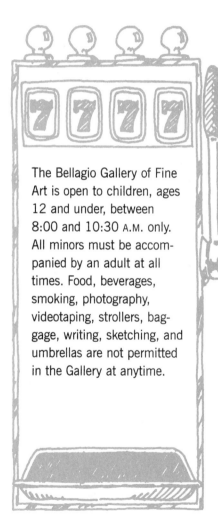

The Bellagio Gallery of Fine Art is open to children, ages 12 and under, between 8:00 and 10:30 A.M. only. All minors must be accompanied by an adult at all times. Food, beverages, smoking, photography, videotaping, strollers, baggage, writing, sketching, and umbrellas are not permitted in the Gallery at anytime.

"The sophisticated, gracious style of the boutiques reflect the overall ambiance of Bellagio," says Steve Wynn, chairman of the board of Mirage Resorts, Inc. This sophistication is obvious, not only in the selection of shops and boutiques at Bellagio, but also in the overall design and layout of the shops themselves. Like everything else at Bellagio, the shopping experience is aimed at a discriminating and upscale audience.

An Old World *porte cochère* leads the way to the elegant Via Bellagio promenade where you'll find the following shops and boutiques:

Chanel—A fashion and fine jewelry boutique offering the complete range of Chanel products, such as the Chanel Ready-to-Wear Collection designed by Karl Lagerfeld, handbags, accessories, shoes, and Chanel Beaute and Fragrances. The Chanel Fine Jewelry Boutique houses the complete collection of fine jewelry designs based on Mademoiselle Chanel's own artistic heritage and passion for jewelry.

Giorgio Armani—This boutique carries the Giorgio Armani Borgonuovo collections for men and women that include tailored clothes, dresses, sportswear, evening wear, and accessories. You'll also find the Giorgio Armani Neve (ski wear), Giorgio Armani Golf, and Giorgio Armani Sposa collections displayed here. Personal shopping appointments, professional wardrobe consultations in the privacy of your hotel room, expert alterations, and a multilingual staff are some of the added amenities available to shoppers.

Prada—Shoppers can choose from ready-to-wear accessories and footwear as well as the new line of Prada sports clothes offered at this boutique.

Tiffany & Co.—Modeled after Tiffany & Co.'s famous Fifth Avenue (New York) store, shoppers will find a full selection of Tiffany's classic merchandise, including fine and engagement jewelry and the jewelry designs of Elsa Peretti, Paloma Picasso, and Jean Schlumberger, plus watches and clocks, china, crystal, sterling silver flatware, stationery and writing instruments, fragrances, and personal accessories. Special services offered include personal shopping assistance, bridal and children's registries, repair and engraving services, and corporate sales services.

Moschino—Designer apparel, shoes, ties, and fragrances are among the offerings under the Moschino label.

Fred Leighton–The fine jewelry at this boutique includes a rare collection of diamonds, rubies, emeralds, and sapphires, plus estate and antique jewelry. The boutique offers items from the collection of the Duchess of Windsor, as well as works from the Art Deco period, including the jewels of Cartier, Van Cleef & Arpels, Mauboussin, Boucheron, and Belperron.

Hermés–This boutique features sportswear and leather goods from the popular French designer.

Gucci–This shop offers Gucci's trademark handbags, luggage, small leather goods, shoes, ties and scarves, women's and men's clothing, watches, household items, jewelry, eyeglasses, and perfumes.

In addition to the boutiques and shops you'll find along the Via Bellagio promenade, other shops within the resort include:

- Lobby Shops–Here you'll find a selection of designer accessories.
- D. Fine–A men's clothing shop.
- Tutto–Bellagio merchandise, gifts, and sundries are sold here.
- The Cirque du Soleil Store–A wide selection of souvenirs from one of Las Vegas's most popular shows is available here, including the soundtrack from the show, clothing items, and other unique gifts.
- Capri–A selection of swim and active wear are offered at this shop.
- Tesorini–A fine jewelry and watches boutique.
- Bellagio Gallery of Fine Art Store–Art posters, note cards, and other gift items are available here, many based on works of art displayed in the gallery itself.

A free monorail runs from the Bellagio to the Monte Carlo. As with all of the Las Vegas resorts along the Strip, a taxi stand can also be found at the resort's main entrance.

Banquet, Function, and Convention Services

Information: (888) 744-7687

www.planitonline.com

If you're looking to hold a meeting, function, banquet, or other special event for a large or small group, the Bellagio offers a full range of function

facilities and amenities, plus the personalized support you need to plan an event and make it successful.

Wedding Chapels

Information: (888) 987-3344 or (702) 693-7700

Although Bellagio is one of the Strip's newer resorts, its romantic setting has already made it a popular place for couples to get engaged, married, and/or to honeymoon. Bellagio offers two wedding chapels and a wide range of wedding packages, starting at around $1,000. There is, however, a $2,500 minimum fee for weddings (which can include florals and photography).

The basic wedding package at the Bellagio would be considered a deluxe package for most other resorts. It includes 90 minutes of chapel time, an officiant, personalized ceremony video, a bottle of champagne and chocolates, a Bellagio wedding certificate, a wedding gift box with traveling case, a wedding music CD, limousine service to the court house, the services of a personal wedding coordinator, use of a bridal dressing room, rehearsal time, and one-day passes for two to the spa.

Caesars Palace

Theme: Ancient Rome

Room Rate: $$ / $$$ ($51–$250)

Number of Rooms: 2,454 deluxe rooms and suites

Casino: 129,750 square feet (divided into three main casino areas), featuring nearly two thousand slot and video poker machines, over one hundred table games (roulette, craps, blackjack, stud poker, Big Six, Let It Ride, baccarat, Pai Gow, live poker, and Caribbean Stud poker), a keno lounge, and a race and sports book

Dining: Six fine-dining restaurants and several casual restaurants. There are also a handful of dining options within the Forum Shops (including Spago, the Cheesecake Factory, and Planet Hollywood).

Primary Show: *Caesars Magical Empire* dinner show

Special Attractions: Omnimax Theatre, the Spa at Caesars Palace, Venus: The Salon, wedding chapel, the Forum Shops

Reservations: (800) 634-6661

Web Site: *www.caesars.com*

Address: 3570 Las Vegas Boulevard South
Las Vegas, NV 89101

Overall Resort Rating Based on Amenities and Rates

Ages Up to 5	Ages 6–15	Ages 16–20	Ages 21 & Up	Senior Citizens
⚁⚁	⚁⚂	⚁⚂	⚁⚂	⚁⚂

Caesars Palace is among the largest, most fairly priced, and nicest mega-resorts on the Strip. It's also one of the classic Las Vegas landmarks, having been open since August 1966. Catering to just about

everyone, this resort property offers the finest of casinos, plenty of dining options, shopping at one of the most successful and classiest malls in the entire world, tennis, swimming, a full-service spa, comfortable rooms and suites, plus plenty of entertainment-oriented activities.

Whether you're traveling on business or for pleasure, Caesars Palace provides virtually all of the amenities and services you could ask for, yet the room rates aren't overpriced. This is definitely one of the most popular mega-resort properties on the Strip, with over 28 million visitors each year. In fact, the resort has been featured in at least 13 major motion pictures and 70 television programs.

Caesars Palace contains 10 "fantasy suites"—two-story, four-bedroom apartments that are decorated in Roman, Egyptian, or Pompeiian styles. The suites were created in 1984 at a cost of over $1.25 million each. They are usually reserved for VIPs, however, when occasionally made available (usually to honeymooners with a large budget), guests can stay in one of these suites for a mere $3,000 (or more) a night.

Guest Room Accommodations

Many of the 2,400 guest rooms and suites in Caesars Palace offer Roman tubs or whirlpool baths, regally draped beds, cable television (with pay-per-view movies), armoires, irons and ironing boards, hair dryers, in-room safes, and telephone voice mail as standard amenities.

The Palace Tower superior deluxe rooms and Palace Tower petite suites, for example, are 550 to 750 square feet each and are equipped with four phone lines (two voice lines, a data line, and a fax line), plus a handful of additional amenities designed to add comfort and luxury to a guest's stay.

Caesars Palace also offers suites with private dining rooms, spacious parlors, wet bars, in-room saunas and steam rooms, whirlpool tubs, and complete home entertainment systems. For the extra fancy suites, you can expect to pay at lease $500 a night.

All guest rooms and suites are available with one king-size bed or two queen-size beds. In late 1997, all the guest rooms underwent a $495 million renovation, which brought the property up to date, allowing it to compete with the new and ultra-modern mega-resorts.

Fine Dining

With six fine-dining restaurants in the resort itself, plus a handful of additional restaurants within the adjoining shopping area (the Forum Shops), visitors to Caesars Palace have a nice selection of dining options. Reservations are recommended for the fine-dining restaurants.

Hyakumi Restaurant and Sushi Bar ($$$)

Reservations: Strongly recommended, call (702) 731-7731

In English, Hyakumi means *one hundred tastes*, which is exactly what you can expect when you dine at this Japanese restaurant that offers both traditional and contemporary favorites. Seating is available in the Teppanyaki section (where a chef will prepare your dinner at a tableside grill), or the regular dining room (which offers an a la carte menu). There's also a full sushi bar that overlooks the casino.

The restaurant is open for dinner only on Tuesday through Saturday nights. Jackets are considered optional but preferred for gentlemen.

Palace Court ($$$)

Reservations: Strongly recommended, call (702) 731-7731

A la carte French cuisine is the specialty of the house. This is one of the most honored restaurants in the state of Nevada. Jackets are required for gentlemen. Open for dinner only on Thursday through Monday nights.

Bacchanal ($$$)

Reservations: Strongly recommended, call (702) 731-7731

Named after Bacchus, the Roman god of wine and festivities, the Bacchanal offers a six-course *prix fixe* medley of continental cuisine. Wine "goddesses" pour three wines from shoulder height as you're entertained by belly dancers swaying around a misty central pool.

You'll need at least two full hours for this unique dining experience. Open for dinner only, Tuesday through Saturday. Dinner seatings are at 6:00, 6:30, 9:00, and 9:30 P.M. only.

Don't be surprised if you see Caesar and Cleopatra roaming around the public areas of Caesars Palace. These costumed characters are just one of the features that add ambiance to the whole ancient-Roman motif.

$ = entrees under $10; $$ = under $20; $$$ = over $20

Empress Court ($$$)

Reservations: Strongly recommended, call (702) 731-7731

Overlooking the spectacular Garden of the Gods swimming pools and gardens, the Empress Court was inspired by dining destinations in Hong Kong. Order a la carte, or select one of two multicourse meals. The menu spotlights varied Asian fare, including Malay, Thai, and Indonesian delicacies. Giant freshwater and saltwater aquariums hold daily seafood shipments that often include live rock cod, Dungeness crab, and lobster. Jackets are suggested for gentlemen. Open for dinner only, Thursday through Monday.

Neros ($$$)

Reservations: Recommended, call (702) 731-7731

An a la carte selection of prime steaks aged to perfection, fresh seafood (flown in daily), lamb, chicken, and veal spotlight the talents of Nero's master chef, Mario Capone, and his talented culinary team.

Neros serves dinner seven nights weekly. Suggested attire: country club casual (dress shorts acceptable May through September only).

Terrazza ($$$)

Reservations: Recommended, call (702) 731-7731

Terrazza (pronounced tear-ahtz-ah) is the name of the 220-seat restaurant and lounge in the Garden of the Gods pool area. Italian for *terrace*, Terrazza is located on the pool level, at the juncture of the Roman Tower and the Palace Tower. The dining room features country rustic Italian cuisine.

The dining facility features an exhibition kitchen, plus a wood burning, brick pizza oven and both interior dining and dining alfresco on a poolside terrace.

Open for dinner only, Terrazza's glass-enclosed pavilion offers a full view of the pool and gardens. Terrazza's plush lounge features live jazz trios Wednesday through Sunday evenings.

If you're looking for a delicious yet casual meal, check out the Stage Deli for a wide assortment of extra-large sandwiches. The dining room itself is rather crowded, but the food is excellent and not too expensive. Planet Hollywood also offers an excellent theme-oriented, family-dining experience.

$ = entrees under $10; $$ = under $20; $$$ = over $20

Casual Dining

La Plazza ($ / $$)

This food court offers nine outlets: an international bakery (which serves flaky croissants and freshly baked cinnamon rolls); a New York–style deli; the American Grill; a pasta and pizza stop; Chinese, Japanese, and Mexican eateries; a salad bar; and an ice cream fountain.

Café Roma ($)

Open 24 hours and overlooking the Palace Casino, Café Roma offers the ambiance of an eclectic, New York–style eatery. It's the kind of place where you can get chicken soup with matzo balls, Japanese miso, Spanish gazpacho, a juicy hamburger, beer, and American breakfast favorites. Complete dinners (with selections from fish to beef to chicken) are also available, as is a buffet breakfast, lunch, or dinner.

24-hour room service is available to all hotel guests.

Palatium ($)

The Palatium buffet offers an array of fresh salads, bread, vegetables, fine meats, hot entrees, and luscious desserts. Offering a double-line food service center, two carving stations, two dessert islands, and two frozen yogurt sundae buffets, there's enough food here to feed the entire Roman empire (or a bunch of hungry vacationers). The buffet offers separate breakfast, lunch, and dinner menus on Monday through Friday, with special brunch menus on weekends and holidays. A champagne brunch is offered every Saturday and Sunday. Selected ethnic themes highlight the dinner menu.

Special Attractions

With entertainment experiences for the entire family, Caesars Palace truly is a full-service, world-class resort designed to keep visitors entertained throughout their stay. Even if you're not staying at this resort, many of the attractions and activities are open to the general public and are well worth experiencing. For example, if you enjoy shopping, the Forum Shops is one of the most popular malls in the world. If you want to relax and be pampered, there's no better place than the Spa at Caesars Palace, one of the best world-class spas located on the Strip.

$ = entrees under $10; $$ = under $20; $$$ = over $20

The following are some of the major attractions offered at this resort complex:

Omnimax Movie Theatre

Show Times: Ongoing

Information: (800) 445-4544 or (702) 731-7900

Offering an ever changing lineup of movies (shown throughout the day and evening), the Omnimax Theater provides a spectacular, "you are there" movie-going experience. Playing only 70-mm Omnimax movies, the screen is 57 feet high and is accompanied by a sound system with 89 speakers. The typical Omnimax movie lasts 45 to 60 minutes. Most movies are suitable for people of all ages, however, certain documentaries are more suited for older viewers.

Caesars Magical Empire

Ticket Price: $75.50 per person

Show/Dinner Times: Seatings begin at 4:40 P.M., with the last one at 10:00 P.M. (Tuesday through Saturday)

Tickets and information: (702) 731-7333 or (800) 445-4544

Get ready for an evening of mystery and fun that's unlike anything you'll experience at another Las Vegas resort. This is a full evening of dining and entertainment, all for one price.

Caesars Magical Empire presents mystery, fine dining, and grand-scale illusions, all reminiscent of Caesar's world two thousand years ago. Enter through the Celestial Court—the gateway to this enchanting new world. Your adventure begins in the Chamber of Destiny, where the story of Caesars Magical Empire is told as you experience an environmental illusion that takes you along an underground catacomb.

You'll then be guided through the catacomb maze, past intriguing artifacts and through mysterious doorways to one of 10 dining chambers of the gods. Here a sumptuous three-course meal is served to the 24 chamber guests in a group dining experience.

Once you've finished dining, visitors are free to explore the many dazzling attractions in Caesars Magical Empire. The center court, Sanctum Secorum, is

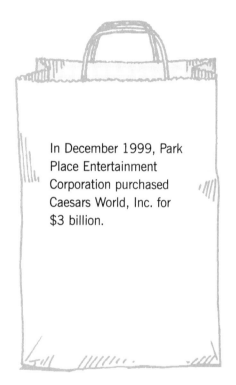

In December 1999, Park Place Entertainment Corporation purchased Caesars World, Inc. for $3 billion.

home to many environmental illusions, plus the Luminaria show (a combination of sound, light, and dancing fire).

Adjoining the Sanctum Secorum is a pair of elegant lounges. The Grotto Bar lies inside a cavelike demon's mouth, and the Spirit Bar is nestled between two seance rooms. The two live-entertainment theaters emphasize audience participation.

The Secret Pagoda is an intimate 75-seat theater featuring masters of "close-up" magic. The opulent Sultan's Palace theater, which seats 150, headlines top prestidigitators and their startling illusions.

After you have been charmed by all the wonders of Caesars Magical Empire, pass through the Infinity Hallway—a final phantasm that transports you back to modern reality.

Caesars Magical Empire

Ages Up to 5	Ages 6–15	Ages 16–20	Ages 21 & Up	Senior Citizens
Not Admitted	⚀ ⚁	⚀ ⚁ ⚂	⚀ ⚁	⚀ ⚁

Race for Atlantis

Box Office: (888) 910-RACE or (702) 733-9000

Hours: 10:00 A.M. to 11:00 P.M. (Sunday through Thursday)
10:00 A.M. to midnight (Friday and Saturday)

Ticket Prices: $9.50 (adults), $8.50 (seniors), $8 (students and Nevada residents), and $6.75 (children). Visitors can experience this attraction a second time (on the same day) for an extra $4.50.

Located within the Forum Shops is Race for Atlantis, the world's first giant-screen (82 feet in diameter) IMAX 3-D motion simulator ride. Passengers are "chosen by the gods" to race against a fierce field of competitors—including Neptune, the reigning monarch, and Ghastlius, champion of evil—in a flight to the finish that will determine the ruler of Atlantis for the next millennium.

Passengers are seat-belted into four 27-seat motion simulators that thrust riders six degrees in any direction. Each guest is provided an electronic headset equipped with the IMAX "personal sound environment" system and liquid crystal shutters that synchronize with IMAX's proprietary

The Premium Adventure Pack allows people to experience five Las Vegas rides and attractions for $37.95, a savings of $14. Attractions include Race for Atlantis, *Star Trek: The Experience* (at the Las Vegas Hilton), the Big Shot (Stratosphere thrill ride), the High Roller (Stratosphere roller coaster), and the Celebrity Encounter (at the Venetian). This is an excellent deal for young people looking to experience a full day of entertaining rides and attractions. Transportation to and from each of these attractions, however, isn't provided.

3-D projection technology. The marriage of IMAX's large-format filmmaking with state-of-the-art computer animation is the key to the ride-film's extraordinary clarity.

The adventure begins with a video introduction by actor Michael Geeter and continues with a four and a half minute ride. Cutting-edge sound engineering and high-tech motion simulation equipment combine to immerse the riders in a multisensory experience that brings the mythical kingdom of Atlantis to life.

Warning: Race for Atlantis is a fast-paced thrill ride. Anyone with back problems, a heart condition, who is pregnant, or suffering from any other physical disability should avoid this ride.

Tickets are available for same-day purchase (no advance reservations needed) at Caesars Palace box offices and at the Race for Atlantis box office. Although the ride can accommodate 1,000 riders an hour, be prepared for waits up to one hour (or more) during peak periods. The busiest time to see this attraction is immediately after the Festival Fountain Show finishes.

Special discount offers are available that allow you to experience Race for Atlantis plus one or more of the Strip's other rides and attractions, such as *Star Trek:* The Experience, which is at the Las Vegas Hilton. Check with the box office for details before purchasing your ticket.

If you're looking for a refreshing snack, the Dippie Dots Ice Cream stand located in the lobby area of Race for Atlantis offers a unique treat in a variety of flavors.

In addition to the fitness center and spa, Caesar Palace guests can enjoy the resort's Garden of the Gods, a lavishly landscaped 4.5 acre area that includes three swimming pools, two outdoor whirlpools, and six tennis courts.

Race for Atlantis

Ages Up to 5	Ages 6–15	Ages 16–20	Ages 21 & Up	Senior Citizens
Not Suitable	⚀⚁⚂	⚀⚁⚂	⚀⚁⚂	⚀⚁

Spa, Health Club, and Salon

The Spa at Caesars Palace

Hours: 6:00 A.M. to 8:00 P.M. (daily)

Appointments: (702) 731-7791

This world-class spa offers 28 treatment rooms and a staff of professionals trained to offer a wide range of massages (reflexology, Shiatsu, and Swedish) and other therapeutic treatments. Moor mud baths, seaweed body masks, sea salt treatments, and loofahs are just some of the services offered. All treatments should be scheduled in advance.

In addition to offering individualized treatments, the spa features eucalyptus scented saunas and steam rooms, hydrotherapy treatment baths, a Zen meditation/relaxation chamber, a television lounge, and a juice bar.

Venus: The Salon at Caesars Palace

Hours: 8:00 A.M. to 8:00 P.M. (daily)

Appointments: (702) 731-7791

Hair stylists, makeup artists, and other professionals are available to provide a wide range of services in a luxurious and state-of-the-art facility. Makeup lessons, makeovers, and waxing services are available. Appointments should be made in advance.

Fitness Center

Hours: 6:00 A.M. to 8:00 P.M. (daily)

In conjunction with the many services offered at the Spa, guests of Caesars Palace can enjoy the resort's 6,500-square-foot fitness center, which offers stationary bikes and stair steppers, along with a variety of weight machines and other high-tech fitness equipment. There's also a rock-climbing treadmill. Personal trainers are available for individualized fitness guidance.

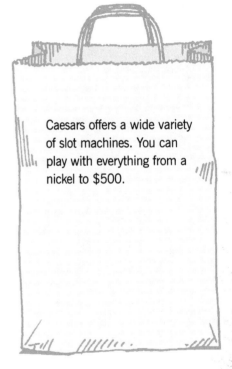

Caesars offers a wide variety of slot machines. You can play with everything from a nickel to $500.

As a member of Caesars Emperors Club, you'll be able to earn points redeemable for cash above and beyond any money you win in the casino. When you play the slots, simply slip your membership card into a scanner mounted on the side of your slot machine. It's good on all slot machines, from quarters on up to $500, reel and video machines alike, including video blackjack, video keno, and video poker. Be sure to request a free membership card when you check into the hotel, or contact the information desk within the casino for details.

Casino

Several of the finest casinos in Las Vegas are found in Caesars Palace. The Palace Casino features 8 craps tables, 25 blackjack tables, 7 roulette tables, 5 baccarat tables, 2 mini-baccarat tables, 665 slot machines, 2 Pai Gow poker tables, and a keno lounge.

Caesars Palace's second main casino offers a race and sports book, 4 craps tables, 26 blackjack tables, 2 Caribbean Stud poker tables, 2 Let It Ride tables, 1 casino war table, 1 Spanish 21 table, 5 roulette tables, 1,167 slot machines, 1 Big Six game (played like *Wheel of Fortune*), and 1 Pai Gow poker table.

The smaller Palace Court casino area contains three blackjack tables, a roulette table, and three baccarat tables, and the Forum Shops casino area contains 102 slot machines.

Since Caesars' casinos cater in part to an upscale clientele, many of the table games require high minimum wagers. The slot machines range from nickel slots to $500 a spin. If you're looking to place small bets at the table games, you may have to search the casinos a bit. Caesars Palace is also known for its live poker, where players go against each other rather than the "house."

Shopping

When it comes to shopping, Caesars Palace offers one of the most exciting and upscale shopping experiences in the world. Between the Forum Shops and the Appian Way shops, you'll find a wide range of specialty shops, boutiques, and restaurants. Exploring the Forum Shops alone can take a half day or a complete evening.

The Appian Way

Hours: 10:00 A.M. to 11:00 P.M. (Sunday through Thursday)
10 A.M. to midnight (Friday and Saturday; some establishments open later)

Within the actual Caesars Palace resort is a shopping promenade known as the Appian Way. This shopping area is distinctive for its corridors of imported fine marble and its giant statue of David, an exact replica of Michelangelo's masterpiece. Here you'll find the following upscale shops, boutiques, and restaurants:

- Ancient Creations (rare coins and unique jewelry)
- Art in Crystal
- Bernini Couture (fine apparel)
- Brittany & Company
- Caesars Exclusively!
- Carina
- Cartier
- Ciro
- Colosseum Cigars
- Cuzzens
- Emperors Essentials (sundries)
- Galerie Michelangelo
- Godiva Chocolatier (gourmet chocolates)
- Oculus (fine opticians, designer eyewear)
- Paradiso (designer swimwear and lingerie boutique)
- Paul & Shark Yachting
- Piazza del Mercato (fine resort apparel and gifts)

The Forum Shops

Information: (702) 893-4300

Hours: 10:00 A.M. to 11:00 P.M. (Sunday through Thursday) 10 A.M. to midnight (Friday and Saturday; some establishments open later)

You'll find more than one hundred upscale merchants and restaurants in the Forum Shops at Caesars. These include such high-fashion boutiques as Gucci, Bernini, Versace, and Guess, plus unique specialty shops such as Caesars Exclusively, Magic Masters, Just for Feet, and more. You'll also find world-class restaurants, like Spago and the Palm.

This shopping mall routinely welcomes more than fifty thousand people a day, while holiday visitor volume often exceeds seventy thousand shoppers in a single day, making this one of the most successful and popular malls in the world.

Within the Forum Shops is a synchronized Festival Fountain show featuring animated statues, lighting effects, and "dancing" water fountains. This is a free show, held hourly throughout the day and evening. There's also a 50,000 gallon saltwater aquarium within the mall. On weekend afternoons a marine biologist and a scuba-diving aquarist gather visitors and describe the marine life in the aquarium.

Experience the Forum Shops from home by checking out the Mall's Web site at www.shopcaesars.com. Online shopping is available.

The Forum Shops

- A/X Armani
- Abercrombie & Fitch
- Alfred Dunhill
- Allstate Ticketing & Tours
- Amen Wardy (home collections)
- Animal Crackers
- Ann Taylor
- Antiquities
- Avventura
- Banana Republic
- Bank of America ATM / Cash
- Bath & Body at Home
- Bebe
- Bernini
- Bernini Collections
- Bertolini's
- Beyond the Beach
- Brookstone
- Bvlgari
- Cache
- Caesars World
- Caviarteria
- Chinois (a Wolfgang Puck restaurant)
- Cheesecake Factory
- Chocolate Chariot
- Christian Dior
- Cinema Ride
- Crystal Galleria
- Cuzzens
- Cyber Station
- Davante
- Diesel
- The Disney Store
- DKNY

- El Portal
- El Portal Luggage
- Emporio Armani
- Endangered Species
- Escada
- Estée Lauder
- Express
- FAO Schwarz
- Fendi
- Field of Dreams
- Footworks
- Foto Forum
- Fred Joaillier
- Galerie Lassen
- Galleria di Sorrento
- Gap/Gap Kids
- Gianni Versace
- Gucci
- Guess
- Hugo Boss
- Hyde Park Jewelers
- Ice Accessories
- Images by Crazy Shirts
- Just for Feet
- Kenneth Cole
- Kids Kastle
- The Knot Shop
- La Coste
- Lalique
- La Salsa
- Louis Vuitton
- M.J. Christensen Jewelers
- Magic Masters
- Magnet Maximus
- Max Mara
- The Museum Company
- N. Landau Hyman

- Niketown
- Opals & Gems
- The Palm Restaurant
- Planet Hollywood
- Planet Hollywood Superstore
- Polo/Ralph Lauren
- Porsche Design
- Roman Times
- Rose of Sharon (size 14 & up)
- Salvatore
- Shauna Stein
- Shooz at the Forum
- Sloane's Lingerie
- Spago
- Sports Logo
- St. John Knits
- Stage Deli
- Structure
- Stuart Weitzman
- Sunglass Hut
- Swatch Store
- Sweet Factory
- Swensen's Ice Cream
- Valet
- Vasari
- Versace Jeans Couture
- Via Veneto
- Victoria's Secret
- Victoria's Secret Bath and Fragrance
- Virgin Megastore
- Warner Brothers Studio Store
- West of Santa Fe
- Zero Gravity

Business Center

Business travelers will find a wide range of services available to them at the Business Center, including fax machines, copiers, and the ability to ship packages via UPS or FedEx. The concierge staff is also available to assist with many types of business related needs.

Banquet, Function, and Convention Services

As you'd expect from any world-class resort, especially one in Las Vegas, Caesars Palace offers a wide range of meeting rooms, banquet facilities, convention areas, and ballrooms, plus services and support personnel capable of managing virtually any type of event, large or small.

The Colosseum Complex is the resort's original conference facility, while the newer Palace Tower Convention Area features over 110,000 square feet of additional conference space that can be subdivided to accommodate groups of 10 to 5,000.

Wedding Chapel

Information/Reservations: (702) 731-7422

The elegant Neptune's Villa Wedding Chapel opened in 1998 and offers wedding ceremonies and packages ranging in price from $775 to several thousand dollars, depending on the services you request. Bridal consultants, photography packages, floral packages, live music, and even having Caesar and Cleopatra (with members of their royal court) attend your wedding are all available options. In addition to the chapel, larger ceremonies (up to two thousand guests) can be held in the resort's ballrooms.

Circus Circus

Theme:	A circus big top
Room Rate:	$$ ($51–$100)
Number of Rooms:	3,770 rooms (all renovated in 1998) plus 130 suites
Casino:	101,286 square feet, featuring 2,220 slot machines (including video poker, keno, and 21), 52 blackjack tables, 4 craps tables, 7 roulette tables, 1 Big Six game, 4 Pai Gow poker tables, 1 Caribbean Stud poker table, 2 Let It Ride games, 1 casino war game, and 10 poker tables. There's also a keno lounge and a race and sports book.
Dining:	Six restaurants, a food court, and six bars/lounges
Primary Show:	Ongoing free circus acts
Special Attractions:	The Adventuredome, the Midway Stage
Reservations:	(800) 444-CIRCUS or (702) 734-0410
Web Site:	*www.circuscircus-lasvegas.com*
Address:	2880 Las Vegas Boulevard South Las Vegas, NV 89109

Driving to Circus Circus? The resort offers plenty of free parking (5,719 parking spaces) as well as valet parking.

Overall Resort Rating Based on Amenities and Rates

Ages Up to 5	Ages 6–15	Ages 16–20	Ages 21 & Up	Senior Citizens
⚁⚁	⚁⚁⚂	⚁⚂⚃	⚁⚁	⚀

Since opening October 18, 1968, Circus Circus has been the ideal resort for families visiting Las Vegas. It was the first to cater to couples traveling with young children and teens—not just to business travelers, adult vacationers, and gamblers.

While this resort offers a full casino and other amenities you'd expect from a casino and resort in Las Vegas, it also caters to younger guests with a wide range of activities. From the indoor theme park (Adventuredome) and the arcade to the continuous circus acts, Circus Circus offers guests (both young and old) plenty to see and do. Over the years, Circus Circus has continued to expand. The latest round of renovations (completed in 1998) ensured that all of the older guest rooms and facilities were brought up to date.

Circus Circus continues to be one of the least expensive resorts along the Strip and is ideal for budget travelers or those looking for a casino and resort that offers a fun-filled atmosphere for the young at heart.

Guest Room Accommodations

Circus Circus is divided into multiple towers and contains a total of 3,770 guest rooms and 130 suites. The Casino Tower is a 15-story building with 773 guest rooms. This tower is located in the center of the Circus Circus property and features two casinos, a race and sports book, the circus arena, a carnival midway, video game arcade, multiple dining facilities, a wedding chapel, and retail shops. Located above the main casino in this tower is the Midway Stage, which is the largest permanent circus big top in the world.

The 29-story Skyrise Tower contains 1,188 guest rooms, its own casino and pool, and an indoor connection to the resort's shopping promenade. The West Tower is the resort's newest building. The 35-story tower contains 999 guest rooms. Circus Circus Manor is a set of five three-story buildings with 810 guest rooms, a pool, and its own parking lot. The Manor is considered the resort's "budget area."

The basic guest rooms at Circus Circus are 460 square feet and offer air conditioning, a color television (with cable TV and pay channels), direct dial telephones, and 24-hour room service. Nonsmoking and wheelchair accessible rooms are available upon request. As mentioned earlier, Circus Circus is one of the Strip's more affordable resorts. The rooms don't offer many of the luxuries of other resorts located along the Strip, but the rooms are comfortable, clean, and available with one king-size or two double beds.

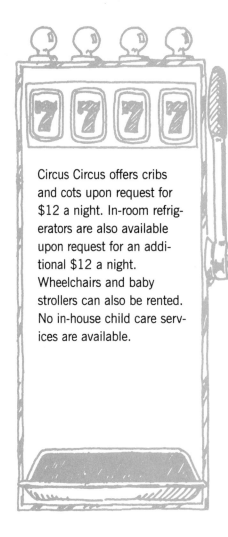

Circus Circus offers cribs and cots upon request for $12 a night. In-room refrigerators are also available upon request for an additional $12 a night. Wheelchairs and baby strollers can also be rented. No in-house child care services are available.

If you're an RV owner, consider parking your vehicle at Circusland Recreational Vehicle Park—the only park of its kind located along the Las Vegas Strip. This area features 399 spaces with full hookups, pool, general store, video game arcade, and a self-service, coin-operated laundromat available 24 hours a day. Guests of Circusland are given full access to all Circus Circus amenities and facilities.

The Skyrise Tower and West Tower guest rooms are decorated in rich tones of deep purple, green, dark blue, or rust. The Casino Tower rooms are decorated in earth tones with a renaissance flair. All of the tower rooms have European-style furniture. The Manor rooms are decorated in bright circus colors. All rooms have a bathtub/shower combination (with the exception of wheelchair accessible rooms which offer roll-in showers).

Eating under the Big Top

Circus Circus features a few fine-dining restaurants, such as the Steak House and Stivali Italian Ristorante; however, the majority of the eating establishments at this resort offer casual and affordable dining experiences suitable for the entire family. In addition to the restaurants, Circus Circus has several bars and lounges that cater to adult guests.

The Steak House ($$ / $$$)

Reservations: Required, call (702) 794-3767

Ranked as one of the top steakhouses in Las Vegas, this fine-dining restaurant serves the best quality Midwestern beef, aged to perfection in a glass enclosed aging room, showcased in the seating area of the dining room. Prime cuts are then prepared for all to see over an exhibition-style, open-hearth mesquite charcoal broiler. The portions are plentiful.

The Steak House is open daily for dinner from 5:00 P.M. to midnight. On Sunday, a champagne brunch is served during three separate seatings (9:30 A.M., 11:30 A.M., and 12:30 P.M.). Reservations for dinner or brunch are required. The dress code is casual, and the average meal cost is about $25 per person.

Stivali Italian Ristorante ($$ / $$$)

Reservations: Strongly recommended, call (702) 691-5820

In 1997, Circus Circus opened this fine Italian restaurant, which rivals the Steak House in terms of food quality and topnotch service. During the restaurant's first year in operation, it won the *Las Vegas Review-Journal* reader's poll for "Best Italian Restaurant."

$ = entrees under $10; $$ = under $20; $$$ = over $20

The menu includes many classic Italian dishes, plus some of the chef's personal favorites like stuffed portabella mushrooms filled with bay shrimp, imported cheeses, and seasoned bread crumbs. There is also a large selection of pizzas and the restaurant's specialty, called Pizzette, which is a pizza appetizer.

Stivali Italian Ristorante is open Sunday through Thursday, from 5:00 to 11:00 P.M., and Saturday and Sunday from 5:00 P.M. to midnight. Monday through Friday, between 3:00 and 5:00 P.M., the restaurant offers "Take of Stivali," during which free appetizers and drink specials are served. Reservations for dinner are strongly recommended. The dress code is casual.

Circus Buffet ($)

Reservations: Not accepted

With a dining room that seats over a thousand people, the Circus Buffet serves over ten thousand customers daily. Enjoy this inexpensive, all-you-can-eat extravaganza, which recently underwent a $9.5 million renovation. A large selection of entrees is offered during every meal period. The buffet is open Monday through Friday for breakfast (6:00 to 11:30 A.M.), lunch (noon to 4:00 P.M.), and dinner (4:30 to 11:00 P.M.). On weekends, a brunch is served from 6:00 A.M. to 4:00 P.M. Seating is on a first-come basis.

Promenade Cafe ($ / $$)

Enjoy a large selection of American dishes at this 24-hour restaurant.

The Pink Pony ($ / $$)

This cafe, located near the main casino and under the big top, is open 24 hours a day. Every evening (after 5:00 P.M.), a Chinese menu is also available.

Pizzeria ($)

Freshly baked pizzas, calzones, and salads are the specialty of this casual restaurant. Open every day from 11:00 A.M. to midnight, this is a great (and affordable) place to bring the entire family for lunch or dinner.

Sorry, but like all of the resorts located along the Strip, Circus Circus does not allow pets to stay in the guestrooms. The Animal Inn Pet Kennel (702-736-0036) is one of the local area kennels.

$ = entrees under $10; $$ = under $20; $$$ = over $20

Snack Bars ($)

For a light snack or a quick meal, check out the various fast-food establishments in the Circus Circus complex, including the Westside Deli, Skyrise Deli, McDonald's, and the Adventuredome Snack Bar. These places are inexpensive and offer table service (or nearby seating).

Bars and Lounges

If you're looking for a light snack or want to enjoy a drink, Circus Circus has six bars and lounges. Some offer live entertainment, while others feature TV screens to watch sporting events. Several of these bars and lounges simply offer a friendly atmosphere to enjoy a drink with friends, relatives, business associates, or loved ones. Your choices include the Sports Bar, West Casino Bar, Steak House Bar, Stivali Bar, Skyrise Lounge, and the Horse-A-Round Bar. Hours of operation vary. All of these bars and lounges offer full bar service with counter, booth, or table seating.

Special Attractions

Circus Circus has several entertainment areas designed for the entire family. The Adventuredome is an indoor theme park, complete with rides and attractions, while the Midway area combines traditional carnival-style games with state-of-the-art arcade games. Throughout these areas, clowns, jugglers, mimes, and magicians wander around entertaining guests.

The Adventuredome

For recorded information, call (702) 836-6617

This $90 million indoor theme park opened in 1993 and is ranked among the top 25 most popular theme parks in North America. In its first five years, over ten million people experienced the Adventuredome's rides and attractions. When driving along the Strip, it's impossible to miss seeing the Adventuredome. Its five-acre glass dome is over one hundred fifty feet high, so there's plenty of room for the park's thrill rides.

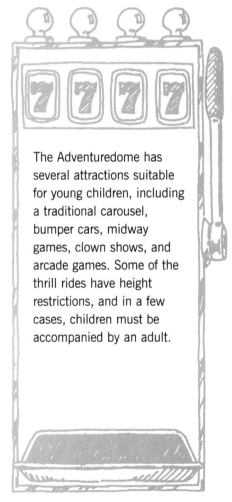

The Adventuredome has several attractions suitable for young children, including a traditional carousel, bumper cars, midway games, clown shows, and arcade games. Some of the thrill rides have height restrictions, and in a few cases, children must be accompanied by an adult.

$ = entrees under $10; $$ = under $20; $$$ = over $20

Set in a Grand Canyon–styled motif, the theme park is open every day of the year. Since it's indoors (unlike the theme park at the MGM Grand), weather has no impact on a guest's ability to enjoy a fun-filled day on the rides. It's always a comfortable 72 degrees.

The Adventuredome is open Monday through Thursday, from 10:00 A.M. to 6:00 P.M., Friday and Saturday from 10:00 A.M. to midnight, and Sunday from 10:00 A.M. to 8:00 P.M. Admission to the park is free (including its shows), but each ride costs between $2 and $5. You can buy a one-day pass and experience all the rides, as often as you wish for $12.95 for kids and $16.95 for adults.

The Adventuredome features the following attractions:

The Canyon Blaster—The world's largest indoor, double-loop, double-corkscrew roller coaster awaits you in the Adventuredome! Travel at speeds up to 55 miles per hour and experience both positive and negative G-forces before the 1 minute and 45 second ride comes to an end. (Riders must be at least 48 inches tall.)

The Canyon Blaster

Ages Up to 5	Ages 6–15*	Ages 16–20	Ages 21 & Up	Senior Citizens
Not Suitable	⚀ ⚁ ⚂	⚀ ⚁ ⚂	⚀ ⚁ ⚂	Not Suitable

Must be over 48" tall

The Rim Runner—Enjoy this wet and wild boat ride (water flume) that ends with a giant splash as you drop down a 60-foot waterfall while traveling at over 40-feet-per-second. This is the most exciting ride in the Adventuredome. (Riders must be at least 48 inches tall.)

The Rim Runner

Ages Up to 5	Ages 6–15*	Ages 16–20	Ages 21 & Up	Senior Citizens
Not Suitable	⚀ ⚁ ⚂	⚀ ⚁ ⚂	⚀ ⚁ ⚂	Not Suitable

Must be over 48" tall

Fun House Express—This state-of-the-art IMAX motion simulator ride uses computer-generated images to portray a fun-filled roller coaster ride.

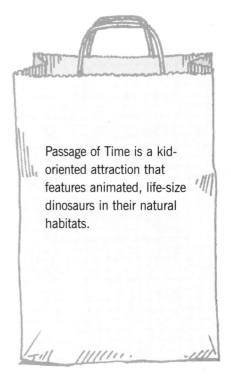

Passage of Time is a kid-oriented attraction that features animated, life-size dinosaurs in their natural habitats.

This ride is extremely turbulent, but much less intense than a traditional roller coaster ride that allows riders to experience actual drops or spin upside down. (Riders must be at least 42 inches tall.)

Fun House Express

Ages Up to 5	Ages 6–15*	Ages 16–20	Ages 21 & Up	Senior Citizens
Not Suitable	⚀ ⚁ ⚂	⚀ ⚁ ⚂	⚀ ⚁ ⚂	Not Suitable

Must be over 42" tall

Lazer Blast Laser Tag Arena—This 7,500 square-foot, black-lit arena is where people go head-to-head in laser tag battles. Guests are equipped with specially designed vests and laser guns. The red team and the green team battle one another for the highest individual and team score. Each game is five minutes long. The arena is filled with physical obstacles that provide hiding places and opportunities to launch surprise attacks or ambushes against opponents. (Participants must be at least 42 inches tall.)

Lazer Blast Laser Tag Arena

Ages Up to 5	Ages 6–15*	Ages 16–20	Ages 21 & Up	Senior Citizens
Not Suitable	⚀ ⚁ ⚂	⚀ ⚁	⚀ ⚁	Not Suitable

Must be over 42" tall

Road Runner—This is a mini Himalayan ride suitable for people of all ages.

Sand Pirates—This giant pirate ship swings back and forth across the Adventuredome giving riders a thrill. People who suffer from motion sickness should refrain from eating before experiencing this ride.

Xtreme Zone—This is one of the Adventuredome's newest attractions. It allows guests to experience wall climbing and a giant trampoline. The wall climb is suitable for beginners or advanced climbers.

Canyon Cars—Experience a traditional bumper cars ride.

Thunderbirds—This children's ride allows guests to fly around in circles in replicas of 1920s airplanes. (Only people over 33 inches and under 54 inches tall can ride Thunderbirds.)

Drifters—This traditional ferris wheel ride features cars shaped like hot air balloons and is suitable for people of all ages.

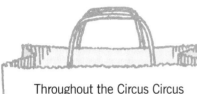

Throughout the Circus Circus resort, especially in the Midway area, don't be surprised if you run into clowns, mimes, jugglers, and magicians strolling throughout the property and entertaining guests day and night. Some clowns make balloon animals for passersby. Look for the Face Painting by Patches the Clown area where kids can have all kinds of designs painted on their faces.

BC Bus–This ride is designed for young people but open to everyone. It's a giant school bus that moves up, down, and around in circles. It's much less intense than the Sand Pirates ride.

Cliffhangers–This children's play area features tunnels to crawl through, balls to jump in, plus slides and nets to climb on. Sorry parents, this attraction is for kids only.

Miner Mike–Kids ride in coal bins along a track. It's a roller coaster designed for young people. (Only people over 33 inches and under 54 inches tall can ride Miner Mike.)

Inverter–A thrill ride for adults. Get ready to be inverted! Ride 50 feet into the air then flip 360 degrees.

Circus Carousel–Ride on the animal of your choice as you experience this classic carousel ride that is suitable for people of all ages.

Pikes Pass Miniature Golf Course–This 18-hole indoor miniature golf course offers a fun-filled activity for the entire family.

The Midway

The carnival-like atmosphere of Circus Circus comes alive in the Midway area, which contains over two hundred games and a state-of-the-art arcade. The Midway surrounds the world famous circus stage where free circus acts are performed every day, twice per hour, between 11:00 A.M. and midnight. Test your skills and try to win a prize at one of the many carnival games that cost $.50 to $2 each. (Some of the games offer small prizes to all kids who play.) The arcade games cost $.25 to $1 per play. Classic arcade games, like Ms. Pac-Man, are mixed with state-of-the-art arcade games.

If you get hungry while exploring the Midway, you'll find a McDonald's (look for those famous golden arches) near the circus stage area. Another option is the Horse-A-Round Bar, which looks like a carousel with booth seating.

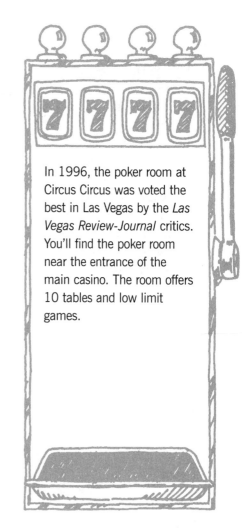

In 1996, the poker room at Circus Circus was voted the best in Las Vegas by the *Las Vegas Review-Journal* critics. You'll find the poker room near the entrance of the main casino. The room offers 10 tables and low limit games.

Pools

Circus Circus features three outdoor, heated swimming pools (with accompanying Jacuzzis). They are located behind the Manor building, at the RV park, and at the Skyrise Tower.

Circus Circus provides personal gaming lessons for guests who would like to improve their table game playing skills. Lessons are held in the main casino Monday through Friday (excluding holidays). Blackjack lessons are held at 10:30 A.M. and 3:00 P.M. Roulette lessons are at 11:00 A.M. Craps lessons are held at 11:30 A.M., and guests can participate in poker lessons at noon. All lessons are free of charge and open to guests 21 and over.

Unlike many resorts along the Strip, Circus Circus does not offer a spa or health club facility. There is, however, an independently owned and operated health club near the resort called the Sporting House; it is open to Circus Circus guests for a small daily fee.

Casino

While the kids are having fun at the Midway or Adventuredome, adults (over the age of 21) can try their luck in the casinos at Circus Circus. The resort offers three separate casinos containing a total of 2,220 slot machines (including video poker, keno and 21), 52 blackjack tables, 4 craps tables, 7 roulette tables, 1 Big Six game, 4 Pai Gow poker tables, 1 Caribbean Stud poker table, 2 Let It Ride games, 1 casino war game, and 10 poker tables. There's also a 160-seat keno lounge (on the main level of the Casino Tower), and a race and sports book.

The casino's race and sports book offers wagering on horse and greyhound racing as well as major sporting events. All races eligible for wagering are simulcast live from the tracks and shown on big-screen televisions. Sports fans can watch their favorite teams on one of the 14 television monitors. Fans can also keep up with sports results throughout the country via the sports book's electronic display board. This race and sports book is open from 8:30 A.M. until the last major event of the day.

Shopping

Keeping the carnival atmosphere alive, the shopping promenade at Circus Circus offers a fun-filled shopping experience that allows you to take some of the circus fun home with you in the form of souvenirs. The retail shops within Circus Circus include:

Exclusively Circus Circus—All kinds of adult and children's clothing imprinted with the famous Circus Circus logo is offered here. Mugs, glasses, postcards, and other souvenirs with the casino's logo are also available.

Circus Spirits—This is Circus Circus's in-house liquor store. It features a large selection of mini-liquor bottles, soft drinks, bottled water, milk, juices, snack food items, sundries, film, and tobacco products.

Circus Gifts—If you're looking for souvenirs that scream "Las Vegas," chances are you'll find them here. This shop is located in the Main Tower and offers Circus Circus items as well as other Las Vegas memorabilia.

Magnetized—Refrigerator magnet collectors will think they've died and gone to heaven when they see the selection of magnets—in every size and shape—offered at this shop.

Market Express—Find snack foods, newspapers, sundries, film, candy, soda, and bottled water at this convenience store, which is located in the Main Tower.

Circus Jewels—A large selection of jewelry is offered.

Under $10—For shoppers on a budget, check out this Under $10 store. Las Vegas souvenirs and other keepsakes are offered. As the name suggests, everything at this store is priced at $10 or less.

Photo Shop—One-hour film processing is offered here along with a large selection of film, camera accessories, and batteries. If you forget your camera, you can purchase one here as well.

Personalized—Souvenirs that are personalized with a name, date, or other sentimental message can be purchased here. Mugs, pictures, key chains, T-shirts, plates, and other items can be personalized in less than five minutes to create a one-of-a-kind keepsake or gift.

Houdini's—Amaze your friends and family members by performing a magic trick. Houdini's features hundreds of tricks that anyone can perform. Located along the promenade, this magic shop features ongoing magic demonstrations by professional magicians. Plan on spending some time watching these magic shows—they're entertaining and absolutely free. All tricks performed during the demonstrations can be purchased.

LYCNSPL8—All kinds of merchandise based on licensed cartoon characters is available here.

Gold Castle—This jewelry store, located in the Main Tower, specializes in fine karat gold jewelry.

Sweet Tooth—Ice cream and candy are the specialty of this shop that will satisfy anyone's sweet tooth. Ten different ice cream flavors are

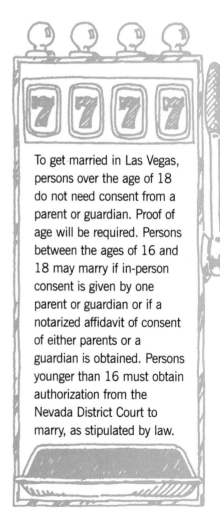

To get married in Las Vegas, persons over the age of 18 do not need consent from a parent or guardian. Proof of age will be required. Persons between the ages of 16 and 18 may marry if in-person consent is given by one parent or guardian or if a notarized affidavit of consent of either parents or a guardian is obtained. Persons younger than 16 must obtain authorization from the Nevada District Court to marry, as stipulated by law.

Don't forget to obtain a marriage license! Before getting married in Las Vegas, you must obtain a marriage license at the Clark County Courthouse (located at 200 South 3rd Street in Las Vegas). The courthouse is open Monday through Thursday from 8:00 A.M. to midnight. Starting Friday at 8:00 A.M., the courthouse is open continuously until midnight on Sunday. It's also open during all legal holidays. There is a $35 fee for this license. No blood tests are required, and there is no waiting period to get married in the state of Nevada.

served, along with popcorn, bulk candies, and cotton candy. You'll find this shop along the promenade.

Headliners–This newspaper and convenience store is located along the promenade. Film, sundries, candy, soda, and inexpensive souvenirs are sold here.

Marshall-Rousso–Casual and dress clothing and shoes for men and women are available here.

Circus Kids–Children's clothing, toys, and other items for kids are available from this shop located along the promenade.

Frozen Fusion–Located along the promenade, Frozen Fusion blends fresh fruit and frozen yogurt to create tasty treats.

Celebrity Sport Arena–A large selection of sports and celebrity memorabilia is sold here, including many autographed items.

Banquet, Function, and Convention Services

Catering Department: (702) 836-6514

All types of functions can be held at Circus Circus in its 8,000 square feet of banquet facilities, whether your event is for eight, eighty, or eight hundred people. Full catering and event planning services are offered.

The Chapel of the Fountain Wedding Chapel

Information/Reservations: (800) 634-6716 or (702) 794-3777

Circus Circus was the first Las Vegas casino and resort to offer an in-house wedding chapel. Thousands of brides and grooms have declared their vows in this quaint and picturesque chapel. Everything a couple needs to create a memorable wedding experience is available at the Chapel of the Fountain, including photography, video, and floral services. Special wedding packages, some including accommodations, are available at prices starting at $135.

The chapel office is open Sunday through Thursday from 9:00 A.M. to 6:30 P.M., and from 9:00 A.M. to 9:00 P.M. on Friday and Saturday. Contact the chapel in advance to reserve the date and time for your wedding.

Excalibur

Theme:	A medieval castle circa King Arthur's era
Room Rate:	$$ / $$$ ($51–$250)
Number of Rooms:	4,008 rooms (all refurbished by August 1999)
Casino:	100,000 square feet, featuring 2,475 slot and video poker machines, and a large selection of table games, plus a race and sports book and 150-seat keno lounge
Dining:	Five fine-dining restaurants, plus five casual eating establishments
Primary Show:	*Tournament of Kings*
Special Attractions:	The WCW Nitro Grill, the Dragon Battle, the Fantasy Faire, the Glockenspiel Fairy Tale
Reservations:	(800) 937-7777 or (702) 597-7777
Web Site:	*www.excalibur-casino.com*
Address:	3850 Las Vegas Boulevard South Las Vegas, NV 89109

Overall Resort Rating Based on Amenities and Rates

Ages Up to 5	Ages 6–15	Ages 16–20	Ages 21 & Up	Senior Citizens
⚁⚀	⚀⚁⚄	⚀⚁⚄	⚀⚀	⚀⚀

When this medieval-themed resort opened in 1990, it was the largest hotel and casino in the world with its two 28-story towers containing over four thousand guest rooms. Owned and operated by Circus Circus Enterprises, Inc. (which also owns and operates Circus Circus and the Luxor), it's impossible to miss this massive resort on the southwest corner of the Strip, about one mile from McCarran International Airport and diagonal from the MGM Grand.

Excalibur continues to be a favorite Las Vegas destination for families traveling with young children and teens. In addition to the *Tournament of Kings* dinner show, the entire 117-acre complex features décor from medieval times, plus actors dressed as knights, kings, and other members of the royal court roaming throughout the complex entertaining guests on an ongoing basis.

According to legend, Excalibur was a magical sword embedded in stone. During a period of unrest and disunity in post-Roman Britain, it was proclaimed that whoever could pull the sword from the stone would be crowned King of England. After countless knights failed to free the sword, Arthur, a mere squire, succeeded. King Arthur's reign gave birth to the tales of Camelot. The Knights of the Round Table and the Arthurian legend inspire much of Excalibur's décor and excitement.

Recently Excalibur added a children-and-teen-oriented attraction that takes guests "back" into the present. The WCW Nitro Grill is a theme-oriented restaurant and gift shop based on the mega-popular World Championship Wrestling franchise. Professional wrestlers from the WCW make regular appearances at this restaurant, which is a must-see attraction for any teen wrestling fan. There's also a large arcade (the Fantasy Faire) containing two motion simulator rides, an assortment of carnival-style games, and a variety of other attractions suitable for young people.

For adults, the casino is large and well equipped to handle almost anyone's gambling pleasures, plus there are plenty of shops designed to help you part with your winnings. The legend of King Arthur and the Excalibur sword comes alive right before your eyes as you enter the Excalibur property.

Guest Room Accommodations

All rooms at Excalibur offer air conditioning, color television (with pay-per-view movies), and direct-dial phones. Nonsmoking and/or Jacuzzi suites are also available, as are rooms with various bed configurations. When making your room reservation, discuss your room needs with the representative to ensure you receive the proper accommodations upon your arrival. Room service is available 24 hours a day and free parking is available to all guests. Most rooms offer only basic amenities, so you don't find things like data jacks, wet bars, or bathtubs (as opposed to showers). The in-room furnishings are functional, yet much of it is made from imitation wood. What this resort lacks in luxury, it makes up for in overall atmosphere. Children and teens in particular will enjoy the festive surroundings that Excalibur offers. For families traveling with children, adjoining guest rooms are available.

Fine Dining

Unlike some of the fancier hotels along the Strip, the fine-dining restaurants at Excalibur are family-friendly (children are allowed in the dining rooms), and the prices are reasonable. The dress is "dressy casual" for these restaurants, and reservations are recommended. Most of these restaurants are on the second level in the main casino building.

The Steakhouse at Camelot ($$$)

Reservations: Recommended, call (702) 597-7449

Whatever the occasion, people of all ages will enjoy this American-style restaurant, which offers an extensive wine selection and a cigar room. This restaurant offers a selection of top-quality steaks plus an extensive dessert menu. Live piano music is presented from 6:00 to 11:00 P.M. nightly.

Sir Galahad's Prime Rib House ($$)

Reservations: Recommended, call (702)-597-7448

Open for dinner only, this Tudor-style prime rib house offers delicious prime rib carved tableside, in addition to a nice selection of other entrees. Creamed spinach and Yorkshire pudding complete Sir Galahad's dining experience. If you're planning a party, private dining rooms are available for up to twenty people.

Regale Italian Eatery ($$)

Reservations: Recommended, call (702) 597-7443

Open for dinner only, you'll find a menu chock full of Italian entrees such as pizzas and pastas, served in an Italian village setting. This restaurant is headed by Tuscany-born Chef Edoardo Bucci. Live music is performed nightly from 5:00 to 10:00 P.M. (except on Wednesday and Thursday nights).

If you're celebrating a special occasion, special gift baskets, balloons, champagne, and other items can be ordered through room service and delivered directly to your room or suite.

Casual Dining

As a family-oriented resort, Excalibur offers a handful of less expensive, less formal dining options, including the WCW Nitro Grill, which is especially popular with boys.

Round Table Buffet ($ / $$)

This newly remodeled buffet offers a wide selection of entrees, salads, and desserts at one price that's extremely reasonable. Since this is an all-you-can-eat establishment, bring a hearty appetite! Open for breakfast, lunch, and dinner, service is on a first-come basis, so be prepared to wait for seating during peak meal times.

$ = entrees under $10; $$ = under $20; $$$ = over $20

WCW Nitro Grill ($$)

Information: (702) 64-NITRO or (702) 597-7394

Dining at the WCW Nitro Grill is the next best thing to being ringside at a WCW wrestling match! The menu features a combination of steak and grill items, and is priced much like any other theme restaurant, such as the Hard Rock Cafe, Planet Hollywood, or the Rainforest Cafe, located elsewhere in the Las Vegas area. Connected to this restaurant is a retail shop offering exclusive WCW and Nitro Grill merchandise. Every week at least one WCW wrestler makes a live appearance at the WCW Nitro Grill, signs autographs, and does a wrestling demonstration. All WCW events are also televised in the restaurant.

WCW's wrestling superstars include Hollywood Hulk Hogan, Bill Goldberg, Warrior, Diamond Dallas Page, Kimberly, and the Giant. For more information about WCW wrestling, check your local TV listings or visit The Nitro Grill Web site at *www.nitrogrill.com*.

Sherwood Forest Cafe ($ / $$)

Located on the casino level, near the resort's front desk area, Sherwood Forest Cafe is open 24 hours a day. This is the place to go for an inexpensive meal or snack. This cafe offers an extensive coffee shop menu, with breakfast, lunch, and dinner items served all day and night. There's also a selection of Chinese specialties available in the evening, and a separate children's menu offered throughout the day and night. Full table service is provided, but no reservations are accepted.

The Village Food Court ($)

In addition to the fine-dining and casual restaurant options at Excalibur, if you're looking for food that's fast and cheap, there's no need to go any farther than the Village Food Court. Here you'll find a central seating area and the following food options:

- Cafe Espresso—Gourmet coffees, cappuccino, espresso, and a full array of pastries are the specialty here.
- Wetzel's Pretzels—Freshly baked pretzels are served throughout the day (no pretzel sits longer than 30 minutes). Several toppings are available, including salt, butter, and cinnamon.
- Krispy Kreme Doughnuts—Here you'll find doughnuts in many varieties.
- Cold Stone Creamery—Soft-serve and traditional ice cream treats are served here.

$ = entrees under $10; $$ = under $20; $$$ = over $20

- McDonald's—Just look for those famous golden arches. Need anything more be said? If you're traveling with kids, chances are this will be a regular stop at mealtime. It's the perfect dining option for families on the go.

Special Attractions

When the sun sets, the knights come out at Excalibur—a resort that offers a wide range of ways to have fun. Eat, drink, and gamble the night away.

The Dragon Battle

Every hour, on the hour, from dusk until midnight (weather permitting), an exciting fire-breathing dragon appears in the moat outside the front entrance of Excalibur and does battle with none other than Merlin the Magician.

With all of his legendary powers at his disposal, Merlin must face his greatest nemesis, a 51-foot dragon. This free show is exciting for people of all ages. It features a state-of-the-art robotic dragon, pyrotechnics, and plenty of medieval action.

Tournament of Kings

Reservations: (702) 597-7600

Ticket Price: **$34.95 per person (includes dinner)**

Show Times: **6:00 P.M. and 8:30 P.M. (nightly)**

If you're expecting to see a typical Las Vegas style show at Excalibur, you're in for a shock. There are no showgirls, no big dance numbers, and no master illusionists or comedians. Instead, get ready to get your hands dirty (literally) as you participate in *Tournament of Kings*, an exciting, interactive dinner show that's presented nightly.

Medieval jousting, invading armies, dragons, fire wizards, and plenty of brave knights on horses will entertain you as you dine on a medieval-style dinner. (Sorry, no flatware is provided. You'll be using your hands to eat this meal.) Special effects, pyrotechnics, and highly detailed costumes all add to the ambiance.

Tournament of Kings is a lavish, $1-million production that takes place in a custom-designed dinner theater/arena. The main star of the show (aside from the knights, acrobats, and horses) is the audience itself, which is led through a chorus of cheering and singing as the action unfolds before them.

This show offers an evening's worth of exciting entertainment for people of all ages, but it will particularly appeal to kids. A multicourse dinner, which includes soup, chicken, and dessert, is included.

Since this show stars real-life horses, the best seating is several rows away from the stage/arena area. This will help avoid having sand from the arena kicked up by the horses into your food.

Tournament of Kings

Ages Up to 5	Ages 6–15	Ages 16–20	Ages 21 & Up	Senior Citizens
Not Suitable	⚀ ⚁ ⚂	⚀ ⚁ ⚂	⚀ ⚁	⚀

The Glockenspiel Fairy Tale

This free show involves a large clock with audio-animatronic characters. It is presented over the giant clock at the rear entrance of Excalibur every hour between 10:00 A.M. and 10:00 P.M.

Pool

The Excalibur pool area offers the perfect place to relax or enjoy a swim. Hours of operation vary by season, however, the resort offers two heated swimming pools, a 16-seat spa, waterfalls, water slides, and a shaded dining area nearby. The snack bar and cocktail bar in the pool area are open daily. The pool is open to all guests of the resort.

Health Club, Spa, and Salon

Hours: 8:30 A.M. to 5:00 P.M. (Monday through Saturday)
                9:00 A.M. to 4:00 P.M. (Sunday)

Appointments: (702) 597-6595

Kristina's Salon, located on the third level of the Castle building, offers a full range of services for men and women, including haircuts, shampoo, perms, and nail care. Appointments should be made in advance.

"It took nine months to construct the beast," said animation supervisor Scott Kessel, who worked with the California-based company that created the robotic dragon that stars in the Dragon Battle. "We really wanted to make the dragon look lifelike." The animators were able to recapture the finest details of this mythical creature with hand-painted murky-green scales, glowing yellow eyeballs, and a blood-red smile that truly makes the monster an intimidating competitor for any knight, or in this case, Merlin the Magician, who is also robotic. While the dragon may look and act real, he's really constructed of silicone, stainless steel, fiberglass, and rubber.

Casino

While Excalibur may have all of the amenities and charm of a family-oriented resort, it also offers a rather impressive, full-service casino designed for adult guests. One of the nice things about this casino is that there are plenty of low minimum bet gaming tables and many $.05 and $.25 slot machines. Thus, the casino caters to casual gamblers as well as high rollers. Within Excalibur's 100,000-square-foot gaming area you'll find:

- 2,475 slot, video poker, and video keno machines (Slots range from $.05 to $25.)
- 59 blackjack tables (including five handheld, single-deck tables and 49 shoe-dealt tables)
- 7 roulette wheels
- 4 craps tables with double odds
- 3 Pai Gow poker tables
- 2 Caribbean Stud poker tables
- 2 Let It Ride tournament tables
- 1 mini-baccarat table
- 1 Big Six wheel
- 1 casino war
- 11 poker tables (featuring 7-car stud and Texas hold 'em)
- A 150-seat keno lounge (plus the ability to play keno in the restaurants)
- A 150-seat race and sports book with big screen TVs and interactive wagering

As with virtually all of the casinos in Las Vegas, free gaming lessons are available daily. If you've never gambled in Las Vegas before, it's an excellent idea to participate in free lessons to learn the basic rules of each game as well as the etiquette before putting your money on the line.

Shopping

In keeping with the medieval theme of Excalibur, many of its shops are located in the Medieval Village area on the second level, which is where you'll find restaurants, the wedding chapels, a pub, the food court, and a cast of costumed characters interacting with visitors. The Court Jester's Stage, which offers free entertainment at scheduled times throughout the day and evening (between 10:00 A.M. and 10:00 P.M.) is also found here. Juggling,

Wedding Chapels

Information:
(800) 811-4320

Excalibur offers two lovely wedding chapels and a range of different wedding packages (including accommodations, meals, etc.). If you want to experience a theme wedding, medieval attire is available for the bride and groom. Each chapel averages about 10 weddings a day.

magic, and comedy acts are the types of things you'll experience when you visit the Court Jester's Stage.

Shops include: an airbrush/caricature kiosk, Castle Keepsakes (featuring Excalibur merchandise), Dragon's Lair (offering crystals and shining armor), Merlin's Mystic Shoppe (offering a touch of magic to each shopper), and Marshall-Rousso (fine men's and women's clothing). There's also Sweet Habits (offering candy, chocolate, and fudge).

Banquet, Function, and Convention Services

Information: (800) 811-4316

Like many of the other resorts along the Strip, Excalibur offers a one-stop shop for planning and holding virtually any type of function, banquet, or meeting. The property offers 12,000 square feet of meeting space located on the third level of the main building. "The facilities consist of one large room, which can be broken down into as many as eight smaller rooms, depending on the needs of a group," explained Excalibur's director of food and beverage, Cyndi Bennett. A full-service catering kitchen surrounds the facilities, and a large catering menu and staff are available. An event planning staff is also available. "Our staff is able to coordinate all food, beverage, room, audio, and visual requirements at the same time. From a simple meeting to an elaborate wedding reception, we can handle all of the details," added Bennett.

The banquet and convention facilities are decorated in shades of cream, burgundy, gold, and green. The divider walls are a neutral cream color.

The Crown Club, Excalibur's players' club, can be joined free of charge by visiting the casino. Members earn rewards for their casino play which include cash and complimentary show tickets, meals, and rooms. Rewards are based on how much you gamble in the casino. Call extension: 7417 for details or visit the Crown Club desk in the center of the casino.

Flamingo Hilton

Theme: A traditional Hilton resort complex, but with a Hawaiian motif

Room Rate: $$ / $$$ ($51–$250)

Number of Rooms: 3,642 guest rooms and suites (including two super-suites, 24 luxury parlors, 150 mini suites, and six conference suites)

Casino: 77,000 square feet, featuring 2,100 slot and video poker machines, plus 64 table games

Dining: Nine restaurants, including a buffet, coffee shop, and several fine-dining establishments

Special Attractions: *The Great Radio City Spectacular* and *Forever Plaid* (musical shows)

Reservations: (800) 732-2111

Web Site: *www.Hilton.com/hotels/LASFHHH/*

Address: 3555 Las Vegas Boulevard South
Las Vegas, NV 89109

Overall Resort Rating Based on Amenities and Rates

Ages Up to 5	Ages 6–15	Ages 16–20	Ages 21 & Up	Senior Citizens
⚁⚁	⚁⚁	⚁⚁	⚁⚁	⚁⚁

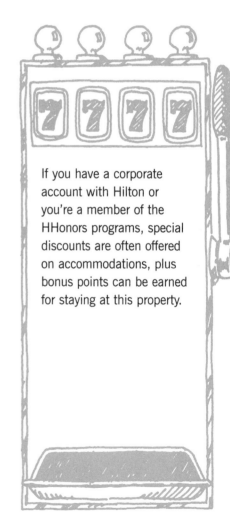

If you have a corporate account with Hilton or you're a member of the HHonors programs, special discounts are often offered on accommodations, plus bonus points can be earned for staying at this property.

One of the best known companies in the hotel industry is definitely Hilton. Around the Las Vegas Strip area, Hilton operates the Flamingo Hilton and the Las Vegas Hilton, both of which offer all of the amenities you'd expect from a topnotch Hilton resort property. In fact, many tourists confuse these two Hilton properties.

The Flamingo Hilton is located on the Strip, while the Las Vegas Hilton is located a few blocks off of the Strip. The Flamingo Hilton is definitely a family-oriented hotel that also caters to business travelers and vacationers. You'll find this resort in what is called the famous "Four Corners" of the Las Vegas Strip. It's within walking distance of Caesars Palace, The Mirage, and Bally's, and within three-and-a-half miles of McCarran International Airport (about a 10-minute taxi ride) and three miles from the Las Vegas Convention Center.

Visitors of all ages can enjoy the hotel's tennis courts, pool, fitness center, and video game arcade, while adults can enjoy the fully equipped casino. *The Great Radio City Spectacular* show features the world famous Rockettes. The show is presented nightly as the resort's headline entertainment.

Guest Room Accommodations

The Flamingo Hilton offers standard rooms, double rooms, king rooms, and suites. Single king-size beds, two queen-size beds, and connecting rooms are available. The suites contain a wet bar as well as an additional telephone in the bathroom. The rooms offer cable TV with an in-house television station that offers an ongoing video tour of the property plus free gaming lessons. Rollaway beds, cribs, and other amenities are available upon request to accommodate families.

Fine Dining

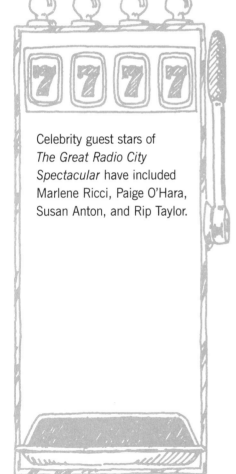

Celebrity guest stars of *The Great Radio City Spectacular* have included Marlene Ricci, Paige O'Hara, Susan Anton, and Rip Taylor.

The Flamingo Hilton is walking distance from several well known mega-resorts, including The Mirage, Treasure Island, Bally's, and Caesars Palace (and the Forum Shops, which contains several restaurants). Nevertheless, the Flamingo Hilton features a handful of fine-dining establishments offering America, Italian, and Chinese cuisine.

To make reservations for any of the resort's fine-dining restaurants, call (702) 733-3333. Room service is available 24 hours a day, however, a limited menu is available between 11:00 P.M. and 6:00 A.M. A full kosher menu is available.

Conrads ($$ / $$$)

Reservations: (702) 733-3333

Steak, prime rib, and fresh seafood are the house specialties here. Open for dinner only, from 5:30 to 11:00 P.M., this is considered the Flamingo Hilton's most upscale restaurant. Proper attire is required.

Peking Market ($$)

Reservations: (702) 733-3333

Features a full Chinese menu.

$ = entrees under $10; $$ = under $20; $$$ = over $20

Alta Villa ($$)

Reservations: (702) 733-3333

Traditional and contemporary Italian cuisine is offered here. Open for dinner only, from 5:30 to 11:00 P.M.

Hamada of Japan ($$)

Reservations: (702) 733-3333

Traditional Japanese cuisine is served here. Open for breakfast (6:30 to 10:30 A.M.), lunch (11:00 A.M. to 2:30 P.M.), and dinner (5:00 P.M. to 12:30 A.M.). Breakfast and lunch prices range between $11.50 and $23.50 a person, while dinner entrees cost from $15 to $25 each.

Casual Dining

Lindy's Coffee Shop ($)

Open 24 hours, this coffee shop offers a diverse menu.

Bugsy's Deli ($)

Deli sandwiches and hamburgers are typical menu items found at this casual and inexpensive restaurant.

Paradise Garden Buffet ($)

Open for breakfast (6:00 A.M. to noon, $6.75 per person), lunch (noon to 2:30 P.M., $7.75 per person), and dinner (4:30 to 10:00 P.M., $9.95), this is an all-you-can-eat buffet. On Friday, the buffet offers the "Seafood Spectacular" from 4:30 to 10:00 P.M.

Flamingo Room ($ / $$)

A typical coffee shop menu is offered for breakfast. For dinner, however, American and continental cuisine is served. Breakfast is served from 7:00 A.M. to noon. Dinner is served from 5:00 to 11:00 P.M. The average meal price is $15 to $20 a person.

Pool Grill ($)

This snack shop, located by the pool, offers a limited menu.

$ = entrees under $10; $$ = under $20; $$$ = over $20

Shopping

The Flamingo Hilton has a few shops and boutiques on-property (including: D'Finess, Promanda Gift Shop, Flamingo Apparel, Mesa, Kidz Clubhouse, and Alta Ville Gift Shop). As mentioned earlier, however, the hotel is just two blocks from the Forum Shops at Caesars Palace and about five blocks from the Fashion Show Mall.

Banquet, Function, and Convention Services

Information:
(702) 733-3111

Wedding Chapel:
(800) 933-7993

The Flamingo Hilton offers a wide range of meeting, function, and banquet facilities, plus a staff of professional meeting planners. The resort also offers a wedding chapel. The Garden Chapel seats up to fifty guests and features a stunning outdoor gazebo. For meeting space, the property offers 50,000 square feet of flexible space that includes a grand ballroom (the Sunset Ballroom) offering an impressive view of the Strip.

Casino Snack Bar ($)

This snack shop, located in the casino, also offers a limited menu.

Special Attractions

The Rockettes from Radio City Music Hall are the stars of their own Las Vegas musical show, while the cast of *Forever Plaid* performs a selection of mega-hit songs from the 1950s. Combine these shows with the resort facilities at the Flamingo Hilton and you'll find plenty to see and do, especially if you're a business traveler or adult traveling for pleasure. If you're traveling with teens, *Forever Plaid* is a suitable show.

Live Flamingos

The Flamingo Hilton is more than just a name. A flock of live Chilean flamingos live on-property and can be seen daily. The resort is also the home of other exotic animals, including penguins. Check out the Flamingo Habitat area located in the rear of the resort. You'll also see ducks, swans, cockatoos, macaws, Koi, goldfish, turtles, and other creatures living in a lovely landscaped area. This is a free attraction suitable for all ages.

The Great Radio City Spectacular

Show Times: 7:45 P.M. (except Friday) and 10:30 P.M.
(Thursday, Saturday, Sunday, and Monday nights only)

Ticket Prices: $42.50 (cocktail show) or $52.50 (dinner show)

Box Office: (702) 733-3333

New York's Radio City Rockettes have a secondary home at the Flamingo Showroom. These high-kicking showgirls perform nightly (except for Friday) and are joined onstage by a special celebrity guest star (who changes periodically) as well as a handful of specialty acts. This is a musical performance featuring full production numbers. The Flamingo Showroom, where this show takes place, has a 600-seat main floor area, plus a 140-seat balcony. The 7:45 P.M. performance includes a full dinner, while drinks only are served at the later show.

The Great Radio City Spectacular

Ages Up to 5	Ages 6–15	Ages 16–20	Ages 21 & Up	Senior Citizens
Not Suitable	Not Suitable	⚀ ⚁	⚀ ⚁	⚀ ⚁

Forever Plaid

Show Times: 7:30 and 10:30 P.M. (except Monday)

Ticket Prices: $24.15

Box Office: (702) 733-3333

This nonstop tribute to 1950s music is performed in an intimate 200-seat auditorium. The show comes straight from its successful off-Broadway run. You'll be clapping your hands to the music in this high-energy musical performance.

Forever Plaid

Ages Up to 5	Ages 6–15	Ages 16–20	Ages 21 & Up	Senior Citizens
Not Suitable	Not Suitable	⚀ ⚁	⚀ ⚁ ⚂	⚀ ⚁ ⚂

Spa, Health Club, and Salon

Hours: 8:00 A.M. to 8:00 P.M. daily (spa)

Available to all guests, the Flamingo Hilton Health Spa offers a fitness center (complete with exercise equipment), four lighted tennis courts, a sauna, spa, and two Olympic-size swimming pools (plus a kids' pool). The facility is professionally staffed and offers separate men's and women's health club facilities.

Lockers, towels, sandals, and a frozen juice bar are all included in the $17 per day facilities fee. Special spa services, such as massages or the use of tanning beds, cost extra and should be scheduled in advance. A 30-minute Swedish massage, for example, is priced at $45 (plus tip) but includes the use of the spa facilities. Next to the spa are a beauty salon and a barber shop.

Casino

Over two thousand slot and video poker machines plus 64 gaming tables (including poker, Pai Gow poker, craps, roulette, Big Six wheel, blackjack, Sic Bo, progressive Caribbean Stud, and Spanish 21) are among the gaming options available at the Flamingo Hilton's casino. There's also a keno lounge and sports book.

The Flamingo Hilton Tennis Club, with its four lighted courts, enables guests to play anytime during the day or evening hours. The Club features a complete pro shop and practice court, and a tennis pro is available to give private lessons.

Golden Nugget

Theme:	Nineteenth century Victorian design
Room Rate:	$$$ / $$$$ ($101+)
Number of Rooms:	1,907 guest rooms, 27 luxury apartments, and 6 penthouse suites
Casino:	36,000 square feet, featuring table games and slots, plus a race and sports book
Dining:	Five fine-dining restaurants and several casual-dining options, including a buffet
Special Attractions:	The Spa, the Hand of Faith Gold Nugget, the Fremont Street Experience
Reservations:	(800) 634-3454 or (800) 8-GOLDEN
Web Site:	*www.goldennugget.com*
Address:	129 East Fremont Street Las Vegas, NV 89101

While Golden Nugget offers luxury accommodations, its location in downtown Las Vegas, as opposed to the Strip, makes it less desirable among business people or convention goers. While the downtown area has undergone recent revitalization, it continues to be less of a tourist area than the Strip.

Overall Resort Rating Based on Rates

Ages Up to 5	Ages 6–15	Ages 16–20	Ages 21 & Up	Senior Citizens
⚀	⚀	⚀ ⚁	⚀ ⚁	⚀ ⚁

Owned and operated by Mirage Resorts, Inc. (the company behind Bellagio, The Mirage, Treasure Island, plus several properties outside of Las Vegas), the Golden Nugget is a Las Vegas landmark with a rich tradition spanning over fifty years. This casino and hotel first opened its doors August 30, 1946, as the largest and most luxurious casino in town.

Located in downtown Las Vegas (not along the Strip), Golden Nugget has received the Mobil "Four Star" award and the AAA "Four-Diamond" award for 15 and 22 consecutive years, respectively. While this property doesn't offer any high-tech theme parks or attractions, it does offer a taste of luxury and a look into Las Vegas's past.

The Golden Nugget pioneered the concept of creating an impressive entertainment extravaganza on Fremont Street. The $70-million Fremont Street Experience is a four-block-long pedestrian walkway equipped with 2.1 million computer programmed lights and more than 540,000 watts of stereo sound.

Getting to Downtown Las Vegas

Fremont Street in downtown Las Vegas is easy to reach by car, taxi, shuttle bus, or trolley. On the eastern end of Fremont Street (on the corner of Fourth and Carson streets) is a 1,400-space parking garage. Validated parking is free for up to five hours. The covered lot is open 24 hours a day.

Taxis are available at the main entrance of all hotels along the Strip. There's also the Citizens Area Transit (CAT) bus service that travels between the Strip and Fremont Street. Take the Route 301 or 302 (express) service. The fare each way is $1.50 for adults and $.50 for children, seniors, and people with physical disabilities.

Every fifteen minutes the downtown trolley also delivers visitors to the Fremont Street Experience. Trolley service runs between 11:00 A.M. and 2:00 A.M., and provides service to major hotels on the Strip. The fare is $1.35 per person. Keep in mind that it's necessary to transfer from the Las Vegas Strip trolley to the downtown trolley at the Stratosphere. This method of transportation isn't the fastest, but riding the trolley offers a mini-tour of the Strip and downtown Las Vegas.

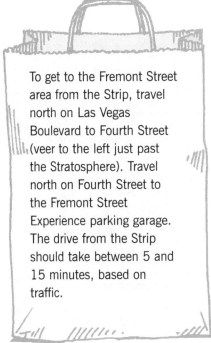

To get to the Fremont Street area from the Strip, travel north on Las Vegas Boulevard to Fourth Street (veer to the left just past the Stratosphere). Travel north on Fourth Street to the Fremont Street Experience parking garage. The drive from the Strip should take between 5 and 15 minutes, based on traffic.

Guest Room Accommodations

The Golden Nugget offers a variety of guest rooms, suites, and apartments to fit most mid- to-high-range travel budgets. The hotel's three towers contain 1,907 one- and two-bedroom suites, luxury apartments, and penthouse suites (each equipped with a whirlpool bath).

All of the guest rooms and suites have recently been refurbished to feature warm beige and brown tones. All guest rooms provide a selection of custom bath amenities. Most rooms also include hair dryers, irons and ironing boards, in-room safes, and lighted makeup mirrors.

The Golden Nugget's towers overlook the pool terrace, downtown Las Vegas, or the Sierra Nevada Mountains. Rooms are available for nonsmokers and the physically challenged upon request. This hotel's high employee-to-guest ratio allows it to provide top quality service. Other amenities include express checkout, safe deposit boxes, fax service, cable TV (with pay-per-view movies), and same-day laundry/valet service.

Fine Dining

In addition to the following two fine-dining restaurants, 24-hour room service is available to hotel guests. As with all of the fine-dining restaurants located in resorts and casinos throughout Las Vegas, formal attire is acceptable but not required.

Stephano's ($$$)

Reservations: Suggested, call (800) 634-3454

Featuring a romantic Italian countryside atmosphere, Stephano's offers fresh seafood and pasta entrees. Indulge in Stephano's most popular dish, Osso Bucco, or one of many Northern Italian specialties.

Lillie Langtry's ($$$)

Reservations: Suggested, call (800) 634-3454

Serving traditional Szechuan and Cantonese cuisine, Lillie Langtry's décor is soft and surreal, allowing diners to savor the aromas of ancient Chinese cuisine. Specialties include Mongolian beef, lobster Cantonese, and stir-fried lobster. The restaurant also serves prime mesquite broiled steaks.

Casual Dining

Golden Nugget guests and visitors can enjoy a relatively inexpensive meal at one of the hotel's casual-dining establishments.

The Buffet ($)

Lunch and dinner feature freshly carved turkey, roast beef, and ham, plus entree selections, a salad bar, and a dessert bar. Most lavish is the all-day Sunday champagne brunch, featuring dishes such as eggs Benedict, blintzes, pancakes, creamed herring, and smoked fish.

Caron Street Cafe ($$)

Dine in a European sidewalk cafe amidst handpainted murals of a topiary garden, lush plants, and flower arrangements. Breakfast, lunch, and dinner are served 24 hours.

$ = entrees under $10; $$ = under $20; $$$ = over $20

The Neon Museum

Las Vegas is known for its flashing lights and neon, so it's fitting that an entire museum is dedicated to classic and vintage neon signs. The Neon Museum is an interesting attraction for people of all ages and worth the stop if you're already planning to explore the downtown area.

California Pizza Kitchen ($$)

Tandoori chicken, shrimp scampi, and Peking duck are just a few of the 32 varieties of gourmet, wood-fired pizzas served at the California Pizza Kitchen. A wide array of delectable pastas, grilled items, garden-fresh salads, and specialty desserts is also offered. Open for lunch and dinner. The Caesar salad with chicken is excellent either as a side dish or main meal.

Casino Snack Bar ($)

Located in the heart of the casino is a snack bar that serves a limited menu.

Lounges

The Sports Lounge, located inside the race and sports book, is a full-service bar and lounge built with the sportsman in mind. Relax in the spacious lounge and catch the action on eight 35-inch TVs showing the major race and sporting events of the day. In the evening, the lounge turns into a nightclub, featuring a variety of live bands from 8:30 P.M. to 1:30 A.M. every night, except Monday.

Claude's Bar, in the heart of the casino, serves a variety of assorted beer, wine, and well drinks from its "long" bar.

The International Beer Bar offers 38 different types of beers—from the windswept hops of Holland to the distilleries of Japan—to satisfy even the most discriminating connoisseur.

Special Attractions

Downtown Las Vegas has gone through many transitions over the years, but the most recent revitalization efforts have been designed to bring tourist traffic back to the downtown area. Being located in the heart of the downtown area, Golden Nugget guests can easily enjoy the area's various attractions, shops, and shows.

Pool

Dip into the Golden Nugget's Olympic-size pool amid the shade of leaning palm trees and the resort's outdoor misting system. White alabaster

For a listing of phone numbers for other hotels and casinos located in the downtown area, see Chapter 3, "The Las Vegas Strip at a Glance."

$ = entrees under $10; $$ = under $20; $$$ = over $20

swan statues and bronze fish sculptures throughout the attractive landscaping add a touch of elegance to the pool terrace. Unwind in the whirlpool spa or bask in the sun while sipping an exotic cocktail. Pool attendants are on-hand to accommodate you with complimentary usage of lounge chairs and towels. Cocktail service, a snack bar, and pool products such as tanning oil, sunglasses, and visors are available.

The Hand of Faith Exhibit

The Hand of Faith is the largest gold nugget on display in the world. It was discovered near the Golden Triangle in Australia and weighs 27.2 kilograms (61 pounds 11 ounces or 875 troy ounces). The gold nugget is appropriately displayed near the main entrance of the Golden Nugget.

The Fremont Street Experience

Information: (800) 249-3559 or (702) 678-5777

Admission: **Free**

www.vegasexperience.com

Every evening after dark (around 6:00 P.M.) until midnight, the Fremont Street Experience offers a different hourly light and sound show utilizing 540,000 watts of sound and 2.1 million computer synchronized lights. Admission is free and the shows are open to everyone. Rising 90 feet in height and stretching the length of five football fields along Fremont Street, this attraction is visually stunning.

The Fremont Street Experience

Ages Up to 5	Ages 6–15	Ages 16–20	Ages 21 & Up	Senior Citizens
⚀	⚀ ⚁ ⚂	⚀ ⚁ ⚂	⚀ ⚁ ⚂	⚀ ⚁ ⚂

Spa and Salon

Like most of the luxurious resorts and hotels and casinos in Las Vegas, the Golden Nugget offers a full-service spa and salon designed to pamper guests. This spa offers separate facilities for men and women and a staff of specialists who can provide anything from a massage to personalized

Banquet, Function, and Convention Services

Information: (702) 386-8220

Golden Nugget offers 12 rooms, totaling 25,000 square feet of convention area and meeting room space that can accommodate up to five hundred people. Two of the banquet rooms overlook the pool area (which features tropical landscaping).

fitness instruction. The facility is equipped with whirlpool baths, steam rooms, and saunas, plus a Swedish shower, and a wide range of exercise equipment.

The salon also offers personal care and attention for men and women, providing complete hair care services, manicures, pedicures, facials, skin care programs, and body waxing.

Appointments are required for all special services offered at the spa and salon, and advanced appointments are also needed. A flat daily fee is required to use just the spa facilities.

Casino

When the Golden Nugget opened over fifty years ago, it was exclusively a luxurious, 5,000-square-foot "gaming hall" (casino). Since then, the casino has expanded dramatically. It now encompasses 36,000 square feet and offers many popular types of gaming tables, including: blackjack, craps, roulette, Pai Gow, and Pai Gow poker. The casino also offers plenty of slot machines, video poker machines, a keno lounge, and a race and sports book.

The times may have changed, but the Golden Nugget continues to cater to an upscale clientele. One way it does this is by offering a VIP High Limit Salon area, featuring a wide array of $5 and above slot and video poker machines, plus extra amenities designed to offer comfort. This area is decorated with handwoven carpets, imported marble, European velvet fabrics and draperies, and crystal chandeliers. Look for the VIP High Limit Salon adjacent to the 24 Karat Club Booth in the main casino area.

For people planning to gamble primarily at the Golden Nugget, the casino offers a club allowing gamblers to earn points based on the amount of money they gamble. Points can be redeemed for free rooms, meals, discounts, show tickets, etc. For more information, visit the 24 Karat Club's Web site at *www.24karatclub.com* or call (800) 777-0135.

Shopping

The Gift Boutique, located just off the hotel's main lobby, offers a wide array of fine jewelry, designer clothing, leather items, and fashion accessories. The Gift Shop features an assortment of Golden Nugget merchandise, casual sportswear, children's wear, toys, and other gift items.

Hard Rock Hotel & Casino

Theme:	Rock 'n' roll like a Hard Rock Cafe restaurant, only much bigger
Room Rate:	$$$ / $$$$ ($101+)
Number of Rooms:	668 rooms and suites
Casino:	30,000 square feet, including the Peacock Lounge—a private high-limit gaming area, and a race and sports book
Dining:	Seven restaurants, including the Sports Deluxe sports bar, plus 24-hour room service
Primary Show:	The Joint concert venue, where top-name music acts appear regularly
Special Attractions:	RockSpa, the world's largest Hard Rock Store, Baby's Nightclub, and the extensive rock 'n' roll memorabilia collection displayed throughout the property
Reservations:	(800) 693-7625
Web Site:	*www.hardrockhotel.com*
Address:	4455 Paradise Road Las Vegas, NV 89109

To get a close-up look at this resort before leaving home, be sure to check out the Hard Rock Hotel and Casino's Web site (*www.hardrockhotel.com*). It features animated tours of the property and live video shots, allowing you to view the action day or night.

Overall Resort Rating Based on Amenities and Rates

Ages Up to 5	Ages 6–15	Ages 16–20	Ages 21 & Up	Senior Citizens
⚀	⚀	⚀ ⚁	⚁ ⚂ ⚄	⚀

The Hard Rock Hotel and Casino is truly unique. This hotel and resort property is located off of the Strip (about a three-minute drive away), and is also a three-minute drive from McCarran International Airport. From a décor standpoint, the Hard Rock Hotel is very much like any Hard Rock Cafe restaurant/bar, only on a much flashier and larger scale.

This resort caters to young adults, Generation Xers, and middle-aged people who are music fans. This is very much a destination with an attitude, not to mention a priceless collection of rock 'n' roll memorabilia

displayed throughout all public areas. You'll find costumes and instruments from the biggest names in the recording industry, gold records, photos, and other personal items from people who have dominated the music industry. Much of the memorabilia is autographed.

The Hard Rock Hotel is definitely suitable for college students, young business travelers, and vacationers. The resort doesn't cater to children or older people (especially those who aren't music fans).

The Hard Rock Hotel is easily identifiable from a distance. You'll know it by the 90-foot neon Fender Stratocaster guitar perched on the roof. Once inside, you won't hear that same old elevator music that many of the casinos play. Instead, you'll hear music from people like Bob Seger, Eric Clapton, Nirvana, and Chrissie Hynde.

Meanwhile, as you begin to explore this property, you'll be surrounded by some of the most incredible rock 'n' roll memorabilia ever assembled—literally thousands of items, from Elvis Presley's gold lamé jacket and a Beatles "Wall 'O' Merchandising," to a fragment of Otis Redding's fateful plane and Madonna's cone-shaped bra.

While some Las Vegas area resorts have a theme, the Hard Rock Hotel makes rock 'n' roll a way of life, which is why it can truly be called the world's first rock 'n' roll resort.

The resort features memorabilia that takes you from the very beginnings of rock 'n' roll to the absolute cutting edge of today's music. Overall, the accommodations and amenities are topnotch, providing a comfortable environment with plenty to see and do. If you're staying at this resort, yet want to explore the Strip, it's only a short taxi ride away.

> Because this resort is so unique and incredibly popular among music fans (and music industry insiders visiting Las Vegas), it's often booked solid, so make your reservations as early as possible, especially if you're planning on being in Las Vegas during a peak travel period. Even if you can't get a room here, it's worth checking out the property if you're a music fan. Guests must be at least 21 to make a reservation or to stay at the resort without being accompanied by an adult.

Guest Room Accommodations

The Hard Rock Hotel has 670 rooms, including 68 luxury suites. Each room and suite features French doors that open to views of the hotel's pool, the Strip, or the surrounding mountains. Rooms are appointed with leather headboards on king- or queen-size beds, parchment and iron lamps, stainless steel bathroom sinks, and various musical touches (such as curtains with a musical instrument motif and framed photographs of legends including Jimi Hendrix and Janis Joplin).

Basic rooms are approximately 450 square feet and include one king- or two queen-size beds, a desk, a table with two chairs, a 27-inch television, and a marble covered bathroom. Additional in-room amenities include:

- Trinitron color TVs in each room and suite (suites contain full entertainment centers with cable TV, VCR, and a CD player)
- Individually controlled thermostats
- A wide selection of cable channels including in-house movies
- Four all-music channels with different themes: Passion Zone, Legends, Rock, and Alternative
- Direct dial phones with data/fax port
- Some suites contain in-room Jacuzzis

Fine Dining

While many consider the food at Hard Rock Cafe restaurants to be average (most people go for the atmosphere), the dining options at the Hard Rock Hotel and Casino offer excellent cuisine at fair prices. The fine-dining restaurants are certainly equivalent in atmosphere and quality to anything you'll find at the nicest of Las Vegas resorts.

A.J.'s Steakhouse & Piano Bar ($$$)

A.J.'s, a modern but sentimental tribute to the classic Vegas steakhouses of the 1960s, is Peter Morton's loving homage to his father, famed Chicago restaurateur Arnie Morton. The eatery features dark wood finishes, translucent curtains, curved leather booths, a grand piano, an elevated bar, and an open cook line. Live piano music is presented nightly. Main entrees range from a 20-ounce prime center cut New York strip sirloin and double cut lamb chops to horseradish encrusted Alaskan salmon and broiled Maine lobster.

Nobu ($$$)

Nobu, Chef Nobu Matsuhisa's groundbreaking temple of Japanese cuisine with Peruvian influences, has already set unmatched standards of excellence in Los Angeles, New York, and London. From squid pasta to a

$ = entrees under $10; $$ = under $20; $$$ = over $20

miso-inflected cod, Chef Matsuhisa has fashioned a completely original dining establishment.

Mortoni's ($$ / $$$)

Mortoni's, a Hard Rock Hotel original, has been immensely popular since the resort first opened. Offering a casually elegant spin on Morton's—Peter Morton's famous celebrity-filled Los Angeles restaurant—Mortoni's serves meticulously prepared Northern Italian fare in a relaxed yet opulent setting.

Casual Dining

The atmosphere may be less formal (thoroughly casual), and the prices may be low, but the food served at these casual-dining restaurants is top-notch.

The Counter ($ / $$)

Breakfast, lunch, and dinner is served 24 hours a day. The menu is extensive and includes everything from eggs, to salads and sandwiches, to burgers.

Pink Taco ($$)

The Pink Taco is an authentically hip restaurant offering celebrated California Chef Tacho Kneeland's fresh and modern take on Mexican classics. A full-service bar serves a wide variety of margaritas and tequilas. As the name suggests, tacos are the house specialty.

Mr. Lucky's 24/7 ($ / $$)

Open 24 hours a day, this upscale coffee shop serves breakfast, lunch, and dinner entrees anytime. The atmosphere is a bit loud (there are TVs throughout the dining room tuned to sporting events), but the prices are surprisingly low and the food is very good. Sandwiches, burgers, soups, salads, appetizers, and a full breakfast menu are offered. Beer and wine is also served. You'll find Mr. Lucky's located right off the casino floor.

$ = entrees under $10; $$ = under $20; $$$ = over $20

Banquet, Function, and Convention Services

Group Sales: (800) 693-7625

Over 60,000 square feet of event space is available at the Hard Rock Hotel. This includes a 6,000-square-foot conference center, an executive boardroom, and extensive banquet facilities to accommodate a wide range of group sizes. Penthouse suites, the Beach Club area, and some of the restaurants can also be reserved for private functions.

Lounges

The Hard Rock Hotel and Casino offers several cutting-edge lounges and bars, designed to provide guests and visitors alike with a comfortable place to relax, socialize, and have fun.

Sports Deluxe is one of the best equipped sports bars in Las Vegas. Located next to the sports book, Sports Deluxe was designed like a theater so that the maximum amount of tables and booths have a clear view of the several state-of-the-art flat screen monitors above the bar. In addition, each booth has its own TV, so you and your friends can choose to watch the screens above the bar or, if you prefer, tune your personal TV to a station of your choice.

Palapa Bar & Grille is a full-service bar located poolside, which offers a light menu. You can also relax and enjoy a fine cigar at the hotel's Cuba Libre Cigar Bar.

Special Attractions

Nearly everything there is to see and do at the Hard Rock Hotel and Casino centers around music or rock 'n' roll.

The Joint

The Joint is Hard Rock Hotel's live concert venue that features an ongoing series of concerts and other special events. With seating for up to 1,400 guests, the Joint has played host to hundreds of live concerts from current and past music stars.

For concert information, call any TicketMaster office [Las Vegas: (702) 480-3232], visit TicketMaster online (*www.ticketmaster.com*), or call the Hard Rock Hotel at (800) HRD-ROCK.

Baby's Nightclub

This is one of Las Vegas's newest and trendiest nightspots. Dance, drink, and party the night away! This club definitely appeals to a younger, hipper crowd.

Pool

Part of the Hard Rock Hotel's recent $100-million expansion plan included building a lovely two-acre addition to the Pool and Beach Club area. The Beach Club offers sandy beaches, oceanlike pools, underwater music, and deluxe private cabanas. Some of the newer features added include swim-up gaming (blackjack), plus a poolside bar and grill.

Spa, Health Club, and Salon
RockSpa

Hours: 6:00 A.M. to 8:00 P.M. (daily)
            Treatments are available from 8:00 A.M. to 7:00 P.M.

Appointments: (702) 693-5554

In addition to offering a complete workout facility, RockSpa is a full-service spa offering a wide selection of massages, including:

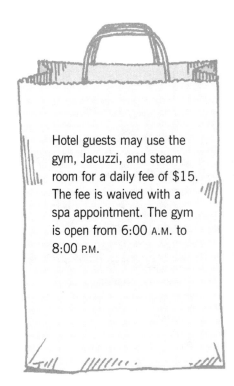

Hotel guests may use the gym, Jacuzzi, and steam room for a daily fee of $15. The fee is waived with a spa appointment. The gym is open from 6:00 A.M. to 8:00 P.M.

- Aromatherapy—A gentle massage using light, long flowing strokes with an individually selected essential oil, which through inhalation and application to the skin surface is used to relax, sedate, or stimulate bodily functions, promote intuition and creativity, and release emotional stress. (60- or 90-minute treatment.)
- Swedish—The "basic" massage, this treatment incorporates a variety of strokes, including kneading, stroking, tapping, and shaking, to induce relaxation in the body, with some special attention to a trouble area or two, promoting overall circulation and well-being. (60- or 90-minute treatment.)
- Integrative Deep Tissue—Used to release chronic muscular tension, a licensed therapist uses a variety of advanced techniques with greater pressure and on deeper muscles, tailored to your body for the ultimate massage experience. (60- or 90-minute treatment.)
- Mini Massage—Designed for a specific problem area, for people short on time, or to add to another body treatment, this chair massage is perfect to work out your neck and shoulders, lower back, or specific sports-related problem areas. (Available at the pool or in the gym at $2 per minute.)

- Reflexology—A form of therapeutic foot and/or hand massage that uses specific pressure techniques on precise reflex points and nerve endings corresponding with all body parts. The therapist breaks up the crystallizations and moves blocked energy.

In addition to massages, the following body wraps and other treatments are available at RockSpa (as well as at many of the full-service spas at other Las Vegas mega-resorts). The following is a listing of the types of body treatments available at many of these spas:

- Moor Mud Wrap—A revitalizing European therapy using authentic thermal Moor mud to heal, soothe, and rejuvenate tired muscles, joints, and dull skin, remineralizing, softening, and purifying the face and body.
- Spirulina Body Wrap—Using live spirulina algae that is harvested from pure salt lakes in Southern California, this seaweed treatment imparts essential protein, vitamins, minerals, and enzymes to nourish, stimulate, detoxify, and revitalize the face and body.
- Essential Oil Wrap—A luxurious application of aromatherapy oils mixed with a therapeutic cream rich in minerals and trace elements. Relieves tension, provides moisture to dry skin, and promotes overall detoxification.
- Thermal Mineral Bath—From a Hungarian spring that's over two thousand meters deep, the crystals in this thermal mineral water contain large quantities of biologically active minerals and trace elements that are absorbed through the skin during bathing, aiding in detoxification of the body. Especially beneficial for sore muscles and aching joints, relaxing the body, and inducing a restful night's sleep.
- Thalassobath Bath—A purifying algae bath using fresh dried fucus seaweed and seawater crystals. This treatment is rich in vital minerals and algae that both stimulate circulation and accelerate the body's natural rate of perspiration, which aids in overall detoxification.
- Aromatherapy Bath—The finest essential oils, containing thermal mineral bath crystals and trace elements, produce a soothing or invigorating effect, depending on the bath selected.
- Herbal Bath—An old German natural remedy, these baths use a potent aromatic oil solution made from rich botanicals that are still used in Germany for medicinal purposes.

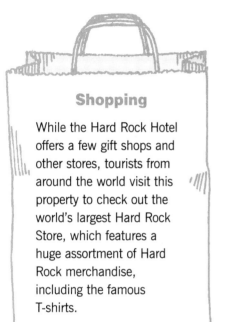

Shopping

While the Hard Rock Hotel offers a few gift shops and other stores, tourists from around the world visit this property to check out the world's largest Hard Rock Store, which features a huge assortment of Hard Rock merchandise, including the famous T-shirts.

- Turkish Scrub—An exhilarating thermal salt exfoliation using salt rich in minerals and trace elements, followed by a loofah scrub with a thermal mineral shower/bath gel, and completed with an application of a moisture balancing lotion.
- Thermal Mineral Scrub—A deep cleansing body exfoliation using granulated pumice stone, thermal minerals, and aromatherapy oils in a gel base, followed by a loofah scrub with a thermal mineral shower/bath gel, and completed with an application of a moisture balancing lotion.
- Chamomile Scrub—An exfoliation using a granulated pumice stone in a cream base, followed by a loofah scrub with a chamomile shower/bath gel that is rich in botanicals, and completed with a softening chamomile body spray.
- Refresher Facial—A deep cleansing introductory facial using Hungarian Moor mud, which refines and remineralizes dull skin. Includes a skin analysis and a short massage of the face and shoulders, as well as a heated hand treatment.
- Traditional European Deep Cleansing Facial—A purifying treatment for any skin type, this facial includes a gentle exfoliating peel to remove dull surface skin cells, a luxurious massage, a deep cleansing mask and botanical extracts to rejuvenate and nourish the skin. A heated hand treatment completes the experience.
- Aromatherapy Facial—A purifying treatment for normal, dry, or mature skin that takes advantage of the rejuvenating benefits of essential oils, which work to relax, detoxify, and soothe facial muscles, while simultaneously hydrating the skin and promoting the flow of lymph. This treatment includes a peel and a luxurious, relaxing massage, specifically chosen according to your skin type. Beneficial for those with sinus problems, or for those seeking to relieve stress.
- Cellular Repair Facial (with acupressure lifting massage)—A luxurious hydrating facial to nourish and tone the skin through the combined action of the rejuvenating products with a 20-minute contour lifting massage and acupressure exercise. Includes an RNA/DNA or vitamin C ampoule treatment to improve the color and texture of the skin, and is especially beneficial for sun-damaged and mature skin.
- Glycolic Facial—This facial gently refines and smoothes the texture of the skin, diminishes fine lines, and improves skin color, restoring the

If you want a massage, but you're not interested in making a trek to the RockSpa, in-room and at-the-pool massage service is available for an additional fee.

skin's natural glow. Through a state-of-the-art glycolic peel, the skin is gently exfoliated then nourished with vitamins, minerals, and other essential elements. Includes a luxurious contour lifting massage and acupressure exercise.

- Gentleman's Facial—A deep cleansing, therapeutic facial designed specifically for the special skin care needs of men. Relaxes the skin as it refines pores. Includes a luxurious massage and deep cleansing mask. Specifically addresses sensitivity and razor burn.

Salon

Hours: 9:00 A.M. to 7:00 P.M. (daily)

Appointments: Recommended, call (702) 693-5522

The Hard Rock Hotel features a full-service salon that offers a wide variety of hair and nail services.

Casino

Although the casino within the Hard Rock Hotel is smaller than many of the casinos along the Strip, the casino here is certainly fully equipped, offering all of the slots, video poker machines, and table games gamblers look for. Table games at the upscale casino (which doesn't offer many tables with low minimum bets) include blackjack, Caribbean Stud poker, craps, Let It Ride, mini-baccarat, Pai Gow poker, and roulette.

Harrah's Las Vegas

Theme: A classic Las Vegas casino and hotel with a Carnaval theme

Room Rate: $$ ($51–$100)

Number of Rooms: 2,672 rooms and 94 suites located in three towers

Casino: 86,664 square feet, featuring 76 table games, 8 poker tables, 1,983 slot and video poker machines, a race book, and a separate sports book

Dining: Seven restaurants and two lounges

Primary Show: *Spellbound* (a show featuring music, dance, comedy, and illusions)

Special Attractions: The Improv comedy club, Carnaval Court (outdoor street fair), the hotel's spa, health club, and salon

Reservations: (800) HARRAHS or (702) 369-5000

Web Site: *www.harrahsvegas.com*

Address: 3475 Las Vegas Boulevard South
Las Vegas, NV 89109

Overall Resort Rating Based on Amenities and Rates

Ages Up to 5	Ages 6–15	Ages 16–20	Ages 21 & Up	Senior Citizens
⚀	⚀ ⚁	⚀ ⚁	⚀ ⚁ ⚂	⚀ ⚁ ⚂

Located in the true heart of the Las Vegas Strip (directly across the street from The Mirage and Caesars Palace, Harrah's Las Vegas is one of the older and more classic casino and hotels, opening in 1973 as the Holiday Casino. Catering primarily to adults (as opposed to family vacationers), Harrah's is competitively priced and offers all of the standard amenities you'd expect from a casino and hotel on the Strip. The only two amenities that might interest children are the video arcade and outdoor swimming pool.

Guest Room Accommodations

The overall design of Harrah's incorporates music, icons, and artwork from Carnaval. The hotel includes three main buildings: the 23-story Mardi Gras North Tower, the 15-story Mardi Gras South Tower, and the 35-story Carnaval Tower. The hotel has 2,672 guest rooms and 94 suites. Basic guest room amenities include:

- 24-hour room service
- One king- or two queen-size beds
- Cable TV, with pay-per-view movies available
- Dry cleaning and laundry services available
- Complimentary valet/garage parking
- Express checkout

Fine Dining

Like so many of the casinos and hotels along the Strip, Harrah's Las Vegas offers a selection of fine-dining experiences with strong influences from around the world. Whether you're in the mood for steak, lobster, spicy kung pao chicken, or veal Parmesan, you'll find it at Harrah's Las Vegas.

The prices at these fine-dining establishments are reasonable. Reservations are highly recommended, especially during peak meal times.

The Range Steakhouse ($$ / $$$)

Reservations: Strongly recommended, call (702) 369-5084

Offering steaks, prime rib, seafood and poultry entrees, this restaurant is open nightly from 5:00 P.M. Most entrees are priced under $20. Nearby is the Range Steakhouse Piano Bar, offering live entertainment nightly from 5:30 to 11:00 P.M. The lounge is an excellent place to relax after dinner. You can enjoy cocktails, premium wines, specialty coffees, appetizers, and fine cigars. The dress code is "upscale casual."

$ = entrees under $10; $$ = under $20; $$$ = over $20

The Cafe Andreotti ($$ / $$$)

Reservations: Strongly recommended, call (702) 369-5084

This traditional Italian restaurant specializes in favorites like veal Parmesan and chicken picatta, in addition to offering a menu chock full of classics. House specials change regularly.

The Cafe Andreotti opens at 5:00 P.M. Wednesday through Sunday. The dress code is casual.

Asia ($$ / $$$)

Reservations: Strongly recommended, call (702) 369-5084

The international flavors of the Orient are found in this restaurant that specializes in Chinese, Asian, Thai, Indian, and Japanese cuisine. A wide range of traditional dishes is offered along with more contemporary menu selections.

The fish tanks in Asia's kitchen contain live fish, shrimp, crab, and lobster, allowing for the ultimate in fresh seafood. Asia opens at 5:30 P.M. on Friday through Tuesday. The dress code is "upscale casual."

Casual Dining

Harrah's fine-dining restaurants all offer quality food at reasonable prices, but if you're looking for a dining experience that's more casual, less expensive, or quicker, check out the hotel's other dining options. Room service is also available to all hotel guests 24 hours a day.

> Harrah's has a reputation for offering world-class casino and resort amenities. Harrah's Entertainment, Inc., operates casinos in every major Nevada and New Jersey gaming market, and in Arizona, Illinois, Indiana, Louisiana, Mississippi, Missouri, North Carolina, and Australia. The company was founded in 1937 as a bingo parlor in Reno, Nevada.

The Garden Cafe ($ / $$)

Open 24 hours a day, seven days a week, this casual restaurant serves breakfast, lunch, dinner, and late-night snacks. Breakfast items range from lighter fare, including fresh fruit or yogurt, to banana pancakes. For lunch, fresh salads, burgers, and sandwiches are available. For dinner, guests can enjoy entrees such as island-style teriyaki chicken, fajitas, prime rib, or seafood fettuccine.

$ = entrees under $10; $$ = under $20; $$$ = over $20

The Fresh Market Square Buffet ($$)

If you're looking for an all-you-can-eat experience that is classical Las Vegas, check out the Fresh Market Square Buffet, which offers fresh food with an international flair (such as Asian, Italian, Mexican, and seafood) that is prepared at individual cooking stations.

The buffet is open daily for breakfast (Monday through Friday, 7:00 to 11:00 A.M. and 7:00 to 10:00 A.M. on weekends), lunch (Monday through Friday from 11:00 A.M. to 4:00 P.M.), and for dinner (from 4:00 to 10:00 P.M., seven days a week). A champagne brunch is served Saturday and Sunday, from 10:00 A.M. to 4:00 P.M. Buffet prices are as follows:

- Breakfast: $7.99 (adults), $4.99 (children)
- Lunch: $8.99 (adults), $5.99 (children)
- Dinner: $12.99 (adults), $7.99 (children)
- Brunch: $12.99 (adults), $7.99 (children)

The Winning Streaks Stadium Cafe ($)

Located in the sports book at Harrah's Las Vegas, guests can enjoy watching their favorite sporting events while eating. Open daily from 11:00 A.M. to 11:00 P.M., a wide range of lighter menu options are available.

Lounges

Club Cappuccino offers a large selection of specialty coffees, espressos, specialty drinks, pastries, sandwiches, soups, and salads. Coffees are also available "to go." Open daily from 5:00 A.M. to 11:00 P.M. (Sunday through Thursday) and 5:00 A.M. to 12:30 A.M. (Friday and Saturday). Prices range from $2 to $4 for coffee and from $3 to $8 for food items.

La Playa Lounge offers a comfortable and relaxed full-service bar (offering tropical drinks) and live music nightly. Open 24 hours a day.

Special Attractions

Aside from gambling, Harrah's Las Vegas offers shows, lounges, a spa, and other facilities designed to help guests relax and be entertained. Whether

---

$ = entrees under $10; $$ = under $20; $$$ = over $20

you're trying to wind down after a long day at a convention or you're simply enjoying a much deserved vacation, there's plenty for adults to see and do at this casino and hotel.

Spellbound

Show Times: 7:30 and 10:00 P.M.

Ticket Price: $39.95, call (800) 392-9002

Combining an entertaining assortment of music, dance, juggling, circus acts, comedy, and illusions, *Spellbound*'s headliner is Mexico's foremost illusionist, Joaquin Ayala. The show offers family-oriented, Las Vegas-style entertainment. This show certainly doesn't compare to *Siegfried & Roy* or Lance Burton's magic shows in terms of entertainment value, but the ticket prices are significantly cheaper and easier to get. Unlike these other shows, this one is more variety show than magic show.

Spellbound

Ages Up to 5	Ages 6–15	Ages 16–20	Ages 21 & Up	Senior Citizens
Not Suitable	Not Suitable	⚀	⚀ ⚁	⚀ ⚁

The Improv Comedy Club at Harrah's Las Vegas

Performances: 8:00 and 10:30 P.M. (Tuesday through Sunday)

Ticket Price: $19.95, call (800) 392-9002

An endless lineup of comedians (often the top names in the business) makes stops at the Improv. Each week, the talent roster changes, so who you'll see performing is anyone's guess. Contact the box office for the current talent lineup. As with any comedy club, strong language may be used by some comedians during their acts.

The Improv

Ages Up to 5	Ages 6–15	Ages 16–20	Ages 21 & Up	Senior Citizens
Not Suitable	Not Suitable	Not Suitable	⚀ ⚁	⚀ ⚁

Spa, Health Club, and Salon

Health club is open daily 6:00 A.M. to 8:00 P.M.

Spa treatments available 9:00 A.M. to 6:00 P.M.

Salon appointments available 9:00 A.M. to 5:00 P.M.

This world-class spa, health club, and salon offers a wide range of services designed to pamper guests and cater to their every need. Massage sessions, for example, last 25, 55, or 90 minutes and range in price from $50 to $105. European facials, body rubs, and other treatments are available by appointment.

The spa is located on the fourth floor of the Carnaval Tower. In addition to offering specialized treatments, the health club features the latest cardiovascular equipment and weight machines. Other amenities include a steam room, whirlpools, and a sauna. The daily fee for using the health club is $15.

Pool

Harrah's Las Vegas offers a large outdoor pool and patio area.

Casino

Harrah's Las Vegas offers a fully equipped casino, complete with 76 table games, 8 poker tables, 1,983 slot and video poker machines, and the Total Gold Players Card (which allows gamblers to earn points that can be exchanged for prizes). There's also a 64-seat race book with 12 TVs and a separate 100-seat sports book with 14 TVs. Table games in the casino include blackjack, craps, roulette, and baccarat. For poker players, the casino offers a separate eight-table room. The casino's keno parlor is open 24 hours a day.

Shopping

Just a short walk from Harrah's Las Vegas are the Forum Shops at Caesars Palace and the Fashion Show Mall, also located along the Strip. Within

During peak periods, be sure to schedule appointments for spa or salon treatments as early as possible to ensure the services you want will be available.

Harrah's, however, you'll find a small selection of shops that offer gifts, souvenirs, and necessities. Shops include:

- Jackpot—Here's where to shop for Las Vegas souvenirs and Harrah's merchandise. You'll also find newspapers, magazines, sundry items, and merchandise from the spa sold here. The shop has two locations: in the main lobby, where it is open 24 hours a day, and at the south end of the property where it is open 8:00 A.M. to 1:00 A.M.
- The Art of Cigars—This store features a large selection of premium cigars and accessories. Humidified storage lockers can also be rented on an annual basis. Located in the hotel's main lobby, the Art of Cigars is open Sunday through Thursday, 9:00 AM to 11:00 P.M. and from 9:00 AM to 1:00 AM on Friday and Saturday.
- Carnaval Corner—Located in the Carnaval Court shopping area, gourmet foods, cookbooks, coffees, liquors, and ingredients from Harrah's restaurants are sold here. This is the place to shop if you enjoy cooking or you're looking for a unique gift.
- On Stage—Merchandise from Harrah's shows, including *Spellbound*, are sold here, along with CDs, picture frames, candles, and other gift items.
- Ghirardelli Chocolate Company—This shop will satisfy anyone's sweet tooth, with an array of ice creams, shakes, sundaes, premium chocolates, coffees, and gift items. You'll find this shop in the Carnaval Court. It's open daily from 10:00 A.M. to 10:00 P.M.
- TCBY—Frozen yogurt is the specialty here.

The casino's high limit gaming area is open Monday through Friday, 11:00 A.M. to 3:00 A.M. (or as needed to accommodate guests). You'll also find this area open 24 hours a day on weekends. Located near the high limit table gaming area is the high limit slot area, featuring $5 to $100 slot and video poker machines.

Banquet, Function, and Convention Services

Information: **(800) 392-9002**

Group Rates: **(800) 537-8370**

With 28,000 square feet of convention facilities, including 21 meeting rooms and a business services area, Harrah's Las Vegas is equipped to handle virtually any type of banquet, function, or convention. The hotel is also conveniently located next to Sands Expo Center.

Imperial Palace

Theme: The Orient

Room Rate: $$ / $$$ ($51–$250)

Number of Rooms: 2,700, including 225 suites

Casino: 75,000 square feet, offering 1,838 slot and video poker machines, 42 table games, a race and sports book, and a keno lounge

Dining: Nine fine-dining and casual restaurants, including the Emperor's Buffet. There are also nine bars and lounges on the property.

Primary Show: *Legends in Concert*

Special Attractions: The Antique and Classic Auto Collection, a Hawaiian Luau, and a walk-in medical center

Reservations: (800) 634-6441

Web Site: *www.imperialpalace.com*

Address: 3535 Las Vegas Boulevard South
Las Vegas, NV 89109

Overall Resort Rating Based on Amenities and Rates

Ages Up to 5	Ages 6–15	Ages 16–20	Ages 21 & Up	Senior Citizens
⚀	⚀⚁	⚀⚁	⚀⚁	⚀⚁

Imperial Palace is the largest independently owned and operated resort casino on the Las Vegas Strip and one of the 15 largest hotels in the world. The property opened in November 1979, but has undergone extensive expansion and remodeling.

This property offers complete resort amenities, but is more competitively priced and targets a more mainstream customer base than many of the other upscale mega-resorts, like the Bellagio or the Venetian. From its excellent location in the heart of the Strip, Imperial Palace primarily caters to adults. It is located about 10 minutes (by car) from McCarran International Airport and about five minutes (by car) from the Las Vegas Convention Center.

Guest Room Accommodations

Imperial Palace has 2,700 rooms and suites that offer comfortable, albeit basic accommodations. Rooms contain a single king-size bed or two queen-size beds, a television, and other furnishings (including a small table/desk with two chairs). Smoking and nonsmoking rooms are available. The suites offer considerably more space and better amenities.

Fine Dining

Enjoy Oriental and American cuisine at the handful of fine-dining restaurants, each offering a different setting. Room service is also available to registered guests.

Ming Terrace ($$)

Reservations: Call (702) 794-3261

Mandarin and Cantonese cuisine is served in an exotic Far Eastern atmosphere. The extensive menu includes abalone, Peking duck, double-cooked pork with cabbage, and many other traditional and contemporary favorites. Open nightly for dinner, starting at 5:00 P.M. This restaurant is located in the dining plaza area, on the fifth floor. Dress is casual.

The Seahouse ($$)

Reservations: Recommended, call (702) 794-3261

Located in the dining plaza area on the fifth floor of the main resort building, the Seahouse offers a selection of fresh seafood dishes. Entrees include lobster, crab, grilled fish, and ethnic seafood delicacies, all prepared in front of you. If you're dining with people who don't enjoy seafood, a small selection of chicken and steak entrees are available. The Seahouse is open Friday through Tuesday, starting at 5:00 P.M. Dress is casual.

The Embers ($$$)

Reservations: Recommended, call (702) 794-3261

For an intimate dining experience at the Imperial Palace, visit the Embers. Diners can select from a diverse menu, which includes steak, prime

$ = entrees under $10; $$ = under $20; $$$ = over $20

Imperial Palace is one of only a few resorts along the Strip to offer CAPS—Certified Airline Passenger Services. When you're ready to check out from the resort, CAPS will check your baggage, transport your bags to the airport, then obtain your seat assignment and boarding pass. To take advantage of this service, from your guest room, call extension #607 two to 12 hours before your departure. Not all airlines currently support this service, so check with the CAPS representative at the hotel. Due to federal security regulations, each traveler must check his or her own bags with CAPS and show photo identification.

rib, lamb, veal, and seafood dishes. The Embers is open for dinner Wednesday through Sunday, starting at 5:00 P.M. You'll find the dining room on the fifth floor of the main resort building, in the dining plaza area. Dress is casual.

The Rib House ($$)

Reservations: Call (702) 794-3261

Dine in a relaxed atmosphere as you enjoy traditional Western fare, such as barbecue ribs and chicken. Original sauces and flavoring add a zestful taste to the house specialties. Most entrees can be prepared blackened or Cajun style. The Rib House is open Tuesday through Saturday for dinner, starting at 5:00 P.M. Like all of the fine-dining restaurants at Imperial Palace, you'll find the Rib House in the resort's fifth-floor dining plaza area. Dress is casual.

Casual Dining

Pizza Palace ($$)

Reservations: Suggested for dinner, call (702) 794-3261

Traditional Italian dishes and pizzas are made to order. Open daily, starting at 11:00 A.M., this restaurant serves generous portions at a fair price, providing for an excellent family-dining experience.

Teahouse / Imperial Buffet ($)

Open 24 hours a day, the Teahouse / Imperial Buffet offers both menu service and a buffet. You'll find this restaurant by taking the escalator near the rear of the casino. Breakfast is served from 7:00 to 11:30 A.M. (the buffet costs $7.45 per person). Lunch begins at 11:30 A.M. and goes until 2:30 P.M. (the buffet costs $7.45 per person on weekdays). A prime rib champagne dinner is served nightly, from 5:00 to 10:00 P.M. ($9.45 per person). On weekends and holidays, a champagne brunch is served from 8:00 A.M. to 3:00 P.M. ($8.45 per person).

Emperor's Buffet ($)

This is a classic, all-you-can-eat buffet, featuring fresh salads, fruits, soups, juices, plus a wide selection of entrees and desserts. Breakfast (7:00 to 11:30

$ = entrees under $10; $$ = under $20; $$$ = over $20

A.M., $6.25 per person), lunch (11:30 A.M. to 5:00 P.M., $7.50 per person), and dinner (5:00 to 10:00 P.M., $8.50 per person) are served daily. Seating is on a first-come basis, so be prepared to wait during peak times. Like so many of the buffets available along the Las Vegas Strip, this one offers an excellent value, so bring your appetite.

Burger Palace ($)

Hamburgers, along with chicken and fish sandwiches, plus salads, doughnuts, pastries, and an assortment of other offerings are served daily from 6:00 A.M. to 1:00 P.M. (Sunday through Thursday), and from 6:00 A.M. to 2:00 P.M. (Friday and Saturday). This is a great place to go for a quick and inexpensive meal or snack.

Betty's Diner ($)

This full-service diner offers a complete breakfast menu along with hot dogs, sandwiches, nachos, ice cream, shakes, malts, and sundaes. An inexpensive and quick dining experience can be found here. Open 24 hours.

Lounges

Throughout the Imperial Palace, you'll find nine full-service bars and lounges. Some offer live music, while others offer a light menu. The Duesenberg Lounge, for example, can be found near the resort's famed auto collection. In the main casino, you'll find the Geisha Bar, the Ginza Bar, the Mai Tai Bar, and the Sake Bar. The Kanpai Bar is located in the satellite casino, while the Sports Bar is next to the race and sports book in the main casino. There's also a poolside bar and a lounge in the resort's fifth-floor dining plaza area.

Special Attractions

The Imperial Palace offers the *Legends in Concert* show, a classic and antique car exhibit, a fitness center, swimming pool, video game arcade, and other activities. The property is a short walk from several of the Strip's best known mega-resorts and shopping areas, so finding exciting

$ = entrees under $10; $$ = under $20; $$$ = over $20

or relaxing ways to spend your time while staying at Imperial Palace shouldn't be difficult.

Legends in Concert

Reservations: (702) 794-3261

Show Times: 7:30 and 10:30 P.M. (except Sunday)

Ticket Price: $34.50

If you're expecting a flashy, special effects–filled extravaganza, you won't find it at Imperial Palace. When it comes to in-house shows, what you will find is *Legends in Concert,* featuring a large cast of extremely talented celebrity impersonators.

During the performance, Elvis, Michael Jackson, the Blues Brothers, Tina Turner, Madonna, Sammy Davis Jr., Buddy Holly, Garth Brooks, Cher, and a host of other music legends will come to life as the impersonators sing and play their own instruments. The show also features a cast of talented Las Vegas showgirls.

This show is suitable for teens and adults alike. It offers light-hearted musical entertainment and a reasonable price. The Imperial Palace has been the permanent home of *Legends in Concert* since May 1983.

Legends in Concert

Ages Up to 5	Ages 6–15	Ages 16–20	Ages 21 & Up	Senior Citizens
Not Suitable	⚁⚁	⚁⚁	⚁⚁	⚁⚁

Imperial Style Hawaiian Luau

Reservations: (702) 794-3261

Show Times: 6:30 P.M. (Tuesday and Thursday)

Ticket Price: Approximately $27

Presented April through October on Tuesday and Thursday evenings, this authentic poolside luau and Polynesian review is presented on the

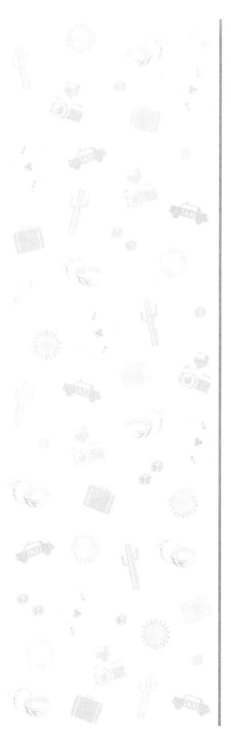

resort's pool deck (in a tropical setting) and includes a seafood dinner buffet. Unlimited mai tais and pina coladas are served (along with nonalcoholic fruit punch). This is an upbeat, family-oriented musical review, complete with the romantic call of the conch shells, the ceremonial lighting of the torches, and the island lei greeting. The show encourages audience participation, so be prepared to hula.

Imperial Style Hawaiian Luau

	Ages Up to 5	Ages 6–15	Ages 16–20	Ages 21 & Up	Senior Citizens
	Not Suitable	⚀ ⚁ ⚂	⚀ ⚁ ⚂	⚀ ⚁ ⚂	⚀ ⚁ ⚂

The Imperial Palace Antique & Classic Auto Collection

Hours: 9:30 A.M. to 11:30 P.M. (daily)

Admission: $6.95 (adults), $3 (children under 12)

This is definitely one of the finest privately owned car collections in the world that is on public display. What began in December 1981 as an exhibit of two hundred automobiles has grown to include more than eight hundred antique, classic, and special interest vehicles, spanning over one hundred years of automotive history. Guests are invited to view the cars at their own pace.

The collection features cars once owned by famous and infamous people, rare vehicles, and some of the most historically significant cars ever produced. While passenger cars are the stars of the Imperial Palace's collection, they are complemented by an assortment of military vehicles, motorcycles, trucks, tractors, taxis, fire engines, and even old-fashioned gas pumps.

Additionally, the auto collection now has a one-of-a-kind attraction—the largest collection of Model J Duesenbergs in the world. Among the Duesenbergs on display are those once owned by film legend James Cagney, chewing gum magnate Phillip K. Wrigley, heavyweight boxing champion Max Baer, band leader Paul Whiteman, razor mogul Col. Jacob Schick, and others.

Presidential cars on display include John F. Kennedy's 1962 Lincoln Continental "Bubble Top," Dwight D. Eisenhower's 1952 Chrysler Imperial,

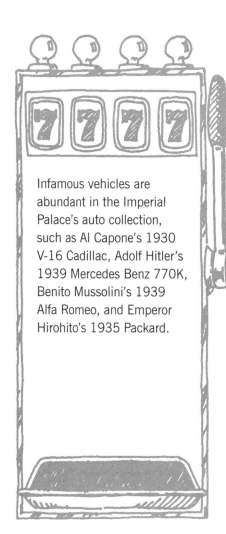

Infamous vehicles are abundant in the Imperial Palace's auto collection, such as Al Capone's 1930 V-16 Cadillac, Adolf Hitler's 1939 Mercedes Benz 770K, Benito Mussolini's 1939 Alfa Romeo, and Emperor Hirohito's 1935 Packard.

Herbert Hoover's 1929 Cadillac, Eleanor Roosevelt's 1932 Plymouth, and Harry S. Truman's 1950 Lincoln. Royalty and foreign presidential rulers are represented with Czar Nicholas II's 1914 Rolls-Royce, the King of Siam's 1928 Delage, and Queen Wilhelmina's 1933 Buick.

Famous celebrities' cars have their niche in the auto collection as well. Among these are Elvis Presley's 1976 Cadillac Eldorado, Tom Mix's 1937 Cord, Liberace's 1981 Zimmer, W. C. Fields's 1938 Cadillac, Howard Hughes's 1954 Chrysler, Jack Benny's 1910 Maxwell, Jack Dempsey's 1926 McFarlan, Leo "Pancho" Carrillo's 1948 Chrysler, and motorcycles owned by Steve McQueen, Clark Gable, and Sammy Davis Jr.

As you leave the auto collection, if you're a car buff, be sure to visit the nearby gift shop, which contains a wide variety of automotive memorabilia and books. The auto collection is interesting, even for noncar buffs. This attraction can provide several hours of entertainment.

The Imperial Palace Antique & Classic Auto Collection

Ages Up to 5	Ages 6–15	Ages 16–20	Ages 21 & Up	Senior Citizens
⚀	⚀ ⚀	⚀ ⚀	⚀ ⚀ ⚁	⚀ ⚀ ⚁

Spa, Health Club, and Salon

Hours: 7:00 A.M. to 7:00 P.M.

Information/Reservations: (702) 731-3311 (ask for the fitness center)

The Imperial Palace's health and fitness center, which includes a coed cardiovascular area with Stairmaster, Lifecycles, treadmills, rowing machines, and aerobics videos, plus free weights, Nautilus and Universal equipment is available to all registered guests for a daily fee of $10. Separate men's and women's locker areas are equipped with steam rooms, dry saunas, showers, and individual lockers. Juice, towels, sandals, and robes are also provided.

For an additional fee, 30- or 60-minute massages are available for $35 and $60, respectively. Massages should be scheduled in advance. Twenty-minute tanning sessions are also available at the health and fitness center.

Pool

The Shangri-La pool is an Olympic-sized heated pool, complete with a waterfall and whirlpool. The pool area also offers a large deck for sun-bathing and poolside cocktail service.

Casino

The Imperial Palace's 75,000-square-foot casino offers 1,838 slot and video poker machines (gamblers can wager between $.05 and $25 per pull on the various slot machines), 42 table games, a race and sports book, and a keno lounge. Table games include all of the traditional favorites, including blackjack, craps, roulette, Pai Gow poker, Caribbean Stud poker, Let It Ride, and mini-baccarat. Complimentary gaming lessons are offered daily. Visit the casino's information desk to register.

The Imperial Palace Casino offers the Daily Wild Times slot tournament. For an entry fee of $20, guests and visitors alike are invited to participate.

The Gallery of Legends within the casino is a non-smoking area that offers a variety of table games and slots.

The main casino also features a fully equipped, 230-seat race and sports book with 250 TV screens. The race and sports book opens at 8:00 A.M. and continues until the final major event of the day is complete. Betting is available on all major sports and on all horse and dog racing at every major track.

A separate keno lounge is also available. For more information about casino events, call (800) 351-7400 extension 1. Like all of the major casinos, Imperial Palace offers the Imperial Player Program. Prizes include complimentary room accommodations, room upgrades, free meals, gift certificates, and other merchandise.

Shopping

The Imperial Palace features several shops on-property that sell souvenirs, resort merchandise, and other essentials. The Forum Shops (at Caesars Palace) and the Fashion Show Mall are a short walk away.

Banquet, Function, and Conference Services

Information: (800) 351-7400, ext. 2

The Imperial Palace's Royal Hall offers 9,600 square feet of banquet and function space. This room serves 650 to 960 people based on its configuration. The resort also contains 17 meeting rooms for 10 to 900 people.

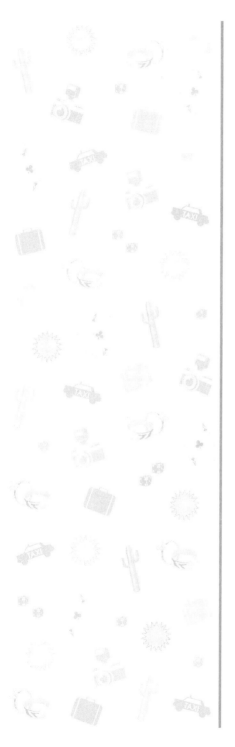

Business Center

In conjunction with the conference services, the Business Center allows guests to send packages, send and receive faxes, make copies, and perform other business-related tasks while staying at the hotel.

Wedding Chapel

Information/Reservations: (702) 346-3373 or (702) 733-0011

The wedding chapel in the Imperial Palace offers a handful of complete wedding packages, starting at $289 (which includes use of the chapel, a candlelight-style ceremony, traditional music, 12 wedding photos, a presentation bouquet, the groom's boutonniere, and other amenities). More elaborate packages are available, including a "Wedding in the Sky" balloon ride, the "Tunnel of Love" drive-thru, and a "Wedding on Wheels" (where the minister comes to your guest room or another location to perform the ceremony).

The wedding planners at the Imperial Palace can also arrange for a wide range of additional services, such as a custom wedding cake, live music, floral arrangements, tuxedo rentals, limo service, and video recording. Ministers are available 24 hours a day; however, advance reservations are recommended if you'd like to use the wedding chapel facilities.

Medical Center

Information: (702) 735-3600

Whether you're experiencing a medical emergency or a headache, the walk-in medical facility in the Imperial Palace offers both doctors and nurses on-staff. This is an independently operated facility located on the eighth floor of the main casino building.

Las Vegas Hilton

Theme: A traditional Hilton resort

Room Rate: $$$ / $$$$ ($101+)

Number of Rooms: 3,174 rooms, suites (including theme suites), and villas

Casino: 67,000 square feet, offering 1,200 slot machines and 75 gaming tables, plus a race and sports book

Dining: Twelve restaurants, including Quark's Bar & Restaurant (a theme restaurant based on the *Star Trek* television series and movies)

Special Attractions: *Star Trek:* The Experience and the Hilton Theater Concert Series

Reservations: (800) 732-7117 or (702) 732-5111

Web Site: *www.lv-hilton.com*

Address: 3000 Paradise Road
Las Vegas, NV 89109

Overall Resort Rating Based on Amenities and Rates

Ages Up to 5	Ages 6–15	Ages 16–20	Ages 21 & Up	Senior Citizens
⚁⚁	⚀⚁	⚀⚁⚂	⚀⚁⚂	⚀⚁⚂

Not to be confused with the Flamingo Hilton, also located in Las Vegas, the Las Vegas Hilton is a full-service resort featuring a wide range of guest room accommodations, plenty of amenities, and reasonable pricing. The Las Vegas Hilton is located several blocks off of the Strip, next to the Las Vegas Convention Center. It's less than a 10-minute drive from McCarran International Airport, making it ideal for business travelers and convention goers.

The original hotel opened in 1969. In 1971, it was bought by Hilton Hotels Corporation. Since then, in 1975, 1978, and 1981, the resort underwent several major expansions, making it the full-service resort it has become. In fact, this hotel serves 2.5 million guests a year.

Guest Room Accommodations

The Las Vegas Hilton is known for its spacious guest rooms and impressive standard amenities, including 24-hour housekeeping, air conditioning, cable TV (with pay-per-view channels), connecting rooms, handheld shower heads, nonsmoking rooms, two phones per room, and telephone voice mail.

In addition to traditional guest rooms, the Las Vegas Hilton offers more expensive accommodation options in the form of suites and villas. The Lanai suites, for example, have private patios opening onto the third-floor recreation deck. The resort also features suites with Hollywood, Gold Coast, Renaissance, and country club themes. For people looking for luxury, the Sky Villas (ranging from 12,600 square feet to over 15,000 square feet) are available to high rollers and anyone else with deep pockets.

Fine Dining

Although 24-hour room service is always available to guests, the Las Vegas Hilton offers a range of fine-dining and casual restaurants.

The Reef ($$$)

Reservations: Recommended, call (702) 732-5755

The Las Vegas Hilton calls this a traditional seafood restaurant with a contemporary flair. The dining room is decorated in a nautical motif, and the menu offers a selection of seafood items. House specialties include the Reef's blackened sashimi, seafood stuffed mushrooms, and macadamia nut calamari. Also featured on the menu are soups (such as Boston clam chowder), salads, stuffed Maine lobster, baked salmon, lobster tails, crab legs, and prime filet. For dessert, don't miss the turtle cheesecake, chocolate mousse, or banana crème brûlé. Open for dinner only, 5:30 to 10:30 P.M. nightly.

Benihana Village ($$$)

Reservations: Recommended, call (702) 732-5755

Dinner at Benihana Village isn't just a meal, it's truly an entertaining experience as talented chefs prepare your meal at your table. Benihana

Other Resort Services

With the goal of being a full-service resort that caters to business people, convention goers, and vacationers alike, the Las Vegas Hilton offers a wide range of services, such as 24-hour valet parking, a hair salon and barber shop, car rentals, and a business center.

$ = entrees under $10; $$ = under $20; $$$ = over $20

Village offers Japanese dining at its best. Steak, chicken, and seafood dishes are the house specialty. All entrees come with salad, soup, rice, vegetables, and tea. Tables seat up to eight people, so if you're dining with a smaller party, you may be seated with strangers, which often adds to the enjoyment of the experience. In addition to the great food, Benihana's Kabuki Lounge provides a perfect opportunity to enjoy a variety of Japanese and Western beverages. While it's a bit pricey, this restaurant is a great place to bring the kids, who will enjoy the show the chefs put on as they prepare each meal. Open for dinner only, 5:00 to 10:30 P.M. nightly.

Bistro Le Montrachet ($$$)

Reservations: Recommended, call (702) 732-5755

The finest in French cuisine with a contemporary flavor and style is what this restaurant offers. The wine list offered at Bistro Le Montrachet features more than four hundred selections. Open for lunch and dinner, except on Tuesday and Wednesday. Dinner is served from 6:00 to 10:00 P.M.

Andiamo ($$$)

Reservations: Recommended, call (702) 732-5755

Flavors of Northern Italy and the Mediterranean coast are on the menu of this restaurant, which also features an exhibition kitchen, allowing guests to watch the chefs at work. Pastas, pastries, and salads are the specialties of the house. Open for dinner only, Tuesday through Saturday, from 5:30 to 10:30 P.M.

Hilton Steakhouse ($$$)

Reservations: Recommended, call (702) 732-5755

Menu selections at this classic steakhouse include quality beef broiled over an open flame. In addition to select types of steaks, rounding out the menu are veal, lamb, pork, chicken, and seafood dishes. All menu items are served a la carte. The main dining room offers rich mahogany booths and chairs, providing an elegant and intimate setting. Open for dinner only, 5:30 to 10:30 P.M. nightly.

Hungry? Every year the Las Vegas Hilton's guests consume 203,370 dozen eggs, 95,130 pounds of bacon, 203,590 pounds of turkey, 410,429 pounds of chicken, 647,213 pounds of beef, 66,815 gallons of milk, 190,288 bottles of wine, 869,085 pounds of fruit, and 171,475 loaves of bread.

$ = entrees under $10; $$ = under $20; $$$ = over $20

For more than seven years and through 837 performances, the Las Vegas Hilton was Elvis Presley's home away from Graceland. He first performed at the Las Vegas Hilton on July 31, 1969. His final show at the resort was on December 12, 1976. While staying at the Las Vegas Hilton, Elvis stayed in the famed 5,000-square-foot "Elvis Suite," located on the 30th floor. This suite has since been renovated and is now where the resort's Sky Villas are located. (Yeah, it's true. Elvis has left the building!)

Garden of the Dragon ($$$)

Reservations: Recommended, call (702) 732-5755

Offering a selection of Szechuan, Peking-style, Northern Mongolian, and Cantonese cuisine, Garden of the Dragon provides diners with a comfortable and intimate setting that overlooks the Benihana Village gardens. Open for dinner only, 6:00 to 10:30 P.M. nightly.

Margarita Grille ($$$)

Reservations: Recommended, call (702) 732-5755

Get ready to cross the border for a truly authentic Mexican feast. Specialties include spinach enchiladas, spicy burritos, chimichangas, crisp tostadas, tacos, and sizzling fajitas. At the bar, a variety of fruit margaritas are served. Breakfast is served 7:00 to 11:30 A.M., lunch 11:30 A.M. to 3:45 P.M., and dinner 4:00 to 10:30 P.M.

Casual and Theme Dining

Even if you don't want to spend a fortune or enjoy a multicourse meal in a fancy setting, the Las Vegas Hilton offers plenty of quality dining options to choose from that are a far cry from traditional fast food.

Paradise Cafe ($ / $$)

Open 24 hours, this cafe offers a broad menu designed to cater to anyone's demanding taste buds, no matter what time it is. It's not exactly fine dining, but it's good.

The Buffet ($$)

The Las Vegas Hilton's answer to an all-you-can-eat buffet can be found at the Buffet, which is open 7:00 A.M. to 11:00 P.M. (weekdays) and 8:00 A.M. to 2:30 P.M. and 5:00 to 10:00 P.M. on weekends. Typical lunch fare includes prime rib, smoked salmon, pasta, lo mein, sushi rolls, broiled steak, and peeled shrimp. For dinner, get ready for an even bigger selection, including crab, shrimp, pasta, wok items, broiled lamb chops, fresh

$ = entrees under $10; $$ = under $20; $$$ = over $20

raw clams, oysters, and turkey. During peak times, be prepared to wait to be seated, since no reservations are accepted and seating is on a first-come basis.

Paddock Snack Bar ($)

You'll feel as if you're at a major league baseball game or some other sporting event when you step into this snack bar and order a hot dog, ice cream, pizza, sandwich, or any other item from the limited menu. This snack bar is located in the SuperBook. It's open daily from 7:00 A.M. to midnight.

Garden Snack Bar ($)

Located outside on the resort's third-floor recreation deck, this snack bar offers a variety of snacks and inexpensive menu items. Open seasonally.

Quark's Bar and Restaurant ($$)

Reservations: (702) 697-8725

Space may be the final frontier, but Captain Kirk would certainly want to dine at Quark's Bar and Restaurant during his shore leave on Earth. While enjoying a variety of Earth-based menu items, ranging from burgers to pasta, you'll feel like you're aboard a Federation space station. Uniformed servers take your order on tricorders as Klingons and Ferengi stroll through the dining room making small talk with guests. Quark's Bar and Restaurant is located within *Star Trek:* The Experience. Next to the restaurant is a full-service bar.

Anyone who is even a casual fan of any *Star Trek* television series or motion picture should make a point to experience *Star Trek:* The Experience and end their intergalactic journey at Quark's Bar and Restaurant for a snack, lunch, or dinner. The food is good and the prices are reasonable, but what makes this restaurant truly special is the *Star Trek* theme. While dining, you can catch some classic moments from *Star Trek* on TVs throughout the dining room.

The Hilton Barron's Club slot club is free to join and allows gamblers to earn points based on the amount of gambling they do in the Las Vegas Hilton's casinos. Points can be exchanged for a variety of rewards and prizes. To join, visit the membership desk located in the hotel's lobby.

$ = entrees under $10; $$ = under $20; $$$ = over $20

Special Attractions

Of all the theme park attractions in Las Vegas, one of the most unique and exciting (at least for *Star Trek* fans) is *Star Trek:* The Experience. This is just one of the entertainment-oriented activities available to guests and visitors at the Las Vegas Hilton.

Star Trek: The Experience

Ticket Prices: $15.95 per person (Nevada residents less)

Information: **(888) GO-BOLDLY** or *www.startrekexp.com*

The Las Vegas Hilton may not offer a full theme park or fancy stage show, but it does offer one of the most incredible experiences any true *Star Trek* fan could ever want. This $70-million attraction was created by the writers, producers, and set designers responsible for the *Star Trek* television series and movies. These people teamed up with those responsible for creating many of the rides and attractions at the Paramount theme parks. The result is an interactive *Star Trek* experience that's unlike anything you can experience elsewhere.

When you step into the *Star Trek:* The Experience, you truly feel like you've stepped into the twenty-fourth century and become a member of Starfleet. Your journey begins as you experience a museum-style exhibit featuring over two hundred *Star Trek* costumes, weapons, makeup, special effects, and props from the TV shows and movies. Your journey then continues as you literally get beamed aboard the Starship Enterprise and partake in your own intergalactic adventure.

The entire experience lasts about 22 minutes, however, you're free to experience the exhibit portion of the attraction at your own pace. The motion simulator/ride aspect of your adventure lasts about four truly exciting minutes. You'll ultimately wind up in a shopping promenade styled after the *Star Trek: Deep Space Nine* space station, where you'll find several stores selling *Star Trek* collectibles and memorabilia.

To get the maximum amount of enjoyment out of this attraction, it's best not to know what to expect. You can be sure, however, you'll experience awesome visual and audio effects, a fast-paced (and turbulent) motion simulator ride, plus other surprises.

The admission price of *Star Trek:* The Experience is $15.95 per person; however, Nevada residents and Star Trek MasterCard holders

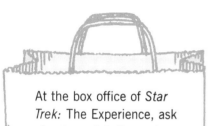

At the box office of *Star Trek:* The Experience, ask about special discounts and package deals allowing you to experience several of Las Vegas's thrill rides and attractions. There's also a special discount if you choose to experience *Star Trek:* The Experience twice in a single day.

receive a discount. Guests must be at least 42 inches tall to experience the motion simulator voyage.

Star Trek: The Experience

Ages Up to 5	Ages 6–15	Ages 16–20	Ages 21 & Up	Senior Citizens*
⚀ ⚁	⚀ ⚁ ⚂	⚀ ⚁ ⚂	⚀ ⚁ ⚂	⚀ ⚁ ⚂

Note: This attraction contains a turbulent motion simulator ride that may not be suitable for people with certain physical disabilities or limitations.

The Hilton Theater

Information: (702) 732-5111

The Hilton Theater presents an ongoing series of concerts, featuring big-name performers. Everyone from Elvis Presley to Melissa Manchester, Lou Rawls, Harry Belafonte, Amy Grant, LeAnn Rimes, Johnny Mathis, Trisha Yearwood, Chaka Khan, Nancy Wilson, and Jamie Foxx have performed here. For additional information about specific shows and concerts, contact the resort's box office.

The NightClub

One of the few nightclubs that target vacationers and tourists in Las Vegas, the NightClub offers nightly live entertainment and dancing, plus what the resort calls the best lighting and sound system in Las Vegas. The dance floor itself is 710 square feet. Live entertainment on Friday and Saturday nights currently features a performer named Louie Louie (*www.louielouis.com*).

Recreation Deck and Spa

On the resort's third-floor roof is an eight-acre recreation deck offering a wide range of outdoor activities, including six lighted tennis courts (with a tennis pro on call), a 350,000-gallon heated swimming pool, a 24-seat outdoor spa, nine-hole putting green, and a full-service health club (offering massages, tanning, etc.).

The adjoining Las Vegas Hilton Health Spa is a fully equipped facility with weight equipment, LifeCycles, steam rooms, saunas, indoor spas, massage

Convention Services

Aside from the Las Vegas Convention Center, one of the largest and best equipped places to hold any type of convention in the Las Vegas area is the Las Vegas Hilton, which offers more than 200,000 square feet of convention space, including the 35,000-square-foot Hilton Ballroom and the 44,130-square-foot Hilton Pavilion. There's also the 70,000-square-foot Hilton Center and many smaller conference rooms. These facilities are equipped with state-of-the-art sound systems and lighting. In-house television production facilities are also available.

Whether you're planning a convention for thousands of people, a business meeting for a dozen people, or some other type of gathering or function, the Las Vegas Hilton's staff can help you plan a successful event.

rooms, and tanning beds. Open seasonally, there's also an outdoor snack bar. There are additional per hour or daily charges for hotel guests to use some of the recreational and spa facilities.

Casino

The 67,000-square-foot main casino offers 75 gaming tables, including baccarat, blackjack, craps, roulette, Big Six wheel, keno, Pai Gow, Pai Gow poker, mini-baccarat, Let It Ride, and Caribbean Stud poker. The casino also offers 1,120 slot machines.

Next to *Star Trek:* The Experience attraction, the Las Vegas Hilton offers the SpaceQuest Casino, which features a futuristic, space theme along with 420 slot machines (from $.05 to $5 machines).

The resort's 30,500-square-foot race and sports book, known as SuperBook, has more than 46 TV screens and one of the most technologically advanced systems in the world, making it the ideal place for sports fans to enjoy popular sporting events and place wagers on them. SuperBook has seating for 400, including 275 semiprivate race book booths.

The VIP Platinum Play room offers amenities catering to high denomination slot players, including a variety of slot machines in denominations from $5 to $500 and video poker from $5 to $100. Hot and cold appetizers are provided to high rollers invited into this special casino area.

Shopping

Throughout the resort complex you'll find a variety of shops, including *Star Trek* theme shops near the exit of *Star Trek:* The Experience. There's also a separate shopping promenade offering a selection of boutiques and shops.

Luxor

Theme:	Ancient Egypt (the building itself is shaped like a 30-story pyramid)
Room Rate:	$$$ ($101–$250)
Number of Rooms:	4,407 rooms and suites
Casino:	120,000 square feet, featuring 105 table games, 2,600 slot machines, video poker, and keno
Dining:	Eight restaurants, a food court, and in-room dining
Primary Show:	*Blue Man Group Live*
Special Attractions:	*Bill Acosta's Lasting Impressions,* Ra: The Nightclub, Nefertiti's Lounge, an IMAX movie theater, King Tut's Museum, In Search of the Obelisk (motion simulator ride)
Reservations:	(800) 288-1000
Web Site:	*www.luxor.com*
Address:	3900 Las Vegas Boulevard South Las Vegas, NV 89119

Overall Resort Rating Based on Amenities and Rates

Ages Up to 5	Ages 6–15	Ages 16–20	Ages 21 & Up	Senior Citizens
⚀	⚀ ⚁	⚀ ⚂ ⚃	⚀ ⚂ ⚃	⚀ ⚁ ⚃

As you approach the Las Vegas Strip, it's impossible to miss seeing the giant pyramid structure that makes up the Luxor. Shining from the top of this massive, 30-story structure every night is the brightest light beam in the world. It can be seen from 10 miles in space.

The Luxor is owned and operated by the Mandalay Resort Group, which also owns and operates Mandalay Bay, the Excalibur, Circus Circus, and the Monte Carlo in Las Vegas, as well as a handful of other casino and resort properties in Reno and other parts of Nevada, in Mississippi, and in Illinois.

This family-oriented hotel has an ancient-Egyptian theme encompassing every aspect of the resort itself, starting with its pyramid shape. This theme is enhanced through the property's décor and shows, helping to create the feeling of being transported from modern day

Las Vegas to ancient Egypt each time you pass through the doors. Just inside the front door, you can't miss the life-sized, 35-foot-tall replica of the Great Temple of Ramses II, one of the truly stunning architectural wonders of ancient Egypt.

In a nutshell, the Luxor offers activities, shows, and attractions for the whole family. It's the adults, however, who will better appreciate the extreme attention to detail that this resort offers in terms of the ancient-Egyptian theme that is present everywhere.

Looking for special room rates that not even travel agents can offer? Check out the official Luxor Web site at *www.luxor.com*. The online reservations area regularly offers special promotions only available on the Web.

Guest Room Accommodations

The 4,400 rooms and suites in the Luxor offer comfort and convenient amenities. Many of the rooms have a stunning view of the Las Vegas Strip, the nearby mountains, or the hotel's pool. Suites with a Jacuzzi and/or concierge and valet service are available.

The Luxor hotel is pyramid shaped, so all rooms in the main building have a slanted wall on the exterior (window) side. The rooms in the towers have square walls. All rooms are decorated in what the hotel calls an "updated Egyptian style." The tower rooms contain both a bathtub and a separate shower, while the rooms in the main pyramid structure contain only a shower.

Fine Dining

You'll be treated like Egyptian royalty as you dine at any of these restaurants located in Luxor's giant pyramid building.

ISIS ($$)

Reservations: Recommended, call (702) 262-4773

The stars shine brightly indoors at this fine-dining establishment that overlooks Luxor's casino from the mezzanine level. Seasonal dishes, Continental cuisine, and calorie-conscious offerings are what you'll find on the menu. Dinner is served nightly from 5:00 until 11:00 P.M.

Sacred Sea Room ($$)

Reservations: Recommended, call (702) 262-4772

Fresh seafood (flown in daily) is the specialty of this fine-dining restaurant. It's decorated lavishly with murals and hieroglyphic reproductions

$ = entrees under $10; $$ = under $20; $$$ = over $20

depicting scenes of fishing on the Nile. Dinner is served nightly from 5:00 until 11:00 P.M.

Luxor Steakhouse ($$$)

Reservations: Recommended, call (702) 262-4778

If you want to dine like a true pharaoh and you're in the mood for nothing less that top quality USDA prime cuts of beef, the Luxor Steakhouse offers elegant dining with specialties including New York strip steak, filet mignon, and roast prime rib. The menu also offers a selection of seafood, chicken, and pork entrees, soups, salads, and, of course, desserts. Dinner is served nightly from 5:00 to 11:00 P.M.

Papyrus ($$)

Reservations: Recommended, call (702) 262-4774

The Luxor may offer a taste of ancient Egypt in terms of its atmosphere, but this restaurant offers many Asian delights including Cantonese and Szechuan cuisine and Polynesian and Pacific Rim specialties. Dinner is served nightly from 5:00 to 11:00 P.M.

Casual Dining
Pharaoh's Pheast Buffet ($)

During your visit to Las Vegas, you'll probably want to experience a classic Las Vegas–style buffet. This particular buffet offers an endless supply of all-you-can-eat entrees, appetizers, salads, and desserts for one price. Breakfast is served from 7:00 to 11:00 A.M., lunch is offered from 11:00 A.M. to 4:00 P.M., and dinner is available daily from 4:00 to 11:00 P.M. No reservations are accepted, so be prepared for a wait.

Pyramid Cafe ($ / $$)

Open 24 hours and located on the casino level of the Luxor, the Pyramid Cafe serves a full-service, sit-down breakfast, lunch, and dinner in a coffee shop–style atmosphere. A full menu is available. If you're looking for a relatively fast and inexpensive meal, this is an excellent dining choice, and a good alternative to the buffet.

$ = entrees under $10; $$ = under $20; $$$ = over $20

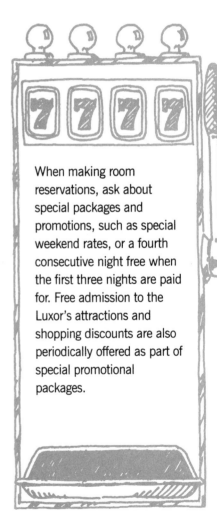

When making room reservations, ask about special packages and promotions, such as special weekend rates, or a fourth consecutive night free when the first three nights are paid for. Free admission to the Luxor's attractions and shopping discounts are also periodically offered as part of special promotional packages.

Nile Deli ($ / $$)

There were no delicatessens in ancient Egypt, but chances are the pharaohs would have enjoyed a classic turkey club sandwich, a potato knish, blintzes, chopped chicken liver, or potato pancakes. The Nile Deli offers "kosher-style" deli foods in a New York–themed setting. Open daily for breakfast, lunch, and dinner, this is an inexpensive dining option suitable for the entire family. The Nile Deli is located on the casino level of the hotel, near the Luxor Theater. Hours of operation are 6:00 A.M. to 10:00 P.M.

Luxor Food Court ($)

When you're looking for fast and cheap food or snacks, look no farther than the Luxor Food Court. It's located on the attractions level of the hotel. Here you'll find many of the fast-food classics you know they never had in ancient Egypt, such as McDonald's, Nathan's, Little Caesar's Pizza, Swenson's Ice Cream, and Luxor Coffee Company. The food court is open daily, from 6:00 A.M. to midnight. It's cheap, it's convenient, and there's enough variety to keep everyone you're traveling with happy.

Lounge

Open seven days a week, Nefertiti's Lounge offers a full-service bar and ongoing entertainment throughout the evening. Whether you need to take a break from the sightseeing, you're gearing up for a night of gambling, or you're meeting friends or coworkers for a nightcap, the lounge offers a place to relax and have a drink.

Special Attractions

The Luxor offers a variety of shows, rides, and attractions. Actors portraying Pharaoh and Nefertiti make appearances in public areas of the resort and are available for photos. Look for them Thursday through Sunday, beginning at noon.

$ = entrees under $10; $$ = under $20; $$$ = over $20

Other Hotel Services

- Business center
- Cable TV
- Cribs and cots
- Dry cleaning service
- Florist
- Free parking
- Hair dryers (in all Tower rooms)
- Newsstand
- Refrigerators (available for $15 a night on a limited basis)
- Rental car service
- Safe deposit boxes (at front desk)
- Show ticket desk/travel desk

Blue Man Group Live

Show Times: 7:00 and 10:00 P.M. (Wednesday through Saturday)
7 P.M. only (Sunday and Monday)

Ticket Prices: $60.50 and $71.50

Reservations: (702) 262-4400

Blue Man Group has a new permanent home at the Luxor. These nonspeaking "performance artists" wear blue makeup from head-to-toe and entertain audiences by performing music using extremely unusual instruments and by doing unusual mime movements. For example, according to the group, "The PVC instrument used during the performance is made from hundreds of feet of PVC tubing. Pitch is determined by the length of the tube. It is by far the coolest instrument ever made, partly because of its sound and partly because it changes color."

The two-hour show is extremely visual, highly unusual, and definitely worth seeing. Because the theater at the Luxor has been custom-designed for this performance troop, the Las Vegas version of the show is more extravagant than what's presented in other cities. *Blue Man Group Live* is suitable for the entire family, but young children (and some adults for that matter) simply may not get it . . . the show is that unusual.

For more information about Blue Man Group, which performs in major cities such as New York, Chicago, Boston, and now Las Vegas, visit their official Web site at *www.blueman.com*.

Blue Man Group Live

Ages Up to 5	Ages 6–15	Ages 16–20	Ages 21 & Up	Senior Citizens
Not Suitable	⚀ ⚀	⚀ ⚁ ⚂	⚀ ⚁ ⚂	⚀ ⚀

Bill Acosta's Lasting Impressions

Show Times: 7:00 P.M. (Tuesday through Sunday)
7:00 and 9:30 P.M. (Tuesday and Sunday only)
No performances are held on Monday

Ticket Price: $24.95

Reservations: (702) 262-4400

When you think of impressionists, Rich Little probably comes to mind. While Little can be seen performing often as a special guest or headliner in Las Vegas, the Luxor offers its own impressive one-man impressionist show—Bill Acosta, a master vocal impressionist. Acosta transforms himself

"Over the years, I have developed a technique I call 'vocal chasing,'" says Acosta, to explain how he shifts gears between voices so rapidly. "It's the way I have trained my vocal cords to move from one voice, pitch, and tone rapidly to another. 'The Twelve Days of Christmas' song I perform during the show is the most challenging, because I repeat each character numerous times. By the end of this 15-minute song I have changed voices 90 times."

into people like Bill Clinton, Ross Perot, George Bush, Katharine Hepburn, Rodney Dangerfield, Arnold Schwarzeneggar, Ray Charles, and Liberace during a fun-filled, high-energy, 75-minute musical show.

The cast of "guest stars" in this show that Bill Acosta re-creates is so large, audiences can expect to see and hear a different impression every minute of the show. Performances take place in the Luxor Live Theater, a 350-seat venue on the hotel's attractions level.

This show is a comedy club–style performance and is more suitable for adults. The show is thoroughly entertaining and is presented in the tradition of the greatest Las Vegas–style comedy and music shows of yesteryear.

Bill Acosta's Lasting Impressions

Ages Up to 5	Ages 6–15	Ages 16–20	Ages 21 & Up	Senior Citizens
Not Suitable	•	• •.	• •.	• •. ⋰

Luxor IMAX Movie

Ticket Prices: $8.95 / $13.50 (double feature)

Information: (702) 262-4555

This family-oriented attraction offers a movie experience seen on a screen measuring nearly seven stories high. The IMAX movie frames are 10 times the size of a conventional 35-millimeter film—resulting in awe-inspiring 2-D and lifelike 3-D images that envelop viewers and pull them into other worlds, from the far reaches of outer space to the lowest depths of the sea.

In addition to the massive screen, the 312-seat theater offers a 15,000-watt, state-of-the-art sound system that is far more advanced than what you'd hear in an average movie theater. The sound in this theater actually surrounds you, creating a totally immersive experience.

Throughout each day, two different IMAX movie presentations are shown, currently *T-Rex: Back to the Cretaceous* and *Mysteries of Egypt*. Younger audiences will enjoy *T-Rex: Back to the Cretaceous*, while adults will likely appreciate *Mysteries of Egypt*, which is more of a documentary-style film produced by National Geographic. Disney's *Fantasia 2000* was also presented here on a limited-engagement basis.

The IMAX theater operates throughout the day and evening. Tickets can be purchased up to five minutes before the show. Special discounts are available for the first showing of *T-Rex: Back to the Cretaceous* every morning.

IMAX: *T-Rex: Back to the Cretaceous*

Ages Up to 5	Ages 6–15	Ages 16–20	Ages 21 & Up	Senior Citizens
Not Suitable	⚀ ⚁ ⚂	⚀ ⚁	⚀	⚀

IMAX: *Mysteries of Egypt*

Ages Up to 5	Ages 6–15	Ages 16–20	Ages 21 & Up	Senior Citizens
Not Suitable	⚀	⚀ ⚁	⚀ ⚁ ⚂	⚀ ⚁ ⚂

Ra: The Nightclub

Information: (702) 262-4400

When the sun goes down, the fun begins at this modern day nightclub with an ancient Egyptian twist. Dance into the night as lasers, lights, and a pulsating sound system go into full gear as nonstop dance music is played. The 19,000-square-foot nightclub offers a spacious dance floor, stage, two large and full-service bars, and plenty of booths and tables. There are also two cigar lounges, a sushi bar, special VIP booths, and a variety of other amenities designed to make every night a memorable party experience.

Wednesday nights, Ra hosts "Pleasuredome," what the Luxor calls "the hippest, sexiest house party on the Las Vegas Strip." It features the best club music from Los Angeles and New York and Ra's provocative cage dancing contest. Thursday night is the weekly Deca Dance party, where music from the 1980s is played.

Live performances by top recording artists also take place throughout the year at Ra. The club is open Wednesday through Saturday from 10:00 P.M. to 6:00 A.M. An upscale dress code is strictly enforced and no minors are admitted. Admission is $10 for men and $5 for women with out-of-town identification. Admission is free to women with local identification.

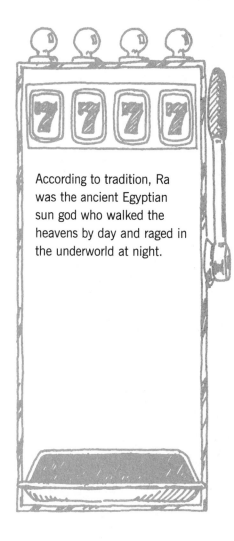

According to tradition, Ra was the ancient Egyptian sun god who walked the heavens by day and raged in the underworld at night.

Midnight Fantasy

Show Times: 10:00 P.M. (daily)

                      10:00 P.M. and midnight (Saturday)

Ticket Price: $22.95

Reservations: (702) 262-4400

The Luxor calls *Midnight Fantasy* "Las Vegas' newest adult review." This adults-only (topless) show will appeal primarily to men. It features singing, dancing, and everything else you'd expect from a Las Vegas–style topless musical review.

Midnight Fantasy

Ages Up to 5	Ages 6–15	Ages 16–20	Ages 21 & Up	Senior Citizens
Not Suitable	Not Suitable	Not Suitable	⚁	⚁

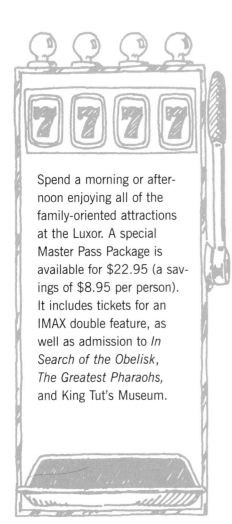

Spend a morning or afternoon enjoying all of the family-oriented attractions at the Luxor. A special Master Pass Package is available for $22.95 (a savings of $8.95 per person). It includes tickets for an IMAX double feature, as well as admission to *In Search of the Obelisk*, *The Greatest Pharaohs,* and King Tut's Museum.

The Greatest Pharaohs Movie

Show Times: Ongoing

Ticket Price: $4

This movie, produced by the A&E television network, explores many of the mysteries of ancient Egypt and the lives of the most famous pharaohs. The first showing is at 9:00 A.M. Shows run every half hour until 11:00 P.M. on Sunday and Monday, and until 4:30 P.M. Tuesday through Saturday. No advance reservations are necessary; however, tickets for later show times can be purchased at the box office.

Save money by buying the "Passport To Egypt" ticket, which includes admission to *The Greatest Pharaohs* and King Tut's Museum, for $6 a person. Visit the theater box office for more information.

The Greatest Pharaohs

Ages Up to 5	Ages 6–15	Ages 16–20	Ages 21 & Up	Senior Citizens
Not Suitable	⚀	⚀	⚁	⚁

King Tut's Museum

Admission: $5

It was in 1922 that Howard Carter discovered the tomb of King Tutankhamen in Egypt—one of the greatest archaeological finds of all time. Since then, the priceless artifacts that were uncovered have toured the world.

King Tut's Tomb and Museum at Luxor is the only full-scale reproduction outside of Egypt of Carter's discovery. During the 15-minute self-guided walking tour, you'll see exact reproductions of the tomb itself as well as the artifacts that were found inside.

The museum is open Sunday through Thursday from 9:00 A.M. to 11:00 P.M., and Friday and Saturday from 9:00 A.M. to 1:00 A.M. An audiotape tour is available in multiple languages. While adults will find this museum fascinating and educational, young children will likely be bored. By visiting this museum, guests will develop a much greater appreciation for ancient Egypt and the artisans of the day.

Save money by buying the "Passport To Egypt" ticket, which includes admission to *The Greatest Pharaohs* and King Tut's Museum, for $6 a person. Visit the theater box office for more information.

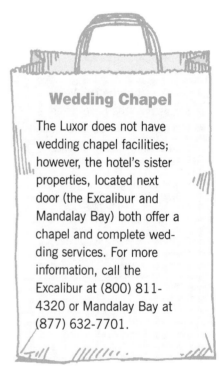

Wedding Chapel

The Luxor does not have wedding chapel facilities; however, the hotel's sister properties, located next door (the Excalibur and Mandalay Bay) both offer a chapel and complete wedding services. For more information, call the Excalibur at (800) 811-4320 or Mandalay Bay at (877) 632-7701.

King Tut's Museum

	Ages Up to 5	Ages 6–15	Ages 16–20	Ages 21 & Up	Senior Citizens
Not Suitable	•	• •	• •	• •	• •

Games of the Gods Arcade

People young and old who enjoy video games will enjoy Games of the Gods, checking out the latest arcade games, virtual reality games, and even trying the karaoke recording studio (to make their own MTV-style music video). This arcade is located on the attractions level of the Luxor. For an even greater arcade experience, check out Sega GameWorks, located a few blocks away from the Luxor.

In Search of the Obelisk

Ticket Price: $6

Ride/Ticket Information: (702) 262-4555

This highly realistic and rather turbulent motion-simulator ride takes passengers on a trip to the dig site of an ancient subterranean civilization. The ride operates throughout the day. It's not suitable for very young children, senior citizens, or anyone with physical limitations.

Pregnant women, people with back or neck problems, etc., should avoid this attraction.

Oasis Spa

Hours:	**This is the only 24-hour spa in Las Vegas**
Appointments/Information:	(702) 730-5720

Based on research conducted by the world's foremost archaeologists, the pharaohs of ancient Egypt led a very pampered and lavish lifestyle. While you're staying at the Luxor, you're invited to treat yourself to royal treatment at the Oasis Spa. This 12,000-square-foot facility features a full range of affordable amenities besides the fitness center, including aromatic steam baths and showers, hot and warm whirlpools, a dry sauna, and an extensive menu of treatments ranging from body wraps and scrubs to massages, facials, hydrotherapy, personal training, and tanning.

The Oasis Spa also features a full-service hair and nail salon (by appointment only). The spa itself is open 24 hours a day; however, appointments for the various treatments and massages book up fast, so schedule appointments in advance. (Appointments can be scheduled up to five days in advance.) Once an appointment is scheduled, plan on arriving 30 minutes early to allow for check-in and time to change. A Spa Facility Day Pass, which provides full access to the spa and fitness center, is included with any spa treatment priced at $35 or more.

Like all of the Las Vegas casinos, the Luxor offers a special rewards club, called the Gold Chamber Club. Participants can win prizes by earning points based on how much they gamble in the casino. Visit any casino information desk in the hotel for details.

Pools

Open year-round (hours of operation vary based on the season), the Luxor's swimming pools are among the largest in Las Vegas. The pools are outdoors, on the west side of the main pyramid. All are heated to 80 degrees and have Jacuzzis. Private cabanas and rafts can be rented. The pool is available to all guests of the hotel, and towels are provided.

Casino

No matter how you enjoy risking your money, when it comes to casino-style games of skill and chance, the Luxor Casino offers all of the popular table games, like blackjack, craps, roulette, baccarat, Pai Gow, Caribbean Stud poker, Let It Ride, poker, and keno. There are also 2,600 slot machines, video poker machines, and video keno machines allowing you to risk between $.05 and $100 dollars a play. Slot players can try to win millions of dollars or cars on progressive games.

If gambling in the hustle and bustle of a busy casino isn't for you, the Luxor offers more comfortable poker rooms, where games of seven card stud and Texas hold 'em are almost always in progress.

Sports fans can bet on their favorite events or sporting competition while watching the 17 giant-screen TVs or 128 individual viewing monitors in the race and sports book area of the casino.

Shopping
Giza Galleria

Open Sunday through Thursday 9:00 A.M. to 11:00 P.M., and 9:00 A.M. to midnight on Friday and Saturday, this mini-mall offers a variety of shopping experiences, including:

- Jewelry shop
- Men's / Woman's store
- Children's store
- Bath and Body store
- Luxor and Las Vegas souvenir store
- Egyptian bazaar
- Tie / Cigar shop
- Ice cream / Candy store
- Egyptian store

Other shops located throughout the Luxor complex include:

- The Luxor Logo shop
- Art and jewelry shop
- The King Tut Museum shop
- Sundry shop
- The Imagine Showroom store

Banquet, Function, and Conference Services

Information: (800) 497-9749

Whether you're planning a small social or business gathering, banquet, meeting, or a convention to be attended by dozens or up to 1,000 people, the Luxor offers 20,000 square feet of meeting space that can be divided into nine different rooms. The function rooms are equipped with sound, lighting, telephone outlets, and other amenities. A full-service business center is also available to handle faxing, mailing, and shipping needs.

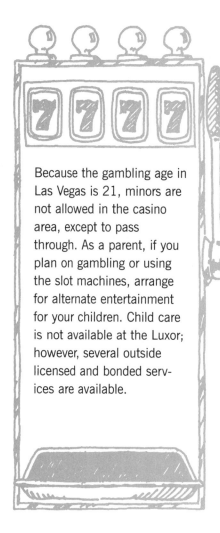

Because the gambling age in Las Vegas is 21, minors are not allowed in the casino area, except to pass through. As a parent, if you plan on gambling or using the slot machines, arrange for alternate entertainment for your children. Child care is not available at the Luxor; however, several outside licensed and bonded services are available.

Mandalay Bay / Four Seasons Hotel

Theme:	The tropics
Room Rate:	$$$$ ($250+)
Number of Rooms:	3,700 rooms and suites, plus 424 Four Seasons rooms and suites
Casino:	135,000 square feet, featuring 122 gaming tables, 2,400 slot machines, and a high stakes gaming parlor. There's also a 300-seat, full-service race and sports book.
Dining:	Fifteen restaurants, including fine-dining and theme restaurants, such as the House of Blues
Primary Show:	*Chicago—The Musical* (Broadway show)
Special Attractions:	Mandalay Bay Events Center, House of Blues, an 11-acre beach area, a 12,200-gallon saltwater aquarium in the registration lobby, the Treasures of Mandalay Bay museum, and Valley of the Waterfalls
Reservations:	(877) 632-7000 or (702) 632-7777
Web Site:	*www.mandalaybay.com*
Address:	3950 Las Vegas Boulevard South Las Vegas, NV 89119

Overall Resort Rating Based on Amenities and Rates

Ages Up to 5	Ages 6–15	Ages 16–20	Ages 21 & Up	Senior Citizens
⚁ ⚁	⚁ ⚁	⚁ ⚁ ⚂	⚁ ⚁ ⚃	⚁ ⚁ ⚃

Mandalay Bay can easily be considered one of the more luxurious casinos and hotels along the Strip. This $950-million resort includes a Four Seasons Hotel on the property that offers its own entrance, parking, check-in, five-star dining, pool/spa, and convention area. The 424 rooms and suites operated by the Four Seasons Hotel are located on the 35th through 39th floors of Mandalay Bay's hotel tower.

Whether you're staying in one of Mandalay Bay's rooms or suites, or one of the rooms or suites operated by the Four Seasons, you're in for a pleasant stay. Guests are treated to a full range of amenities even in the standard rooms.

Joining resorts like Bellagio, Mandalay Bay is designed to appeal to an affluent clientele, including businesspeople, honeymooners, seniors, and couples traveling alone. While children and teens are welcome to stay at the resort, there is little in the way of activities or special attractions that will appeal to them.

It's no surprise that so many major events and attractions, ranging from nationally televised sporting events to concerts are now being held at Mandalay Bay. The majority of the restaurants offer a fine-dining experience, while the spa offers guests a full range of services to pamper both their minds and bodies. Even the entertainment is upscale. Instead of offering a traditional Las Vegas musical revue show, Mandalay Bay brings the excitement of Broadway theater to the Strip with an award-winning, all-star cast presenting *Chicago—The Musical.*

Mandalay Bay is owned by Circus Circus Enterprises, Inc., however, the resort is also managed by Four Seasons Hotels and Resorts.

Guest Room Accommodations

What Mandalay Bay calls a standard room, most of the other resorts along the Strip would call a deluxe room or even a suite. The average standard room is 515 square feet, and includes a master bath and a long list of amenities, including a separate bathtub and shower, robes, makeup mirror, hair dryer, his and hers closets, two phone lines with data ports, a 27-inch television, queen- or king-size beds, floor to ceiling windows, and an iron with ironing board.

The 500 suites at Mandalay Bay are large (between 690 and 6,670 square feet) and offer a wet bar with refrigerator, spa tub, and a handful of other luxuries. There are also special House of Blues–themed rooms (on the 34th floor) and suites decorated with Gothic, Moroccan, and East Indian elements.

When you enter Mandalay Bay's lobby, you'll be treated to a huge aquarium that re-creates beautiful coral reefs that flourish in the Indo-Pacific region and the South Pacific. The tropical fish in the aquarium include Pacific black tip sharks, soldierfish, angelfish, puffers, and butterfly fish. This aquarium is 14 feet tall and contains 12,200 gallons of natural seawater. Another one in the Coral Reef Lounge is 8 feet tall and contains 2,600 gallons of natural seawater.

Fine Dining

Mandalay Bay offers an assortment of truly exquisite fine-dining options. A dress code for some of these establishments is enforced, and reservations are certainly recommended, especially during peak mealtimes.

Aureole ($$$)

Based on his award-winning restaurant in New York City, Charlie Palmer now gives visitors to Las Vegas a chance to experience the seasonal American dishes, created by chefs Joe and Megan Romano (husband and wife team), that made his restaurant famous. Also offered is an extensive selection of rare French and American wines. This is the largest of Mandalay Bay's fine-dining establishments. It's open daily for dinner.

Wolfgang Puck's Trattoria del Lupo ($$$)

The chef to the stars responsible for such restaurants as Spagos and the California Pizza Kitchen has helped to develop a unique Italian restaurant for Mandalay Bay. According to the resort, "The restaurant experience is much like a stroll into a small, secluded piazza in Milan with views of the pasta, charcuterie and bakery production areas as well as wonderful food displays and several communal tables." The menu offers a nice selection of traditional and contemporary dishes adapted from many regions of Northern and Southern Italy. To prepare some of these dishes, a wood-burning rotisserie and pizza oven is used. Open daily for lunch and dinner.

Shanghai Lilly ($$$)

Shanghai Lilly offers a classical selection of Cantonese cuisine with Szechuan specialties. The restaurant features four private dining rooms and chefs who have been brought in directly from the top restaurants in Hong Kong. Open for dinner only.

China Grill ($$$)

Open nightly for dinner, this China Grill location joins sister restaurants in New York City, Miami Beach, and Beverly Hills in bringing

---

$ = entrees under $10; $$ = under $20; $$$ = over $20

diners a wide range of dishes with a distinctly Asian flare. Virtually every dish is prepared on grills or in woks using ingredients gathered from throughout the world.

First Floor Grill (Four Seasons) ($$$)

Offering an ever-changing menu of traditional and contemporary cuisine, the First Floor Grill is owned and operated by Four Seasons. Open daily for dinner, this relatively small and intimate restaurant seats 100 people and offers a private dining room that can seat up to 12 people.

Casual and Specialty Dining

In addition to offering several of the finest of fine-dining establishments in Las Vegas, Mandalay Bay also features a handful of specialty and theme restaurants. Many of these eating establishments are less formal, a bit less expensive, and offer guests even more dining choices.

Other Resort Services

- 24-hour complimentary valet
- 24-hour room service
- Full-service business center
- Lobby concierge

Border Grill ($$)

Adapted from the award-winning restaurant with the same name in Los Angeles, Border Grill is owned and operated by Mary Sue Milliken and Susan Feniger, the popular hosts of the Food Network's *Too Hot Tamales* television series. In 1985, these two chefs took a road trip into Mexico and discovered a wide range of authentic recipes and cooking techniques from home cooks and street vendors, which they took home and later used to influence the various menu selections offered at the Border Grill.

Open daily for lunch and dinner, the restaurant has a reputation for taking traditional Mexican food and successfully "translating" it for the American market.

China Grill's Cafe and Zen Sum ($$)

From the creators of China Grill, this eating establishment is open daily for lunch and dinner. While the focus of this restaurant continues to be preparing every dish on grills or in woks with flavorful sauces, the

---

$ = entrees under $10; $$ = under $20; $$$ = over $20

cafe offers a conveyor dim sum bar that's perfect for a quick and casual meal.

Rumjungle ($$)

Also from the creators of China Grill, Rumjungle combines entertainment with dining as guests are treated to a dancing firewall that transforms into a wall of water immediately upon entering this restaurant. Volcanic mountains of rum and spirits also rise before guests in an illuminated bar. As for the food itself, entrees are prepared over a large open fire pit that serves as a backdrop for a pulsating dance floor.

The menu is mostly tropically inspired, with many items served on flaming skewers, "Rodizio" style. The bar offers a wide assortment of exotic drinks. Whether you're going to eat or drink, you'll be entertained by Latin, Caribbean, and African music until the wee hours of the morning. Open daily for dinner.

Red Square ($$)

If you're looking for something exciting to do at night, Red Square features a frozen ice bar, a wonderful selection of more than one hundred frozen vodkas and infusions, martinis, plus Russian-inspired cocktails. Dining selections include an extensive caviar list and a menu of Russian, French, Italian, and American specialties. Open daily for dinner.

House of Blues ($$)

Combine a full menu with live blues music and you have the Las Vegas location for House of Blues. Menu items include Creole/Cajun staples, such as jambalaya, gumbo, and étoufée, as well as Southern favorites such as fried catfish, barbecued ribs, wood-fired pizza, and burgers. Open daily for breakfast, lunch, and dinner. Like many theme restaurants, this one offers a gift and merchandise shop.

The International House of Blues Foundation Room is a private club open to members and VIP guests. It's also used for special events. Located on the 43rd floor of the resort, this room combines fine dining with a spectacular view of the Las Vegas Strip and surrounding valley.

$ = entrees under $10; $$ = under $20; $$$ = over $20

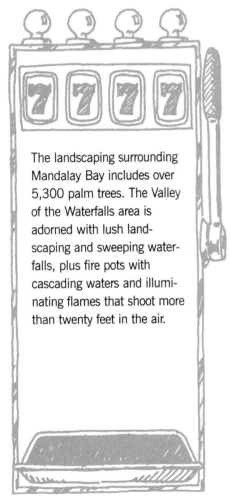

The landscaping surrounding Mandalay Bay includes over 5,300 palm trees. The Valley of the Waterfalls area is adorned with lush landscaping and sweeping waterfalls, plus fire pots with cascading waters and illuminating flames that shoot more than twenty feet in the air.

Other Casual Restaurants

- Raffels Cafe—Open 24 hours, this is an upscale cafe that overlooks the resort's tropical gardens, lagoon, and pools.
- The Noodle Shop—Enjoy a casual meal from a traditional Cantonese noodle kitchen. In addition to a wide range of noodle items, congee, rice, and barbecue dishes are offered at either the restaurant's counter or table seating. Open for lunch and dinner, the Noodle Shop also offers late-night dining. You'll find this restaurant next to the casino's high-stakes gaming area.
- Bay Side Buffet—Open for breakfast, lunch, and dinner, the Bay Side Buffet offers an all-you-can-eat menu at a flat rate. The buffet itself overlooks the resort's 11-acre lagoon.
- Verandah Cafe (Four Seasons)—Both indoor and outdoor seating are available at this cafe, which offers a mix of Mexican, Californian, Italian, and Oriental cuisine. A full breakfast buffet is served daily. Open 24 hours a day.

Lounges

While many of the restaurants and cafes in Mandalay Bay offer full bar service, the resort also features a handful of stand-alone bars and lounges.

- Coral Reef Lounge—Located in the heart of the casino, this full-service lounge/bar also offers a sushi bar.
- Island Lounge—You'll find this lounge on the casino floor. Throughout the afternoon and night, live entertainment is presented.
- Turf Club Lounge—This full-service bar is located next to the race and sports book.
- Orchid Lounge—Live entertainment and exotic drinks are served throughout the afternoon and evening. Every morning, this is one place to stop for a fresh cup of coffee.

Special Attractions

Whether you're visiting Mandalay Bay for pleasure or business, you'll find plenty to do at this resort in addition to gambling. For starters, see a show, relax and pamper yourself at a spa, go shopping, go for a swim (in one of the resort's three pools), or jog along the resort's jogging track.

Chicago—The Musical

Box Office: (877) 632-7400 or (702) 632-7580

TicketMaster: (702) 474-4000

Ticket Prices: $55, $65, and $80

Show Times: 4:00 and 7:30 P.M. (Tuesday through Friday)
               7:00 and 10:00 P.M. (Saturday)
               4:00 and 7:30 P.M. (Sunday)

Additional Information: *www.chicagothemusical.com*

The Tony Award-winning Broadway musical *Chicago—The Musical* has a permanent second home at Mandalay Bay. Not only does this show bring a taste of a full-scale Broadway theatrical production to Las Vegas, but the cast includes well known and highly accomplished talent from stage, television, and the motion picture screen.

Chicago—The Musical is based on the 1926 play by Maurine Dallas Watkins, but has a plot that could be ripped from today's headlines. Roxie Hart is a nightclub dancer who kills her lover and then hires Chicago's shrewdest lawyer, who turns her crime into celebrity headlines.

Ticket prices are $55, $65, and $80 (excluding tax) and are available at the Mandalay Bay Box Office. Although the theater seats 1,800 people, tickets should be ordered in advance.

The Treasures of Mandalay Bay

Admission: $6

Information: (702) 798-1933
               or *www.treasuresofmandalaybay.com*

This museum features a $40-million permanent collection of rare gold and silver coins, colorful and unique Old West bank notes, and historic Nevada mining towns memorabilia, such as nineteenth century gold bars and assay receipts. The museum is open daily and is located off the casino floor, across from Bali Trading Company. Guests are free to roam throughout the 1,100-square-foot museum area at their leisure. For people who enjoy money—collecting it, saving it, spending it, or simply learning the history of it—this museum offers an interesting way to spend a few hours.

House of Blues

Box Office: (702) 632-7600

In addition to offering a unique restaurant, House of Blues is a live music venue that hosts nightly concerts from well known (and not so well known) performers. Bob Dylan, Sheryl Crow, The Blues Brothers, B. B. King, Indigo Girls, Yes, Cheap Trick, Al Green, Stevie Nicks, and Chris Isaak have been some of the performers at this Las Vegas House of Blues location. The venue accommodates 1,800 guests. For an up-to-date concert schedule, contact the box office, TicketMaster, or the House of Blues Web site at *www.mandalaybay.com/house_of_blues.html.*

Surf and Beach Area

Most Las Vegas hotels and resorts offer a few swimming pools, maybe a waterfall or two, and if you're lucky, a whirlpool. Instead, Mandalay Bay offers a lush 11-acre tropical sand-and-surf beach. There are also three swimming pools, nine private bungalows, and 16 cabanas (which can be rented), and a variety of beachside lounges, restaurants, and shops.

Relax on a sandy beach, take a swim in the wave pool, or enjoy a swim in a traditional swimming pool as you experience this oasis in the Las Vegas desert. With 1,700 tons of sand, 1,640,270 gallons of water, and a wave pool that measures 41,178 square feet (with adjustable waves up to 6 feet for boogie boarding and surfing), the surf and beach area of Mandalay Bay is nothing short of impressive.

This area offers a wonderful way to relax and unwind. Surrounding the entire beach area is exquisite landscaping, featuring a tropical motif, complete with palm trees and exotic plants. The adjoining "Lazy River" flows at 2 m.p.h. and allows guests to take a relaxing ride on a raft.

Mandalay Bay Events Center

This 12,000-seat sports and entertainment complex is the setting for many concerts, major sporting events, and television specials that take place

Tickets for House of Blues concerts or events at the Mandalay Bay Events Center can be purchased at the box offices in the resort, or at TicketMaster locations in the Robinsons–May department store, Smith's, and Tower Records. Tickets can also be purchased from TicketMaster using a major credit card or ordered online from the TicketMaster Web site *(www.ticketmaster.com).*

Wedding Chapel

Information:
(877) 632-7701 or
(702) 632-7490

If you'd like to get married on an exotic private island, in a luxurious chapel, surrounded by immaculate landscaping, consider holding your wedding ceremony in one of Mandalay Bay's two chapels. Professional wedding coordinators are on-hand to help you plan the ultimate dream wedding. Photography, videotaping, floral arrangements, and limo service are included in many of the wedding packages. Catering, music, and a full-service banquet staff are also available.

throughout the year. Some of the biggest events in Las Vegas happen at this entertainment complex. For ticketing information and a listing of special events, call TicketMaster at (702) 474-4000 or visit *www.ticketmaster.com* on the Web.

Spa Mandalay

Hours: 6:00 A.M. to 10:00 P.M. daily, but may vary seasonally
Appointments: (702) 632-7220

Staffed exclusively with talented, certified professionals, the spa at Mandalay Bay includes 26 state-of-the-art treatment rooms. Treatments and services range from the classic and traditional therapies of Swedish massage, reflexology, aromatherapy, hydrotherapy, and thalassotherapy. The spa is also equipped with waterfalls, Jacuzzis, and whirlpools, a separate men's and women's facility, and several saunas and steam rooms.

There's also a 4,500-square-foot fitness and personal training center, including a full line of Life Fitness machines for both cardiovascular and circuit training. Personal trainers and group classes in water aerobics and yoga are available. The entrance fee for the spa includes use of an oversized oak locker, robes, slippers, towels, plus a full line of health and beauty products.

Reservations for specific treatments are taken up to three weeks in advance for people planning to stay at the resort. The spa's management reports that weekend appointments typically fill up early, so guests should make their appointments as early as possible, although walk-in appointments are accepted provided slots are open in the schedule.

The daily spa fee (to use the facilities only) is $22 for guests and $27 for nonguests. Treatments such as massages and facials cost extra. Special spa packages are available.

A Robert Cromeans Salon

Appointments: (702) 632-6130

A team of John Paul Mitchell Systems hairdressers staff this exclusive, full-service salon offering what it calls five-star treatment to all of its visitors. Make your appointment(s) as early as possible to ensure the services you want will be available when you want them. Hours of operation are 10:00 A.M.

to 7:00 P.M. (Monday through Friday), 8:00 A.M. to 6:00 P.M. (Saturday), and 10:00 A.M. to 5:00 P.M. (Sunday).

Casino

As you explore the casino area of Mandalay Bay, you'll be surrounded by flowing water, lush foliage, and exotic architecture, not to mention over 2,400 slot machines/video poker machines, 122 table games, a poker room, baccarat, and a race and sports book (with 17 large screens and 300 seats). There's also a high stakes gaming area.

Shopping

Although Mandalay Bay doesn't offer a shopping promenade or mall like other resorts along the Strip, you will find a selection of fine stores offering gifts, souvenirs, clothing, and other merchandise.

- Mandalay Bay: The Store—Mandalay Bay merchandise is offered along with tropical casual wear. Located across from the registration desk in the lobby.
- Rangoon News Bureau—Newspapers, magazines, sundries, and snacks are available at this shop located at the elevator lobby, on the casino level.
- The Wave—Located at the elevator lobby on the casino level, this shop offers golf shirts embroidered with the signature Mandalay Bay wave.
- Bali Trading Company—An assortment of South Seas treasures and gifts are available here, including one-of-a-kind handcarved works of art.
- Stars Memorabilia—If you're looking for celebrity memorabilia, you'll find a large selection of photographs, autographs, and other items here.
- Bombay Cigar Company—This shop specializes in fine cigars and other tobacco products.
- Show Stopper—Souvenir merchandise from *Chicago—The Musical* is available here, including the show soundtrack.
- The Show Shop—Another shop offering merchandise from *Chicago—The Musical.*

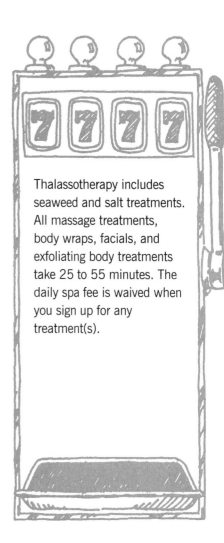

Thalassotherapy includes seaweed and salt treatments. All massage treatments, body wraps, facials, and exfoliating body treatments take 25 to 55 minutes. The daily spa fee is waived when you sign up for any treatment(s).

- Cuzzins—Fine men's clothing, including Brioni suits and other European brands.
- Portfolio—Women's shoes and clothing.
- El Portal Collections—Men's and women's accessories, including leather goods and travel necessities.
- Galerie Renaissance—Fine masterworks of art, glass, jewelry, and sculpture are sold at this upscale gallery. Whether you're an art collector looking to expand your collection, or you just want to browse, you'll find works from creators such as Picasso, Miro, Chagall, Leroy Neiman, and Alexandra Nechita.
- Pearl Moon Boutique—Designer swimwear, spa merchandise, workout gear, hats, sunglasses, and beach footwear are the types of items you'll find at this boutique.
- The Enchanted Flora—This full-service florist offers fresh flowers and arrangements that can be taken with you or shipped anywhere.
- Jungle Juice Spirits—Las Vegas souvenirs and merchandise are available here along with various liquor items.
- Tropical Gifts and Stuff—Logoed merchandise plus a selection of children's playthings are available from this shop, which is located next to the elevator at beach level.

Banquet, Function, and Conference Services

Convention Sales Office: (877) 632-7900

Mandalay Bay Productions: (702) 632-6099

Whether you're planning a party, special event, trade show, or corporate meeting, Mandalay Bay offers a full-service facility for virtually any function. Audiovisual and production services are available, along with a large staff of event planners. Celebrity entertainment, full-stage dance productions, models and showgirls, comedians, musicians, celebrity impersonators, variety acts, and magicians are also available to provide the final touches to your event.

The South Pacific Ballroom, for example, encompasses 44,900 square feet and may be divided into 10 separate sections. The Islander Ballroom, with 31,800 square feet, may be divided into nine sections. Both ballrooms are pillar-less.

MGM Grand Hotel & Casino

Theme:	The Golden Age of Hollywood
Room Rate:	$$ / $$$ ($51–$250)
Number of Rooms:	5,005 (including 751 suites)
Casino:	171,000 square feet, featuring scores of table games, slots, a race and sports book, poker room, and a keno lounge
Dining:	Fourteen restaurants and full in-room dining menu
Primary Show:	*EFX*
Special Attractions:	Grand Adventures family-oriented theme park, Grand Pool and Spa, Studio 54 night-club, and the MGM Grand Lion Habitat
Reservations:	(800) 646-1203 or (702) 891-7777
Web Site:	*www.mgmgrand.com*
Address:	3799 Las Vegas Boulevard South Las Vegas, NV 89109

Overall Resort Rating Based on Amenities and Rates

Ages Up to 5	Ages 6–15	Ages 16–20	Ages 21 & Up	Senior Citizens
⚁	⚂	⚂	⚂	⚂

Located on the Las Vegas Strip, at the corner of Tropicana Avenue (across the street from the New York–New York Hotel and Casino), it's impossible to miss the MGM Grand and its four 30-story emerald green towers. This resort property truly encompasses just about everything a Las Vegas resort could possibly offer, including a wide range of guest room accommodations, a glitzy casino, shows and concerts, restaurants, special events, a full-service pool and spa, and a family-oriented theme park.

The theme of this resort is the Golden Age of Hollywood, showcasing several classic films, including *Wizard of Oz* and *Casablanca.* Looking at this tremendous resort from the outside, it's impossible to miss the 100,000-pound, 45-foot tall, bronze lion statue that guards the property's main entrance. Inside, guests and

Other Hotel Services

A wide range of additional services are offered to guests to assure maximum comfort and convenience. Many of these services are complimentary. Services include:

- A multilingual staff
- Free parking
- Complimentary valet parking
- Rollaway beds and cribs
- Foreign currency exchange
- Safe deposit boxes
- Laundry, valet, and dry cleaning services
- Car rentals
- Tour information
- A full business center
- Voice mail messaging
- Full handicapped accessible facilities and accommodations

visitors alike are treated to an up-close look at real-life lions in the Lion Habitat.

The MGM Grand opened December 18, 1993 and was one of the first Las Vegas resorts designed for the entire family. Built initially at a cost of over $1 billion, the resort is currently undergoing a $575-million enhancement plan. While this 114-acre property offers everything adult vacationers, gamblers, honeymooners, or business travelers could want, families traveling with children of any age will find plenty to see and do on the resort grounds.

This resort is probably best known as the host of many boxing matches and high-profile concerts. The Hollywood Theatre regularly hosts a stable of world-renowned musical performers and comedians, such as Tom Jones, Gladys Knight, Engelbert Humperdinck, the Four Tops, Rodney Dangerfield, and Wayne Newton.

EFX, the resort's flagship show, features over seventy performers, including actors fresh from Broadway and London's West End.

Like so many of the newer resorts in Las Vegas, the MGM Grand offers everything a vacationer, business traveler, or honeymooner could possibly want, all in one location. It really is possible to spend a vacation or business trip at this resort and never have to leave the property. If you do want to venture out, a convenient (and totally free) monorail service links the MGM Grand with Bally's Las Vegas. Each one-way trip takes about three minutes. The monorail operates daily from 6 A.M. TO 1 A.M.

Guest Room Accommodations

The MGM Grand features 5,005 guest rooms in nine price categories. Travelers on a budget will find that the resort's 600 Emerald Tower rooms offer elegant, well equipped, and extremely clean accommodations at affordable rates. Currently, the hotel is in the midst of a year-long room renovation project.

The majority of the rooms at MGM Grand are called "deluxe" rooms. These are approximately 446 square feet, which is larger than comparably priced rooms at most other resorts and casino hotels. Each deluxe room is decorated in one of four Golden Age of Hollywood themes, including *Wizard of Oz*, Hollywood, Southern, and *Casablanca*. Basic amenities include custom black-and-white marble bathrooms, spacious closets, and in-room movies (offered on a pay-per-view basis). Although these rooms are comfortable, like most hotel rooms located in a casino, they're designed to provide a place for guests to sleep, but little more. After all, if you're spending too much time relaxing in your hotel room, you're not in the casino gambling, at a restaurant eating, or taking in a show.

The 751 suites in the MGM Grand Hotel offer many different combinations of amenities, from full kitchens to wet bars, dining and living rooms, and in-room spas. Ranging in size from 675 square feet to over 6,000 square feet, these accommodations offer a variety of options.

The Player Suites are the smallest rooms in this price category. Each offers an oversized bedroom connected to a separate living area. These rooms are available with your choice of two queen-size beds or one king-size bed. Spa Suites are slightly larger than the MGM Grand's Player Suites. Each Spa Suite has a whirlpool and separate shower, a spacious bedroom with a king-size bed, a separate living area, a wet bar, and a dining table with seating for four.

The 775-square-foot Vista Suites offer more space in the bedroom and living area with two entrances to a central bathroom. Two televisions, a wet bar, a king-size bed, and a dining area with seating for four are standard. Lobby Suites are corner-style, "L" shaped, 950-square-foot rooms with one bedroom, a dining area, a bar/snack area, whirlpool, and two televisions.

As the suite prices increase, the amenities and level of luxury increases. The MGM Grand's Glamour Suites boast 1,270 square feet of space. Included in these suites are a wet bar, a dining area with seating for four, two bathrooms, and a large bedroom with a carved sleigh-bed, a marble vanity, and a spacious walk-in closet.

If you're looking for a room with a spectacular view of the Las Vegas Strip, consider reserving one of MGM Grand's Patio Suites. The hotel offers 14 Patio Suites, each has 1,300 square feet of space, two-story vaulted ceilings, and a 786-square-foot outdoor patio area with a private whirlpool. Amenities for these rooms include a big screen television, office areas with two desks, separate dining areas, two baths, his and her sinks, an oversized tub in the master bath, and plenty of closet space.

In 1999, the hotel opened the Mansion, an invitation-only group of 29 private villas. These Tuscan-Mediterranean themed accommodations are modeled after 200-year-old Italian villas and range from 2,400 to 12,000 square feet.

On the Internet, you can view photos and videos of the various rooms and suites at the MGM Grand by pointing your Web browser to *www.mgmgrand.com/lv/ accommodations-rooms.html.*

Fine Dining

No matter what your taste buds are craving, from fast food to fine cuisine prepared under the supervision of one of the world's foremost chefs, you'll find it at MGM Grand. For each restaurant, hours of operation vary and in most cases, reservations are either required or highly recommended, so plan accordingly. Room service is also available 24 hours a day to hotel guests.

Gatsby's ($$$)

Reservations: Required, call (702) 891-3110

With seating for just 70 people, the focus of this restaurant is top-quality service and award winning food, especially dishes with a Pacific Rim flair. Diners are served using the finest crystal, china, flatware, and linens, creating nothing short of a purely elegant dining experience. As for the food, menu specialties include rack of lamb, Kobe beef, seared Ahi tuna in sesame crust, grilled farm-raised ostrich, Dover sole, and fresh abalone. According to the chef, this is one of the few restaurants in America that serves Japanese Kobe beef. The wine list boasts over six hundred selections with wine experts on-hand to help you make the perfect choice.

The first seating on Tuesday through Saturday is at 5:30 P.M., with the last seating at 10:30 P.M. Live entertainment is offered throughout each evening. The restaurant is closed on Sunday and Monday.

The average per-person price for dining at Gatsby's is $55 to $65 (plus alcoholic beverages). While this isn't the best restaurant choice for families traveling with children or teens, if you're looking to spend a romantic evening with a significant other, or planning an intimate celebration or an important business dinner, the atmosphere is ideal.

The Hollywood Brown Derby ($$$)

Reservations: Strongly recommended, call (702) 891-3110

Starting in 1926 and lasting through Hollywood's golden years, the Hollywood Brown Derby was *the* place for celebrities to be seen and to enjoy fine dining. Although the original Brown Derby no longer exists in Hollywood, the atmosphere and menu has been re-created in Las Vegas (as well as at the Disney MGM Studios in Orlando, Florida). It was at the original

Planning to stay awhile? It would take one person 13 years and 8 months to sleep for one night in each of the rooms at the MGM Grand Hotel and Casino. Sweet dreams! To keep each room clean, the resort has the largest privately owned laundry facility in Nevada. This facility washes over 29 million pounds of sheets each year.

$ = entrees under $10; $$ = under $20; $$$ = over $20

Brown Derby restaurant that the Cobb salad was created, and this continues to be one of the restaurant's specialty items.

The Hollywood Brown Derby at MGM Grand is a topnotch steakhouse, featuring large portions. Menu selections include steaks, poultry, lamb, pork, and seafood dishes, a selection of salads and appetizers, and an extensive wine list. The dessert list is equally impressive. The average per-person price for dinner at the Brown Derby is $38 to $45 (not including alcoholic beverages).

In addition to serving dinner every evening (from 5:30 to 11:00 P.M.), the Brown Derby offers a Sunday champagne brunch (from 9:00 A.M. to 2:00 P.M.). The price for this brunch is $10 cheaper if you're seated before 10:00 A.M. Otherwise, plan on spending $32.50 per adult and $12.95 per child.

This is one of the classier restaurants at MGM Grand. While it's suitable for family dining, it's an ideal place to hold a celebration, romantic dinner, or business dinner. Reservations are strongly suggested and proper dress is encouraged.

Emeril Lagasse's New Orleans Fish House ($$$)

Reservations: Recommended, call (702) 891-7374

World-renowned chef Emeril Lagasse offers his signature New Orleans blend of modern Creole and Cajun cooking at this seafood restaurant. Barbecued shrimp, lobster, fresh fish (flown in daily from around the world), and Emeril's famous double-cut pork chops are all featured menu items. Open daily for lunch (11:00 A.M. to 2:30 P.M.) and dinner (5:30 to 10:30 P.M.), the average per-person meal price is $38 to $45 (not including alcoholic beverages).

Mark Miller's Coyote Cafe & Grill Room ($$ / $$$)

Reservations: Recommended, call (702) 891-7349

For Southwestern-style cuisine, drop by celebrity chef Mark Miller's Coyote Cafe & Grill Room, which is open daily from 8:30 A.M. to 10:30 P.M. The restaurant features a desert-inspired décor, giving it the look and feel

The restaurants and dining establishments at the MGM Grand Hotel prepare and serve more than thirty thousand meals a day. In breakfasts alone, this equates to serving 18 million eggs, 292,000 pounds of coffee, and 4.4 million doughnuts a year.

$ = entrees under $10; $$ = under $20; $$$ = over $20

of Santa Fe, New Mexico. On the menu, you'll find specialties like black beans, blue-corn enchiladas, and chicken burritos topped with homemade guacamole along with mild salsas.

The cafe offers a more casual and less expensive dining experience than the Grill Room. (The average per-person meal cost is $15 in the cafe.) The Grill Room offers fancier surroundings and a more extensive menu. (The average per-person meal costs $38 to $45.) This restaurant is suitable for the entire family. Anyone of legal drinking age who enjoys margaritas or daiquiris will appreciate the beverage selection.

Franco Nuschese's Tre Visi Cafe & La Scala Dining Room ($$$)

Reservations: Recommended, call (702) 891-3110

Pastas, chicken, veal, fresh fish, and pizzas are the specialties of this cafe and fine-dining establishment. The cafe is open daily from 5:30 P.M. to 1:00 A.M. and offers meals ranging in price from $20 to $30, while the La Scala dining room serves dinner daily from 5:30 to 11:30 P.M. and offers a more elegant and higher priced menu (averaging $50 per person). The wine list at La Scala features over a thousand selections. When it comes to dessert, the Tre Visi Cafe serves a different flavor of gelato every day of the year.

Both the Tre Visi Cafe and La Scala dining room are suitable for the entire family, but these eating establishments are better suited for more intimate dinners, business dinners, or social gatherings among adults looking for a fine dining experience with an Italian flair.

Dragon Court ($$$)

Reservations: Recommended, call (702) 891-3110

For a taste of the Far East in an intimate setting, Dragon Court offers traditional Chinese cuisine featuring Mandarin and Cantonese specialties. Beef, pork, seafood, poultry, and vegetarian dishes can all be found on the extensive menu.

Dragon Court is suitable for the entire family and is open daily for dinner (from 6:00 to 11:00 P.M.). The average per-person meal costs $35 to $40.

$ = entrees under $10; $$ = under $20; $$$ = over $20

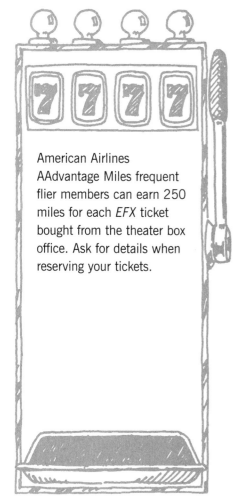

American Airlines AAdvantage Miles frequent flier members can earn 250 miles for each *EFX* ticket bought from the theater box office. Ask for details when reserving your tickets.

Neyla: A Mediterranean Grill ($$$)

One of the newest dining experiences at MGM Grand is the Neyla, which opened in 1999. Offering traditional Mediterranean cuisine and American favorites such as dry-aged strip steak (prepared with a combination of seven spices and stuffed with feta cheese from Bulgaria), this restaurant provides an excellent dining experience no matter what the occasion. Neyla also features a working hookah, which can be used by guests in selected areas of the restaurant.

Casual Dining

Wolfgang Puck Cafe ($$)

Wolfgang Puck, the chef to the stars and owner of Spago's in Hollywood, has opened a chain of restaurants throughout the country specializing in Italian cuisine and pizza. Like all of the restaurants in this chain, this one offers a family dining environment, especially for pizza lovers.

Wolfgang Puck Cafe is open daily from 11:00 A.M. to 11:00 P.M. The average per-person meal costs $15. Seating is on a first-come basis.

Grand Buffet ($$)

Las Vegas is known for its all-you-can-eat buffets, so if you have a big appetite and you're in the mood for a casual dining experience, drop by the buffet for a wide selection of foods at a reasonable price. Open daily for brunch from 7:00 A.M. to 2:30 P.M., and then for dinner from 4:30 to 10:00 P.M., seating is on a first-come basis, so be prepared for a wait.

The Grand Buffet offers an inexpensive dining experience for the whole family. The per-person price for this all-you-can-eat extravaganza is $7.95 (brunch) and $12.95 (dinner). The buffet changes daily, but there's always at least eight main entrees, often including freshly cooked ham, turkey, and prime rib. There's also an extensive salad and dessert bar. The quality of the food at the buffet certainly surpasses fast food, but doesn't touch what's served at MGM Grand's fine-dining establishments. Of course, since you're in a casino environment, you can play keno from your table as you eat.

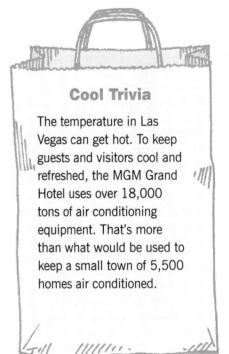

Cool Trivia

The temperature in Las Vegas can get hot. To keep guests and visitors cool and refreshed, the MGM Grand Hotel uses over 18,000 tons of air conditioning equipment. That's more than what would be used to keep a small town of 5,500 homes air conditioned.

$ = entrees under $10; $$ = under $20; $$$ = over $20

Studio Cafe ($)

In Las Vegas, the casinos never close and the nightlife keeps going until the wee hours of the morning. No matter what time of day (or night) it happens to be, if you're hungry, the Studio Cafe is open and ready to serve. The menu offers a wide range of inexpensive American items, plus a separate menu featuring Chinese cuisine. The average per-person meal cost is from $9 to $12. Seating is on a first-come basis, but reservations are accepted for large groups. The Studio Cafe offers an excellent option for sit-down, full-service casual dining that's better than traditional fast food.

Ricardo's Mexican Restaurant ($$)

Reservations: Suggested, call (702) 736-4970

If you're in the mood for Mexican food and a margarita, Ricardo's Mexican Restaurant offers a casual dining experience suitable for the entire family, plus a gift shop featuring themed merchandise. The restaurant is open 10:30 A.M. to 11:00 P.M. Monday and Tuesday, and 11:00 A.M. to 3:00 A.M. Wednesday through Sunday. The average per-person cost for lunch is $9, while the average per-person cost for dinner is $15.

Rainforest Cafe ($$)

Reservations: Recommended, call (702) 891-8580

When you walk through the main entrance of any Rainforest Cafe, you'll find yourself stepping into a lifelike rain forest, complete with trees, waterfalls, rain, audio-animatronic animals, live parrots, and a 10,000-gallon saltwater aquarium. As you dine, don't be surprised if a tropical rainstorm erupts around you. Thanks to flashy special effects, you won't get wet, but the experience truly enhances the dining experience, and kids love it!

The Rainforest Cafes, which are now located throughout the country, offer the ultimate in theme restaurant dining for the entire family. Sure, because this is a theme restaurant (in the same vein as the Hard Rock Cafe, ESPN Cafe, Planet Hollywood, and so many others), the prices are a bit higher than a traditional family-style restaurant, but you're paying for the ambiance. There's also an extensive Rainforest Cafe gift shop chock full of merchandise and souvenirs.

$ = entrees under $10; $$ = under $20; $$$ = over $20

Menu selections include pastas, salads, sandwiches, and a wide assortment of incredible desserts. If you've never experienced a Rainforest Cafe, it's worth checking out either for lunch or dinner. Since these restaurants are basically the same is every city, if you've already dined at a Rainforest Cafe in your home city, you might consider experiencing one of the many other theme restaurants in Las Vegas.

The Rainforest Cafe is open Monday through Thursday, from 8:00 A.M. to 11:00 P.M., and Friday and Saturday from 8:00 A.M. to midnight. On Sunday, hours of operation are from 8:00 A.M. to 11:00 P.M.

Stage Deli ($)

Outside of New York City, finding an authentic New York–style deli sandwich is virtually impossible, but that's exactly what's offered at the Stage Deli at MGM Grand. If you're looking for a delicious, fast, and inexpensive sandwich, this is the place to stop. Pastrami on rye is the specialty, but you'll find turkey, roast beef, and a wide range of other deli meats here. The sandwiches themselves are overstuffed (extra large).

This is a walk-up style restaurant offering sandwiches to go, but seating is available at the race and sports book next to the Grand Theater. You can also take your food back to your room. Open daily 7:30 A.M. to 9:00 P.M.

Special Attractions

EFX

Show Times: 7:30 and 10:30 P.M. (Tuesday through Saturday)

Ticket Price: $51.50 to $72 ($37 for children 5–12)

Box Office: (800) 929-1111

In addition to the hundreds of special events, concerts, and sporting events that take place each year at MGM Grand, one of the resort's biggest attractions is the *EFX* show. Since its debut in 1995, over two million people have experienced this show, which incorporates music, dance, comedy, acrobatics, special effects, and aerialist performances. At the time of this writing, Broadway legend Tommy Tune was starring in *EFX*, which

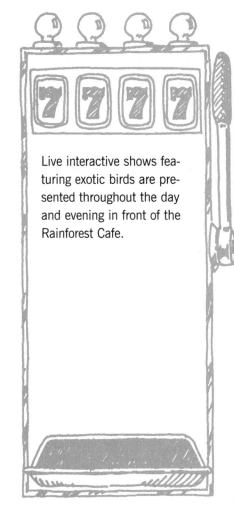

Live interactive shows featuring exotic birds are presented throughout the day and evening in front of the Rainforest Cafe.

$ = entrees under $10; $$ = under $20; $$$ = over $20

in the past has featured other well known performers, including Michael Crawford (*Phantom of the Opera*) and David Cassidy.

Featuring a cast of over seventy performers wearing over 450 costumes throughout the performance, this $45-million show is truly exciting and leaves audience members in awe night after night. You'll quickly see why *EFX* has been dubbed the world's most technologically advanced show. In addition to *Siegfried & Roy* (at The Mirage) and *Cirque du Soleil 'O'* (at Bellagio), this is one of the Las Vegas shows you won't want to miss.

Performances are Tuesday through Saturday nights at 7:30 and 10:30 P.M. in the MGM Grand's *EFX* Theater, which was custom-designed for the show. Tickets should be reserved in advance by calling (800) 929-1111. For group ticket sales, call (800) 456-6114.

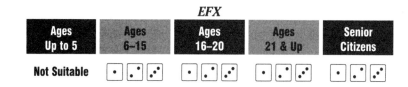

| | ***EFX*** | | | |
Ages Up to 5	Ages 6–15	Ages 16–20	Ages 21 & Up	Senior Citizens
Not Suitable	⚅	⚅	⚅	⚅

Concerts, Sporting Events, and More

Information: (800) 929-1111

Throughout the year, MGM Grand hosts a wide range of concerts, sporting events, and other special events. Recent offerings included World Championship Wrestling, Cher: Live In Concert for HBO, NHL hockey games, 'N Sync in concert, Barbara Streisand: The Millennium Concert, and comedy or musical performances by Rodney Dangerfield, Wayne Newton, and Tom Jones. Andrew Lloyd Webber's Broadway show *Cats* was also presented during a limited engagement at MGM Grand's Grand Theater.

Studio 54

Information: (702) 891-7254

It's a blast from the past at Studio 54 at MGM Grand. The 20,000-square-foot nightclub features three separate dance floors and four bars

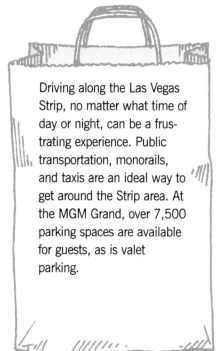

Driving along the Las Vegas Strip, no matter what time of day or night, can be a frustrating experience. Public transportation, monorails, and taxis are an ideal way to get around the Strip area. At the MGM Grand, over 7,500 parking spaces are available for guests, as is valet parking.

that come to life as chart-topping dance music is played on a state-of-the-art sound system. While the original Studio 54 in New York was open only to VIPs, celebrities, and the "in crowd," the velvet rope of this club is open to anyone over the age of 21.

Club hours are 10:00 P.M. to 3:00 A.M. Tuesday, Wednesday, and Thursday, and from 10:00 P.M. to 5:00 A.M. on Friday and Saturday. Admission for men is $10 Tuesday through Thursday and $20 Friday and Saturday nights. Women are admitted free, except during special events. The club has a dress code restricting T-shirts, tank tops, baggy jeans, flannel shirts, hats, tennis shoes, and work boots, so dress accordingly.

If you're looking to relive the 1970s, love to dance, and you're looking for a fun-filled evening, drop by Studio 54 for an after-dinner celebration. The club is available for private parties.

Studio 54

Ages Up to 5	Ages 6–15	Ages 16–20	Ages 21 & Up	Senior Citizens
Not Suitable	Not Suitable	Not Suitable	⚀ ⚁	⚀

The MGM Grand Lion Habitat

Hours: 9:00 A.M. to 11:00 P.M. (daily)

Admission: Free

Lions, tigers, and bears, oh my! The Mirage may offer a stunning display of white tigers, but if you want to see lions up-close, the MGM Grand is the place to visit. This $9-million addition to the resort showcases up to five adult lions daily. These lions are direct descendants of MGM Studios' famous signature marquee lion, Metro. Visitors view the lions from the safety of a transparent tunnel that runs through the lion habitat.

If you have a half hour or so with nothing to do, this is a great activity for people of all ages, and you can't beat the price! Kids especially will have a roaring good time looking at the lion cubs.

Lion Habitat

Ages Up to 5	Ages 6–15	Ages 16–20	Ages 21 & Up	Senior Citizens
⚀ ⚁	⚀ ⚁ ⚂	⚀ ⚁	⚀ ⚁	⚀ ⚁

Grand Adventures

Information: (888) 646-1203

MGM Grand was one of the first Las Vegas resort properties to cater to children and teens as well as adults. While Circus Circus has always presented ongoing free circus acts for guests and visitors, MGM Grand was the first to build a theme park, complete with rides, shows, and attractions. Many of the newer hotels and casinos offer individual thrill rides, but Grand Adventures is a complete theme park.

Open generally from late March to early September, Grand Adventures offers children, teens, and parents a fun-filled afternoon or evening of entertainment. Still, even though it is a full-featured theme park, it's certainly no Disneyland. In addition to the rides, shows, and attractions, you'll find plenty of fast food, including a Burger King, Nathan's Famous, Orient Express, Mamma Llardo's Pizzeria, and a Häagen-Dazs Ice Cream Parlour.

Main attractions at Grand Adventures include:

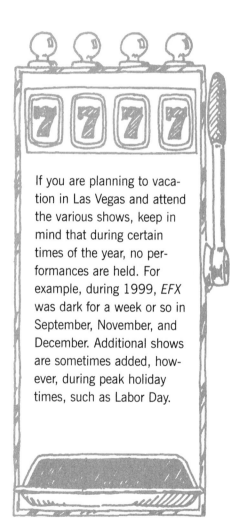

If you are planning to vacation in Las Vegas and attend the various shows, keep in mind that during certain times of the year, no performances are held. For example, during 1999, *EFX* was dark for a week or so in September, November, and December. Additional shows are sometimes added, however, during peak holiday times, such as Labor Day.

- SkyScreamer—The world's largest "skycoaster," this thriller takes riders 220 feet into the air and drops them in a free fall that reaches 70 m.p.h. This ride is not included in the general admission price of the park. To experience SkyScreamer, the cost is $25 per person for triple flyers (3 people at once), $30 each for double flyers (two people at once), or $35 per person for single flyers. This price includes general admission to Grand Adventures; however, reservations must be made in advance at the park's ticket office.
- Lightning Bolt—An outdoor roller coaster.
- Les Bumper Boats—A bumper boat ride for children.
- Over the Edge—A log-flume ride that's guaranteed to cool off riders on a hot day. Riders tour a re-creation of an old saw mill then plummet down 42 feet, ending with a grand splash.
- Grand Canyon Rapids—A free-flowing raft ride.
- Pedalin' Paddleboats—A self-controlled paddle boat ride that's suitable for people of all ages.

As for shows at Grand Adventures, there are ongoing musical performances and dance shows throughout the day on the outdoor stages. For example, the Pirates Cove Theater presents a live-action stunt show. The Magic Screen Theatre and the Gold Rush Theatre also offer shows throughout the day.

Grand Adventures is open daily from 11:00 A.M. to 7:00 P.M. during the following dates:

- March 26th through April 11th
- April 16th through May 30th
- June 4th through September 6th

Admission is $12 per person and includes unlimited access to all rides and shows except for the SkyScreamer. Children under 42 inches tall are admitted free.

Spa, Fitness Center, and Pool

Information: (702) 891-3077

Fitness Magazine named the Grand Spa one of the nation's top 15 hotel spas in 1998, and with good reason. The 30,000-square-foot facility features more than thirty treatment rooms, saunas, steam rooms, whirlpools, and relaxation lounges—everything you could possibly need to pamper your mind, body, and soul. Whether you're in search of a traditional massage, or something a bit more extravagant and unique (such as a facial or sea salt scrub), chances are you'll find it at this full-service spa. There's a daily admission fee for the spa and fitness center. All treatments and services are extra.

The Fitness Center features state-of-the-art exercise equipment, including virtual reality climbers and bikes, treadmills, cross-trainers, free-weights, and computerized circuit-training equipment.

Although the Grand Spa and Fitness Center is geared for adults, anyone of any age will likely enjoy the MGM Grand's huge pool. The 27,000-square-foot Grand Pool is divided into five separate pool areas, including a 1,000-foot gently flowing river "pool." The Grand Pool area features private cabanas, cocktail service, and a poolside restaurant. Use of the pool is free to hotel guests, so don't forget to pack a bathing suit.

Hours of operation vary based on the time of year; however, there's always at least one pool and one whirlpool open year-round. Pool hours will also vary based on weather conditions, but most areas open at 8:00 or 9:00 A.M. and remain open until between 4:00 and 7:00 P.M.

The Grand Spa is open seven days a week. Reservations for massages and other services can be made by hotel guests up to three days in advance. Reservations are strongly recommended.

Youth Activity Center

Information: (702) 891-3200

If you're traveling with children under the age of 12, you should know about the Youth Activity Center, where professionally trained counselors are available to entertain them in a camplike atmosphere. Kids can participate in arts and crafts, video games, table tennis, and board games, or organized outdoor sports (such as basketball). Movies and trips to Grand Adventures are also organized and meals are provided.

Youth Activity Center

Ages 3–5	Ages 6–15	Ages 16–20	Ages 21 & Up	Senior Citizens
⚀ ⚁ ⚂	⚀ ⚁ ⚂	Not Suitable	Not Suitable	Not Suitable

Due to state law, this facility is open to children over three years of age who are completely toilet trained and out of diapers and training pants. For the safety of the children, each room is equipped with video cameras that are monitored continuously. Photo identification is required to retrieve each child. Tours of the facility (for parents) are available only during the first hour of operation each day. The cost for leaving your child at the center varies but it is calculated on a per-child, per-hour basis. The maximum amount of time a child can stay at the facility is five hours per visit. They may return after a two-hour break, however.

Video Game Arcade

While the adults in your group are gambling, younger travelers can spend time in the MGM Grand's video game arcade testing their skills on dozens of the hottest new arcade and virtual reality games. The prices for these games vary. Also, located less than a five-minute walk from the MGM Grand is the Sega GameWorks entertainment center (see Chapter 6 for more details about GameWorks), which is a multifloor arcade featuring hundreds of video games, virtual reality rides, food, and other attractions.

Video Game Arcade

Ages Up to 5	Ages 6–15	Ages 16–20	Ages 21 & Up	Senior Citizens
Not Suitable	⚀ ⚁ ⚂	⚀ ⚁ ⚂	⚀ ⚁	⚀

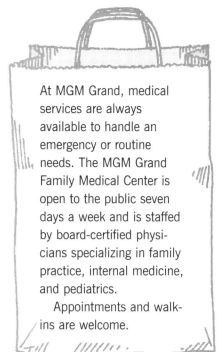

At MGM Grand, medical services are always available to handle an emergency or routine needs. The MGM Grand Family Medical Center is open to the public seven days a week and is staffed by board-certified physicians specializing in family practice, internal medicine, and pediatrics.

Appointments and walk-ins are welcome.

Casino

The MGM Grand offers more than just a simple casino to keep you occupied and entertained. The casino here is huge—equivalent to the size of four football fields. And the space is jam-packed with gaming machines, ranging from $.05- to $500-slot machines. The 165 gaming tables include baccarat, Pai Gow poker, mini-baccarat, Caribbean Stud poker, craps, roulette, blackjack, Let It Ride, casino war, Big Six, and Spanish 21. There's also a poker room, keno lounges, and a race and sports book.

Gamblers who qualify can join the Director's Club to earn valuable bonus points by using their membership cards in slot machines and at gaming tables. Benefits include cash back, exclusive merchandise, discounts or complimentary rooms, food and beverages, room upgrades, show tickets (and preferred seating), express check-in, and invitations to special events.

To join the Director's Club, fill out a registration form at the Director's Club Promotions Booth in the casino. You can begin using your card immediately to earn points, which can then be traded in for awards and prizes.

Shopping

Whether you win a fortune gambling or you have some pocket money burning a hole in your pocket, the MGM Grand offers several shopping areas where you can buy anything from designer fashions and fine jewelry to magic tricks that will amaze your friends. Most of the shops are located along the resort's Studio Walk and in the Star Lane Shops areas.

Banquet, Function, and Convention Services

If you're planning a business meeting, convention, or other professional gathering, the MGM Grand offers a range of meeting room facilities totaling over 380,000 square feet. In addition to 42 meeting rooms for smaller size groups, available space includes:

- The Grand Ballroom (61,388 square feet)
- Premiere Ballroom (49,234 square feet)
- Studio Ballroom (10,120 square feet)

Free gambling lessons are offered to hotel guests. Visit the information desk in the casino for details and to register. If you're new to gambling, taking advantage of these free lessons will give you a slightly better chance to leave Las Vegas a winner if you choose to gamble. You'll also learn basic casino etiquette.

- Vista Ballroom (5,162 square feet)
- Grand Garden Main Level (48,615 square feet)
- Grand Garden Concourse (52,600 square feet)

The Forever Grand Wedding Chapel

One of the newest additions to MGM Grand is the Forever Grand Wedding Chapel. Here you'll find two elegantly decorated, nondenominational chapels and a full-service wedding team that can help you plan the wedding ceremony and celebration you've always dreamed of. Whether you want a quickie wedding or a party for up to fifty of your closest friends and relatives, the Forever Grand Wedding Chapel can accommodate your needs. Minister services, photography, videography, live piano accompaniment, floral arrangements, special hotel accommodations, and reception planning services are all available.

If you want to tie the knot in a different setting, theme wedding packages are available. For example, you can get married on the set of the *EFX* show (surrounded by waterfalls) or say your vows at the Studio 54 dance club with disco lights flashing and 1970s music playing in the background.

Virtually all of the casinos offer some type of free gambling club or promotion. These clubs are designed for people who visit Las Vegas to gamble. From the casino's standpoint, by offering points that can be redeemed for awards, you'll be encouraged to gamble more at a specific casino than other casinos during your trip. Thus, if you're planning to try your luck primarily at one casino, especially over several visits, you could benefit from participating in a program, such as the Director's Club at the MGM Grand.

The Mirage

Theme:	Polynesian
Room Rate:	$$ / $$$ ($51–$250)
Number of Rooms:	3,044 rooms and suites
Casino:	98,000 square feet (designed to represent a Polynesian village), featuring 2,400 slots and video poker machines, keno, 120 table games, plus a separate poker room and a race and sports book
Dining:	An assortment of fine-dining restaurants with an international flair, plus family and casual dining options.
Primary Show:	*Siegfried & Roy*
Special Attractions:	The volcano, Royal White Tiger Habitat, indoor tropical rain forests, and Dolphin Habitat
Reservations:	(800) 627-6667 or (702) 791-7111
Web Site:	*www.themirage.com*
Address:	3400 Las Vegas Boulevard South Las Vegas, NV 89109

Overall Resort Rating Based on Amenities and Rates

Ages Up to 5	Ages 6–15	Ages 16–20	Ages 21 & Up	Senior Citizens
⚀ ⚁ ⚂	⚀ ⚁ ⚂	⚀ ⚁ ⚂	⚀ ⚁ ⚂	⚀ ⚁ ⚂

When it comes to Las Vegas resorts suitable for anyone—business travelers, gamblers, vacationers, convention goers, honeymooners, couples celebrating a special occasion (such as an anniversary), or families—The Mirage truly offers something for everyone, including top amenities at competitive rates.

Owned and operated by Mirage Resorts, Inc., which also owns and operates Bellagio, Treasure Island, the Golden Nugget Las Vegas, and several other resorts and casinos elsewhere in the United States, The Mirage is located between Caesars Palace and Treasure Island, in the heart of the Las Vegas Strip. The resort itself encompasses three, 30-story buildings as well as a cluster of villa apartments and bungalows.

The Mirage isn't just a resort with a focus on luxury. It also offers guests a strong element of entertainment. In front of the property is a lagoon with waterfalls and grottos as well as a volcano that erupts every 15 minutes. Inside, guests and visitors alike are treated to a variety of free and inexpensive attractions, including a 20,000-gallon aquarium in the registration area, a white tiger exhibit, a dolphin exhibit, and what is probably the most popular show in Las Vegas's history—*Siegfried & Roy*.

If you're looking for accommodations that truly represent Las Vegas in the twenty-first century, with all of the luxury, amenities, glitz, and glamour the city has to offer, The Mirage is where you'll want to stay.

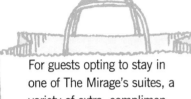

For guests opting to stay in one of The Mirage's suites, a variety of extra, complimentary services are offered, including limo service to and from the airport, fresh flowers on arrival, robes and slippers, turndown service, priority reservations for the *Siegfried & Roy* show, priority reservations at the resort's restaurants, and priority reservations for tee times at several golf courses in the area.

Guest Room Accommodations

As mentioned earlier, no resort in Las Vegas designs its rooms for guests to spend too much time in them (after all, you're supposed to be out gambling, shopping, or seeing the sights). Nevertheless, The Mirage offers extremely comfortable accommodations.

Typical guest rooms offer one king-size bed or two queen-size beds plus a wide range of amenities and fine furnishings. Hospitality Suites feature a bedroom with king-size bed, one-and-a-half baths, and a parlor area. There's also a dining area that can seat six and an adjacent wet bar. The bedroom can be closed off from the hospitality area. Two-bedroom Hospitality Suites are also available. These rooms typically have a king-size bed in one bedroom and two queen-size beds in the second bedroom (making them perfect for families).

The Tower Suites feature a bedroom with a king-size bed and a separate parlor area with a wet bar. Some of the suites also offer two bedrooms, plus a spectacular view of the city. Meanwhile, for the ultimate in luxury, the Penthouse Suites (located on the top two floors of The Mirage tower) offer one or two bedrooms, a separate living/dining area with a wet bar, and a wide range of other amenities.

The Petite Suites offer all of the amenities of the resort's full-size suites, but on a smaller scale. The bedrooms and living areas are separated by a large armoire housing a swivel entertainment center. These suites offer two bathrooms, a wet bar, and a marble entry. Eight villa apartments and six lanai bungalows, each with private pools, are also available.

Fine Dining

In addition to a handful of fine-dining restaurants and other eating establishments that offer more casual, less expensive dining options, 24-hour room service is available to resort guests. Reservations are strongly recommended for all of The Mirage's fancier restaurants. The dress code for these fine-dining establishments is "casual elegance."

Kokomo's ($$$)

Reservations: Strongly recommended, call (702) 791-7223

Kokomo's specializes in steaks and seafood. Although it is located indoors, in the heart of The Mirage's main building, the dining room re-creates a tropical rain forest, making guests feels as if they're outdoors, surrounded by waterfalls and exotic plant life.

The restaurant is open daily for lunch (11:00 A.M. to 2:30 P.M.) and dinner (5:30 to 11:00 P.M.), as well as an a la carte brunch on weekends (from 8:00 A.M. to 2:30 P.M.).

Mikado ($$$)

Reservations: Strongly recommended, call (702) 791-7223

Open nightly for dinner, from 6:00 to 11:00 P.M., Mikado offers a large menu of traditional Japanese foods, including sushi. Other menu items include lobster, steak, chicken, and shrimp cooked and served teppanyaki-style. A complete selection of specially prepared entrees is also available from an a la carte menu as well as a sushi bar located in the garden area of the restaurant. A large selection of wines, including sake, is available with dinner. Appetizers range in price from $5 to $18, while main courses range in price from $17 to $46.

Moongate ($$$)

Reservations: Strongly recommended, call (702) 791-7223

Offering classic Szechuan and Cantonese cuisines from China, this restaurant features a dining room that is decorated using classical Chinese architecture. One of the house specialties is a combination platter of deep-fried prawns, egg rolls, barbecued spareribs, and crab rangoons.

$ = entrees under $10; $$ = under $20; $$$ = over $20

Club Mirage is The Mirage's dollar slot club. As a member (membership is free), whenever you play $1 and above denomination machines, you'll receive Club Mirage bonus points that can be redeemed for cash, complimentary dining, show tickets, and special reduced room rates. To enroll, visit the Club Mirage Service Desk. For more information, call (800) 937-4444 and ask for Club Mirage.

Participating in a slot club at any resort can be beneficial if you're planning to gamble a lot of money at a single casino. Points are awarded based on how much you gamble, so to receive the best benefits, you need to rack up a high number of points.

Moongate is open nightly for dinner, from 5:30 to 11:00 P.M. Appetizers range in price from $5 to $24, while main courses range in price from $17 to $68. A large selection of fine wines is also available.

Onda Ristorante ($$$)

Reservations: Strongly recommended, call (702) 791-7223

Created by Boston-based chef Todd English, Onda offers classic regional dishes from Italy as well as new American cuisine. Menu items include homemade pasta, breads, fresh seafood, and meats. Onda is open nightly for dinner, from 5:30 to 11:00 P.M. A large selection of fine California and Italian wines is available with dinner, which is served in the dining room decorated with imported tiles and marble.

Renoir ($$$)

Reservations: Strongly recommended, call (702) 791-7223

Serving an extensive menu of contemporary French cuisine, Renoir is open nightly (except Wednesday) for dinner, from 6:00 to 10:30 P.M. Appetizers range in price from $16 to $19, while main courses range in price from $28 to $42. A special five-course tasting is available for a flat rate of $90. The décor of this restaurant includes silk covered walls and brocade upholstery, plus artwork from French Impressionist Pierre-Auguste Renoir.

Men are asked to wear jackets when dining at Renoir, which is located next to the Moongate restaurant.

Samba Grill ($$$)

Reservations: Strongly recommended, call (702) 791-7223

This unique Brazilian grill features the "Rodizio" style of cooking, which focuses mainly on entrees consisting of chicken, beef, vegetables, and fish. An all-inclusive dinner menu is priced under $30 per person, however, an a la carte menu is also available. Dinner is served nightly from 5:30 to 11:00 P.M. (Sunday through Thursday). On Friday and Saturday, dinners are served until 1:00 A.M., making this an excellent place for a late night meal. A live

$ = entrees under $10; $$ = under $20; $$$ = over $20

Samba trio performs every night, helping to add an upbeat ambiance to everyone's dining experience.

The Samba Grill offers a beverage list that includes a large assortment of tropical specialty drinks in addition to South American wines. Among the clutter of run-of-the-mill and theme restaurants in Las Vegas, Samba Grill offers an unusual and highly enjoyable dining experience for people of all ages.

Casual Dining

For guests and visitors looking for a more relaxed, less expensive dining experience that's perhaps more suitable for the entire family, the following options are available at The Mirage.

Caribe Cafe ($$)

Open 24 hours a day, this coffee shop offers an extremely diverse menu, including salads, sandwiches, exotic desserts, and all-American breakfasts.

Noodle Kitchen ($$)

A selection of soups, braised noodles, barbecued items, rice dishes, and congees is offered at this restaurant.

Mirage Buffet ($$)

Offering more than 150 menu items each day, this is a classic, Las Vegas–style, all-you-can-eat buffet. It's open daily for breakfast, lunch, and dinner. Due to the popularity of the buffet, be prepared for a wait to be seated, particularly during peak periods.

The California Pizza Kitchen ($$)

Located next to the casino's race and sports book, this chain restaurant offers wood-fired gourmet pizzas and a nice selection of other Southern California–inspired foods.

If you're in the mood for Japanese food and willing to travel by car to another Las Vegas resort property, consider Benihana Village, located at the Las Vegas Hilton, (702) 732-5755. At this restaurant, meals are prepared at your table, making the dining experience thoroughly entertaining.

$ = entrees under $10; $$ = under $20; $$$ = over $20

Coconuts Ice Cream Shop ($$)

A wide selection of desserts are served day and night, including freshly made ice creams, sorbets, and frozen yogurts. There's also a coffee bar (Coffee Express) that serves muffins, cookies, and a variety of gourmet coffees, making it a great place to stop for a quick and inexpensive breakfast or snack.

Paradise Cafe ($$)

Located near the pool area, this cafe offers a light menu. It's an ideal place to stop for a quick and inexpensive snack.

Lounges

The Lagoon Saloon

Located near the rear of the casino, this lounge provides an intimate setting, surrounded by waterfalls and lush, exotic plants. Full bar service and live entertainment is offered.

Baccarat Bar

You'll find this lounge, offering live piano music, at the center of The Mirage's famous casino. Full bar service is available.

The Corner Bar

Located next to Renoir, one of The Mirage's fine-dining restaurants, this lounge offers a light menu (including fried calamari, shrimp scampi, capriccio, and pizetta) along with full bar service and live jazz music.

The Dolphin Bar

Particularly inviting on a hot day, this lounge is located near the resort's pool and offers a large selection of alcoholic and nonalcoholic beverages.

Visit the official *Siegfried & Roy* Web site at *www.sarmoti.com* to learn more about their incredible show and other projects the two world-famous illusionists are working on.

$ = entrees under $10; $$ = under $20; $$$ = over $20

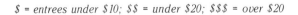

Special Attractions

The Mirage is the permanent home of *Siegfried & Roy*, which is arguably the most visually impressive and awe-inspiring show in Las Vegas and beyond. Although the ticket price is a bit steep, the show offers an entertainment experience like no other. This show is just one of the many attractions that make The Mirage a truly memorable place to stay or visit.

Siegfried & Roy

Ticket Price: $95

Show Times: **Nightly 7:30 and 11:00 P.M.**
(except Wednesday and Thursday)

Box Office: **(800) 963-9634**

Time magazine called *Siegfried & Roy* the show of the century, and with good reason. While Siegfried and Roy are master illusionists, their show is much more than a run-of-the-mill magic show. With a cast of 88 performers, the show takes place in a custom-built theater and features beautiful royal white tigers and white lions of Timbavati that appear and disappear before your eyes. *Siegfried & Roy* is a visual spectacle of lights, costumes, sound, music, dance, and illusion that is truly breathtaking. It is directed by John Napier (the Tony award-winning artist responsible for *Cats, Starlight Express, Les Miserables, Phantom of the Opera,* and other Broadway masterpieces) and Kenneth Feld (the executive producer of *The Ringling Brothers, Barnum & Bailey Circus*). The show will appeal to people of all ages and is well worth the $95 ticket price (which makes it one of the most expensive shows in Las Vegas).

Both Siegfried and Roy have become Las Vegas icons, just as Elvis Presley and the Rat Pack were in years past. The master illusionists, who began performing at The Mirage February 1, 1990, appear Friday through Tuesday for the first five months of the year. They "disappear" for their annual summer hiatus June 5 to June 22, reappearing June 23. They then maintain their twice-nightly Friday through Tuesday schedule until November 28. From November 29 until December 28, the cast takes its annual winter break. Siegfried and Roy complete the year with performances

Seen by well over three million people (approximately 3,000 people each night), *Siegfried & Roy* is probably the most successful and most popular show in Las Vegas. Thus, if you wait until the last minute, tickets will be extremely hard to get. Tickets can be purchased by Mirage guests up to 90 days in advance. Nonguests can reserve tickets with a major credit card up to 30 days in advance by calling the box office. Tickets typically sell out the day of the show early in the morning.

December 29 and 30, followed by a gala New Year's Eve celebration December 31. In case you happen to miss this show while in Las Vegas, their IMAX movie *Siegfried and Roy "The Magic Box"* is currently playing at IMAX theaters around the world.

Siegfried & Roy

Ages Up to 5	Ages 6–15	Ages 16–20	Ages 21 & Up	Senior Citizens
Not Suitable	⚀⚁⚂	⚀⚁⚂	⚀⚁⚂	⚀⚁⚂

Danny Gans (one-man show)

In the spring of 2000, entertainer Danny Gans began his award-winning, one-man show nightly in the 1,260-seat theater in The Mirage. Danny Gans is a singer, impressionist, comedian, and actor who incorporates these talents into a highly entertaining show.

Danny Gans

Ages Up to 5	Ages 6–15	Ages 16–20	Ages 21 & Up	Senior Citizens
Not Suitable	Not Suitable	Not Suitable	⚀⚁	⚀⚁

The Volcano

Admission: Free

In front of The Mirage is a 54-foot volcano that erupts every 15 minutes between dusk and midnight. Flames shoot into the sky, spewing smoke and fire 100 feet above the waters below. The volcano is a free attraction that can be seen from along the Strip by passersby and resort guests alike. It's just one of the attractions that make The Mirage an exciting place to visit.

The Volcano

Ages Up to 5	Ages 6–15	Ages 16–20	Ages 21 & Up	Senior Citizens
⚀	⚀⚁⚂	⚀⚁⚂	⚀⚁	⚀⚁

For a free autographed photo of Siegfried and Roy, write to: Siegfried & Roy Public Relations, 4665 S. Procyon Ave., Suite N, Las Vegas, Nevada 89109. To purchase official Siegfried & Roy merchandise (some of which isn't sold at The Mirage), point your Web browser to *www.sarmoti.com/store/index.html* or call (800) 888-2522.

The Royal White Tiger Habitat

Admission: Free

Open 24 hours a day, this free attraction allows guests and visitors to view some of the royal white tigers raised and trained by Siegfried and Roy. These illusionists have dedicated their lives to preserving this endangered species of tiger. The open-air environment lets guests to view the tigers up-close, while allowing the tigers freedom to roam in a large, open area.

The Royal White Tiger Habitat

Ages Up to 5	Ages 6–15	Ages 16–20	Ages 21 & Up	Senior Citizens
⚀ ⚁	⚀ ⚁ ⚂	⚀ ⚁ ⚂	⚀ ⚁	⚀ ⚁

The Secret Garden

Hours: 11:00 A.M. to 5:30 P.M. (Tuesday through Sunday)

Admission: $10 per adult (includes the Dolphin Habitat)

The Secret Garden is the home to many of Siegfried and Roy's rare animals, including exotic panthers, white lions of Timbavati, and the royal white tigers of Nevada. The largest animal is a ceremonial Thai elephant. By developing this attraction, the illusionists are hoping to increase public awareness of the plight of all endangered animals and foster dialogue about the world's rarest breeds. This attraction demonstrates what is possible when humans and animals work and play together. It also provides guests of all ages a unique opportunity to get up-close to some of the most exotic and beautiful creatures on the planet. The attraction offers an entertaining, thought provoking, and educational experience.

There is a $10 (per adult) admission fee, which includes access to The Secret Garden and the Dolphin Habitat. Children under 10 years of age are admitted free of charge. An audio tour, featuring the voices of Siegfried and Roy is available to guests as they see the various exhibits.

The Secret Garden

Ages Up to 5	Ages 6–15	Ages 16–20	Ages 21 & Up	Senior Citizens
⚀	⚀ ⚁ ⚂	⚀ ⚁ ⚂	⚀ ⚁ ⚂	⚀ ⚁ ⚂

The Dolphin Habitat

Admission: **$10 per adult (includes the Secret Garden)**

This 2.5-million gallon dolphin habitat is home to a family of Atlantic bottle-nosed dolphins. (There are seven dolphins in all.) Four connected pools, an artificial coral reef system, and a sandy bottom replicate the dolphin's natural environment. The facility houses only dolphins that were born at this site or relocated from other facilities. No animals were taken from the wild for this project.

The Dolphin Habitat is an educational facility. Guests are offered a chance to see dolphins in their natural habitat and learn about their role in nature. Guided tours are provided throughout the day. Guests are able to get up-close to the dolphins; however, there is no physical interaction with them. Throughout the day, dolphin experts have spontaneous "interactions" with the animals. This is not a preplanned or rehearsed animal show like you would see at SeaWorld.

The Dolphin Habitat will be of particular interest to children and teens. There is a $10 (per adult) admission fee, which also includes access to The Secret Garden. Children under 10 years of age are admitted free of charge. Be sure to visit the underground area for an underwater view of the dolphins and an excellent photo opportunity.

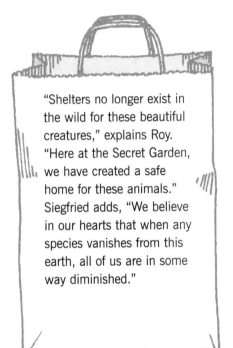

"Shelters no longer exist in the wild for these beautiful creatures," explains Roy. "Here at the Secret Garden, we have created a safe home for these animals." Siegfried adds, "We believe in our hearts that when any species vanishes from this earth, all of us are in some way diminished."

The Dolphin Habitat

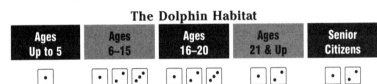

Ages Up to 5	Ages 6–15	Ages 16–20	Ages 21 & Up	Senior Citizens
⚀	⚀ ⚁ ⚂	⚀ ⚁ ⚂	⚀ ⚁	⚀ ⚁

The Aquarium

Admission: Free

When guests enter, one of the first sights they'll notice is a 20,000-gallon saltwater aquarium. Stocked with angelfish, puffer fish, tangs, and other exotic sea creatures, including three different kinds of sharks, the aquarium also houses over 1,000 coral-reef species from around the world. It is one of the most elaborate and technically advanced coral-reef aquariums in the world. The tank itself is 53 feet long with water that is six feet deep. This is a free exhibit, open 24 hours a day.

Video Game Arcade

Hours: 9:00 A.M. to 10:00 P.M. (Sunday through Thursday)
9:00 A.M. to midnight (Friday and Saturday)

Offering about thirty video games, this arcade combines the latest in video gaming with classic games. Most cost $.50 per play. You'll find the arcade near the entrance to the pool area.

Spa and Salon

Spa Reservations: (800) 456-4564 or (702) 791-7472

Salon Reservations: (702) 791-7474

In order to cater to an ever-growing health-conscious clientele, The Mirage features an extensive spa and salon, which offers the latest fitness, health, and beauty programs. At the spa you'll find an aerobic studio, separate men's and women's facilities, sauna, steam bath, whirlpool, private massage rooms, and a juice bar. Personal training sessions are also available.

Spa equipment and services also include stationary bicycles, treadmills, and stair climbers, a full line of CYBEX weight training machines, free weights, aromatherapy, body exfoliation, and seaweed facial masks. Besides the daily fee required to use the fitness and spa facilities, additional fees apply for special services, such as massages, facials, and personal training sessions.

The beauty salon provides a complement of services including hair styling, from cuts to coloring. Nail treatments, facials, and makeup services are also available by appointment.

In 2001, The Mirage will offer an all-new, Broadway-style musical that is currently being written and produced for the resort. Over 100,000 square feet of additional meeting and convention space is also being added.

Pool

The outdoor pool area at The Mirage features a series of lagoons, inlets, and waterfalls surrounded by beautiful tropical landscaping. Private cabanas are available for rental. The pool area is open to all resort guests.

Casino

The large and lavishly decorated casino is designed to represent a Polynesian village. It offers more than 2,400 slot and video poker machines, keno, plus table games like craps, blackjack, and baccarat. There's also a separate poker room and a race and sports book.

Shopping

The Mirage is just a short walk from the world famous Forum Shops at Caesars Palace, but in The Mirage itself you'll find an assortment of fine stores, including:

- D. Fine—Offers a large selection of men's designer fashions.
- Impulse—A selection of gifts, souvenirs, costume jewelry, sundries, and other items are available here.
- The Mirage Shop—Mirage souvenirs as well as *Siegfried & Roy* items can be purchased here.
- The Mirage Collection—Mirage merchandise, souvenirs from *Siegfried & Roy,* and *Cirque du Soleil* merchandise are sold here.
- Shadow Creek—A pro shop for golf enthusiasts.

Banquet, Function, and Convention Services

With two ballrooms—the 40,000-square-foot Grand Ballroom and the 20,000-square-foot Ballroom Mirage—plus dozens of meeting rooms, The Mirage can accommodate groups of five to 5,000. Moreover, in the summer of 2001, The Mirage will open a new convention facility, doubling its current space. The resort also features a fully equipped business center that caters to the needs of business travelers and convention goers.

Monte Carlo Resort & Casino

Theme: The European flair of Monte Carlo

Room Rate: $$$ / $$$$ ($101+)

Number of Rooms: 3,002 guest rooms, including 259 suites

Casino: 102,197 square feet, featuring 2,108 slot machines, 71 table games, a high-limit gaming area, a race and sports book, a keno lounge, and a poker room

Dining: Eight restaurants, including a buffet, as well as a food court

Special Attractions: *Master Magician Lance Burton*, heated outdoor pool, wave pool, and tube ride, and the "Street of Dreams" shopping promenade

Reservations: (800) 311-8999

Web Site: *www.monte-carlo.com*

Address: 3770 Las Vegas Boulevard South
Las Vegas, NV 89109

Overall Resort Rating Based on Amenities and Rates

Ages Up to 5	Ages 6–15	Ages 16–20	Ages 21 & Up	Senior Citizens
1	2	3	3	3

Located between the Flamingo Hilton and the Tropicana (along the Strip), the Monte Carlo is owned and operated as a joint venture between Mandalay Resort Group (which also operates Mandalay Bay) and Mirage Resorts, Inc. This resort opened in June 1996 and is about one mile from McCarran Airport.

From the large fountain near the grand entrance of the Monte Carlo, this resort is classy yet not overly pretentious, making it ideal for business travelers, couples, honeymooners, and families traveling with teens. Lance Burton offers a family-oriented magic show that is extremely entertaining, plus there is plenty of shopping, tennis, a video game arcade, and a swimming pool that will appeal to children and teens.

A free monorail connects the Monte Carlo with the Bellagio, providing fast and easy transportation between the two properties.

Guest Room Accommodations

With 3,002 deluxe rooms and suites, the Monte Carlo features larger than average accommodations decorated with Italian marble and granite finishes as well as brass fixtures. Cherry furniture is used to enhance the turn-of-the-century décor.

In addition to deluxe rooms, one-room suites are available that offer over 700 square feet of space including a seating area with a sofa. One king-size bed or two queen-size beds are available in many of the rooms. Many of the suites offer a full bath with a spa, plus a half bath.

Fine Dining

Steaks and seafood are the specialties of the house at Blackstone Steak House, while Andre's French Restaurant offers an elegant dining experience with a menu influenced by some of France's most famed restaurants. In addition to these restaurants, 24-hour room service is available to resort guests.

Preview Andre's French Restaurant's menu and learn more about this fine-dining establishment by pointing your Web browser to www.andresfrenchrest.com.

Blackstone Steak House ($$$)

Reservations: (702) 730-7777

Choose from prime, aged Midwestern beef that is prepared to order over an open-hearth charcoal broiler, or choose from a variety of fresh seafood or poultry dishes. This restaurant, which is open for dinner from 5:30 to 11:00 P.M. nightly, features entrees priced from $20 to $27. The Surf 'n' Turf special is priced at $38. One house specialty is the hot seafood combo appetizer for two.

Andre's French Restaurant ($$$)

Reservations: Recommended, call (702) 730-9755

This restaurant features a world-class wine cellar (with over 12,000 bottles of wine on-hand), a cigar-friendly lounge, and a menu of traditional French cuisine. The intimate main dining room seats 50 and showcases the Renaissance décor reminiscent of a French chateau's formal dining room—complete with a working fireplace and recessed,

$ = entrees under $10; $$ = under $20; $$$ = over $20

hand-painted ceilings. The tables are accented with fresh flowers, Versace china, sterling silver, and candles.

Menu offerings such as duck foie gras, tuna tartare, Provimi veal, venison, and Muscovy duck breast are typically available. Daily specials often include Maine lobster and other popular seafood dishes.

The dining room is open nightly for dinner, from 6:00 to 11:00 P.M.

Casual Dining

Cafe ($ / $$)

This is one of the best coffee shops you'll find anywhere on the Strip. Open 24 hours, Monte Carlo's cafe offers a wide range of selections, from sandwiches to more elaborate entrees. Freshly baked desserts are also available. So, no matter what time you get hungry, a good meal awaits you at Monte Carlo's Cafe. If you're staying at a nearby resort (such as the Boardwalk Casino or MGM Grand), it's worth taking a walk here to enjoy breakfast, lunch, or dinner. Keno is available in the dining room that overlooks the casino.

Monte Carlo Brew Pub ($$)

This was the first brew pub in Las Vegas. In addition to a full menu (featuring pizza, sandwiches, and pasta dishes) and musical entertainment (a D.J. is featured nightly, from 9:00 P.M. until closing), this establishment offers five specialty ales and the brewmaster's special—all brewed on-premises. The pub is open from 11:00 A.M. until 2:00 A.M. (Sunday through Thursday) and until 4:00 A.M. on Friday and Saturday. On Monday nights, disco music is played.

Dragon Noodle Company ($$)

This Asian restaurant serves many exotic dishes in addition to many traditional favorites, all prepared exhibition style. The dining room itself was designed in accordance with the practices of Feng Shui, which the management states was done to bring diners boundless health, energy, happiness, and good fortune. The restaurant is open for lunch and dinner daily, from 11:00 A.M. until 11:00 P.M. (midnight on Friday and Saturday).

The Monte Carlo Brew Pub is one of the nation's largest breweries, producing over 3,000 barrels (93,000 gallons) per year. Beer is brewed approximately three and a half times a week and is bottled two to three times a month. Six Monte Carlo–labeled beers are produced regularly at the brewery: High Roller Red, Las Vegas Lites, Silver State Stout, Winner's Wheat, Jackpot Pale, and the Brewmaster's Special.

$ = entrees under $10; $$ = under $20; $$$ = over $20

Market City Cafe ($$)

Serving dishes with Southern Italian flair, the portions at this restaurant are large, but the prices are moderate. The antipasto bar features a host of delicacies, such as marinated fennel, grilled eggplant, and fresh mussels. Main courses include homemade pastas, pizzas, and various grilled entrees. Open daily from 11:00 A.M. to 11:00 P.M. (midnight on Friday and Saturday).

Buffet ($)

Located across the casino from the Lance Burton Theater, this is the Monte Carlo's version of an all-you-can-eat buffet. Many of the main entrees are prepared to order, exhibition style. Breakfast is served from 7:00 to 11:00 A.M. ($6.99 per person). Lunch runs from 11:30 A.M. to 3:30 P.M. ($7.25 per person), and dinner is served from 4:00 to 10:00 P.M. ($9.99 per person). A Sunday champagne brunch is served from 7:00 A.M. to 3:30 P.M. ($10.99 per person).

Island Snack Bar ($)

Located by the pool, here you can enjoy a refreshing snack while basking in the sunshine.

Food Court ($)

If you're looking for a fast and inexpensive meal or snack, the food court offers a range of breakfast, lunch, and dinner selections that are perfect for the whole family. In the food court you'll find Golden Bagel & Coffee (serving coffee, bagels, pastries, and more), Sbarro Italian Eatery (serving pasta, pizza, and other Italian specialties), Nathan's (hot dogs and fries are the specialty), McDonald's (if you don't know what's available here, you need to get out more), and Häagen-Dazs (ice cream is the specialty here).

Lounges

- Houdini's Lounge—This is one of the resort's more intimate full-service bars.
- Pool Bar—Located by the pool, a variety of alcoholic and nonalcoholic beverages are served.

To learn more about the Monte Carlo Brew Pub, visit the brewery's Web site at *www.monte-carlo.com/ brewery.html.*

$ = entrees under $10; $$ = under $20; $$$ = over $20

- Showroom Bar—Located in the Lance Burton Theater, this full-service bar caters to show goers before the show and during intermission.
- Sports Book Bar—Enjoy a refreshing drink while watching a variety of televised sporting events simultaneously. This bar is located in the casino's race and sports book.

Special Attractions

Although the Monte Carlo doesn't have any fancy theme park attractions, the resort does offer one of the best magic shows in Las Vegas.

Master Magician Lance Burton

Show Times: 7:00 and 10:00 P.M. (Tuesday through Sunday)

Ticket Prices: $44.95 to $49.95

Box Office: (702) 730-7160

One of the world's foremost magician/illusionists has a permanent home in Las Vegas. While *Siegfried & Roy* offers a visual extravaganza of lights, sounds, dance, and illusion, Lance Burton takes a less flashy approach to his primarily one-man magic show. Lance Burton interacts with the audience in a personal and very entertaining way. At the same time, he performs tricks and illusions that are just as mystifying and breathtaking as anything Siegfried and Roy do in their show.

During his show, you'll see objects (as well as animals and people) levitate, appear, and disappear. Lance is accompanied on stage by dozens of doves and other animals, plus a handful of beautiful assistants. The 1,200-seat theater was custom built for the show, which debuted June 21, 1996. Within three years, one million people had experienced it first-hand at the Monte Carlo.

Although Lance Burton will never reveal the secrets to his tricks, you can meet him after his 10:30 P.M. performance in the Lance Burton Magic Shop next to the theater's main entrance.

No matter how old you are, if you're looking for an exciting, fun-filled, and highly entertaining show while in Las Vegas, you won't want to miss *Master Magician Lance Burton.*

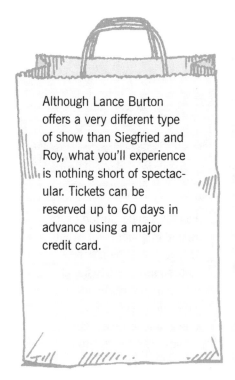

Although Lance Burton offers a very different type of show than Siegfried and Roy, what you'll experience is nothing short of spectacular. Tickets can be reserved up to 60 days in advance using a major credit card.

Master Magician Lance Burton

Ages Up to 5	Ages 6–15	Ages 16–20	Ages 21 & Up	Senior Citizens
Not Suitable	⚀ ⚁ ⚂	⚀ ⚁ ⚂	⚀ ⚁ ⚂	⚀ ⚁ ⚂

Spa, Health Club, and Salon

The Monte Carlo offers a full-service spa and unisex styling salon, plus a 2,000-square-foot exercise room with the latest equipment. The exercise room is open to all guests, while treatments at the spa and salon are available for an additional fee. The spa includes whirlpools, steam rooms, and a sauna. The Monte Carlo also offers three lighted tennis courts that are available to resort guests. Court time should be reserved in advance. Professional private and group instruction is available (for a fee).

Pool

In addition to a heated outdoor pool, the resort offers a 4,800-foot wave pool and a flowing (tubing) river ride.

Casino

Equipped with 2,108 slot machines and video poker machines, plus 71 gaming tables (offering double-deck blackjack, single zero roulette, craps, Pai Gow poker, Caribbean Stud poker, mini-baccarat, and baccarat), the Monte Carlo casino caters to a diverse crowd. The casino also offers a high-limit area, a keno lounge, a poker room, and a race and sports book.

Video Game Arcade

You'll find over sixty of the latest in video games and pinball machines here. If you're too young for the casinos or tired of gaming, and you'd rather be blowing things up or saving the universe, you'll find plenty of high-tech thrills here.

Fans of Lance Burton or magic in general will want to check out the official Lance Burton Web site at *www.lanceburton.com.* From here, you can purchase magic tricks, and videos, and join Burton's official fan club.

Shopping

The Monte Carlo features an indoor, mall-like shopping area known as the "Street of Dreams," which offers about a dozen fine shops and boutiques, including:

- Davante—Designer eyewear and sunglasses.
- Crown Jewels—Fine jewelry and costume jewelry.
- Bon Vivant—Fashions for men and women.
- Beer on Tap—Monte Carlo's Pub & Brewery (which offers a selection of microbrews) offer many of their beers "to go" at this shop.
- Medici Cigar Club—Fine cigars (priced from $3.50 to $25) are sold here, along with a selection of lighters and accessories. Cigar brands include Cohiba, Monte Cristo, Arturo Fuente, Macanudo, and Bahia.
- Brats—Designer clothing for kids.
- Universal Time—Need a watch? Here you'll find a large selection of wristwatches from many designers.
- Pub & Brew Shop—Monte Carlo beer and merchandise is sold here, only to those over the legal drinking age.
- El Portal—A large selection of designer luggage and leather goods.
- Monaco Men's Fashion—Designer clothing for men, from casual wear to fine suits.
- Monte Carlo Classics—Merchandise and souvenirs from the Monte Carlo Resort & Casino.

Beyond the Street of Dreams shops, you'll also find a handful of other shops at the Monte Carlo, including:

- Lance Burton Magic Shop—After experiencing Lance Burton's magic show, you'll want to drop into this shop and maybe pick up a few tricks and illusions to perform yourself. Magic demonstrations are offered throughout the day and night. At midnight (Tuesday through Saturday), Lance Burton himself appears at the shop to meet fans.
- Beach Club Shoppe—Although there's no actual beach nearby, the Monte Carlo does offer a lovely pool area and sun deck. Everything you'll need for a day at the beach (or the pool) can be found here.

- HyperMarket—This well stocked convenience store also offers one-hour film processing. If you're planning an in-room celebration, you can also stock up on wine, champagne, and bottled spirits.
- Nouveau News—Newspapers, magazines, and snack foods are available.
- Club Casino Royale—Merchandise and souvenirs from the Monte Carlo are sold here.

Banquet, Function, and Convention Services

The Monte Carlo has 24,000 square feet of meeting space, with many different sized meeting rooms and ballrooms available for virtually any type of function. The resort's catering and event planning staff offer a wide range of services.

Wedding Chapel

Information: (702) 730-7575

The French Victorian–themed chapel at the Monte Carlo seats 90 guests and is decorated in soft, neutral colors. The chapel itself features French doors, crown moldings, hand-painted murals, and silk floral arrangements. (Fresh flower arrangements can be ordered for an additional fee.) Both religious and civil services can be held in the chapel. Four different wedding packages are available, ranging in price from $205 to over $1,000. Wedding ceremonies can be customized to fit any couple's tastes.

Additional services, such as live music, flowers, photo packages, and videography, are available for additional fees. A $150 nonrefundable deposit is required when booking a wedding date.

Honeymoon Magazine recently named Las Vegas one of the five most romantic cities in the world. Other cities that made the list are San Francisco, New Orleans, New York, and Charleston, South Carolina.

New York–New York Hotel & Casino

Theme:	New York City
Room Rate:	$$$ ($101–$250)
Number of Rooms:	2,033 rooms and suites
Casino:	84,000 square feet, featuring 2,200 slots and video poker machines, 72 table games, keno, and a race and sports book
Dining:	Several fine-dining establishments are joined by a handful of casual and theme restaurants.
Primary Show:	*Michael Flatley's Lord of the Dance*
Special Attractions:	Replicas (most one-third actual size) of New York City landmarks, including the Statue of Liberty, Brooklyn Bridge, and Empire State Building. Surrounding the main resort is the Manhattan Express (a Coney Island–style roller coaster).
Reservations:	(800) NY-FOR-ME or (800)-693-6763
Web Site:	*www.nynyhotelcasino.com*
Address:	2790 Las Vegas Boulevard South Las Vegas, NV 89109

Overall Resort Rating Based on Amenities and Rates

Ages Up to 5	Ages 6–15	Ages 16–20	Ages 21 & Up	Senior Citizens
⚁⚀	⚀⚁⚂	⚀⚁⚂	⚀⚁⚁	⚀⚁⚂

New York (a.k.a. The Big Apple) is known as the city that never sleeps, yet it's the New York–New York Hotel & Casino that really lives up to this reputation. With its restaurants, family-oriented rides and attractions, casino, show, and other activities, you'll find plenty to do, day or night.

The New York–New York Hotel & Casino opened in January 1997, and is a wholly owned subsidiary of MGM Grand, Inc. This resort is across the street from its sister resort, the MGM Grand. The two resorts are linked via a 300-foot-long, 50-foot-high replica of the Brooklyn Bridge that crosses Las Vegas Boulevard.

This entire resort, outside and in, is designed to re-create various aspects of New York City. The main casino, lobbies, shopping, and dining areas resemble various New York attractions including Park Avenue, the Financial District, Central Park, Times Square, the Village, Gourmet Street, as well as Penn and Grand Central Stations. The best thing about visiting New York–New York, as opposed to the real city, is that the resort is clean and safe.

Guest Room Accommodations

The New York–New York Hotel & Casino is an ideal place for families to stay. An assortment of room accommodations and suites are available. The rooms themselves are spacious, offering a single king-size bed or two queen-size beds, a television, seating area, closet, and full bathroom. Some suites contain wet bars, while others offer whirlpool baths and other amenities.

Fine Dining

Gallagher's Steakhouse and Il Fornaio provide the perfect atmosphere for a formal business dinner, intimate celebration, or simply a fine-dining experience. Each restaurant in New York–New York offers a themed menu and atmosphere, combining the favored elements of New York City.

Gallagher's Steakhouse ($$$)

Reservations: (702) 740-6450

The original Gallagher's Steakhouse was founded in 1927. Today, the dry-aged beef and fresh seafood entrees, all cooked to order, are served right here in Las Vegas. Open daily for dinner.

Il Fornaio ($$$)

Reservations: (702) 740-6403

Award-winning Italian cuisine made from authentic regional recipes is offered here. Housemade pastas, rotisserie meats, mesquite-grilled fish, wood-fired pizzas, fresh salads, and hearth-baked bread are among the specialty items found on the menu. The restaurant is open daily, 8:30 A.M. to midnight, for breakfast, lunch, and dinner.

$ = entrees under $10; $$ = under $20; $$$ = over $20

If you play the slot machines, consider joining the New York–New York Slot Exchange, which allows you to earn cash, rewards, complimentary services, and receive special room rates. For more information, or to sign up for the Slot Exchange, call (888) 4-NYNY-LV or visit the casino's Web site to register online at *www.nynyhotelcasino.com.*

Casual Dining

Although New York–New York offers its share of fine-dining establishments, the resort also offers a selection of less formal but equally enjoyable dining options, plus fast-food dining choices for people in a hurry or on a tight budget.

Il Fornaio Panetteria ($$)

An ideal first stop in the morning (or for lunch), this bakery offers a wide selection of pastries, coffees, sandwiches, and salads, along with fresh Italian bread, cookies, and cakes.

Chin Chin Cafe ($$)

Straight from Los Angeles, this popular Chinese restaurant offers a contemporary atmosphere and some of the best fried rice you'll find on the cor tinent. The exhibition-style kitchen allows patrons to watch the skilled chefs prepare a variety of dishes. The food isn't cheap, nor is it fast food, but Chi Chin Cafe offers a casual dining experience the whole family can enjoy for lunch, dinner, or a between-meal snack. An extensive dim sum selection is also offered.

Over 940,000 pedestrians stride Manhattan's real-life Brooklyn Bridge each year, yet over 8 million people crossed Las Vegas's version of the landmark between 1997 and 1999. New York's Brooklyn Bridge is considered one of the greatest architectural accomplishments of the nineteenth century.

America ($$)

Open 24 hours, this restaurant features American cuisine selections from across the country. If you're staying at New York–New York, it's the ideal famil dining restaurant because it's always open and affordable. A selection of American wines and beers is also offered.

Gonzalez y Gonzalez ($$)

If you're in the mood for authentic Mexican cuisine, you'll find it here. In addition to offering traditional New York–style Mexican food items, the restaurant itself is decorated with lanterns, piñatas, and a tequila bar.

Nathan's Famous Hot Dogs ($)

Those world-famous hot dogs and French fries are available from this Nathan's fast-food establishment, located in the Coney Island Emporium area.

$ = entrees under $10; $$ = under $20; $$$ = over $20

Quality fast food suitable for the whole family is served here. It's ideal if you're in a hurry, on a budget, or simply want to enjoy the atmosphere of the Emporium area while having a snack.

Häagen-Dazs Ice Cream ($$)

This ice cream counter offers Häagen-Dazs ice cream and an assortment of other treats.

Schrafft's Ice Cream ($)

This ice cream counter also offers an assortment of ice cream–based treats, including sundaes.

The Village Eateries ($)

The ideal place to go for a quick and cheap bite to eat, you'll find a variety of inexpensive menu options available. Eight small restaurants and food counters make up this dining area found on the main level of the resort. Dining options include deli sandwiches, ribs, chicken, hamburgers, Brooklyn-style pizza, and fish 'n' chips.

The Motown Cafe ($$ / $$$)

Open for breakfast, lunch, dinner, and for late-night snacks, you'll dine in a room filled with Motown memorabilia (such as original Gold Records and costumes) as you listen to world-famous Motown record label artists such as the Four Tops, Temptations, Supremes, and Boys II Men. Enjoy live music performed nightly. After 11:00 P.M., the dance floor opens up, allowing you to enjoy the hits from yesterday and today.

Lounges

If you're not looking for a full meal, but want to relax and have a drink, enjoy live entertainment, or sing along with the entertainment, New York–New York offers several lounges.

$ = entrees under $10; $$ = under $20; $$$ = over $20

Banquet, Function, and Convention Services

Information:
(888) 696-9887

New York–New York can accommodate virtually any type of meeting, convention, or special function. The resort offers meeting rooms, ballrooms, dining rooms, and a wide range of support services.

- Empire Bar—This live entertainment lounge, reminiscent of the 1930s and 1940s, offers an international selection of wines and specialty and after-dinner drinks.
- The Bar at Times Square —This lively bar features dueling pianos and fun-filled sing-alongs for older audiences (you must be of legal drinking age). N.Y.P.D. (New York Piano Duos) perform nightly. The bar itself is modeled after a New York City pub.
- Hamilton's—Actor and cigar aficionado George Hamilton helped to create this upscale lounge and cigar bar. Enjoy nightly jazz entertainment and be sure to try one of the many martini specialties offered from the bar. A light menu and fine cigars are also available. After 8:00 P.M., appropriate attire is required.
- Motown Cafe—Experience the magic, music, and memories of Motown. Live performances are held nightly.

Special Attractions

Like every resort along the Strip, New York–New York offers a casino and many other amenities designed to keep guests comfortable and entertained. This resort also offers a variety of unique entertainment activities, shows, and one of the most thrilling roller coasters in Las Vegas.

Michael Flatley's Lord of the Dance

Show Times: 7:30 and 10:00 P.M. (Tuesday, Wednesday, and Saturday)

9:00 P.M. (Thursday and Friday)

Ticket Prices: $59 (weekdays) and $69 (weekends/holidays)

Box Office: (702) 740-6815

Web site: *www.lordofthedance.com*

The 1,000-seat Broadway Theater, in the heart of New York–New York, hosts *Michael Flatley's Lord of the Dance*. This 90-minute show features over forty dancers and musicians in an incredibly exciting performance that focuses on dance and live music. The most impressive aspect of this show is the perfectly synchronized dancing of the many dancers.

Michael Flatley started dancing at the tender age of 4, when his grandmother, an Irish champion dancer, taught him his first steps. However, it was not until Michael was 11 that his mother Eilish—also an Irish dance champion—took him and his brother and three sisters to dance school. Michael later became the first American to win the World Irish Dance Championships.

This is one of three dance troupes trained by Michael Flatley. This troupe has a permanent home at New York–New York, while the other two troupes tour throughout the United States, Canada, and Europe.

Michael Flatley's Lord of the Dance

Ages Up to 5	Ages 6–15	Ages 16–20	Ages 21 & Up	Senior Citizens
Not Suitable	⚀ ⚁	⚀ ⚁ ⚄	⚀ ⚁ ⚄	⚀ ⚁ ⚄

Manhattan Express: The Coney Island–Styled Roller Coaster

Ticket Price: $8

Hours: 10:00 A.M. to 10:30 P.M. (11:30 P.M. during peak periods)

Imagine a high-speed roller coaster that starts indoors, but through a series of twists, loops, and turns, quickly takes riders outdoors (along the perimeter of the New York–New York resort) as they see the Las Vegas Strip around them. The Manhattan Express roller coaster is one of the fastest and most exciting rides on the entire Strip. With heights of 203 feet and drops of 144 feet, riders travel at speeds up to 67 m.p.h. Experience this high-speed and turbulent ride on one of five, four-car, 16-passenger trains as you blast your way along the 4,777 feet of track. During the ride's first two years, over 5 million people experienced it.

Due to its popularity, if you're planning to ride during peak times (holidays and weekend evenings and nights), be prepared for a wait. For the best view of the Strip, experience the ride at night.

Manhattan Express

Ages Up to 5	Ages 6–15	Ages 16–20	Ages 21 & Up	Senior Citizens
Not Suitable	⚀ ⚁	⚀ ⚁ ⚄	⚀ ⚁ ⚄	⚀

Coney Island Emporium

Guests of New York–New York will enjoy this light-hearted re-creation of Coney Island, complete with kiddie rides, carnival games (that offer prizes), snacks, and state-of-the-art arcade games. Participate in laser tag, ride the bumper cars, or experience a virtual reality game.

The *Lord of the Dance* video is the top selling performance video of all time in the United States with over 3 million copies sold worldwide.

Open Sunday through Thursday, 9:00 A.M. to 1:00 A.M., and Friday and Saturday, from 9:00 A.M. to 2:00 A.M., the Coney Island Emporium is located on the resort's second level, next to the Manhattan Express. This area offers ongoing, hands-on entertainment for children, teens, and adults alike.

Pool, Spa, and Fitness Center

New York–New York offers an outdoor swimming pool along with an adjacent snack bar, bar, and retail shop. Other recreational areas of the resort include a 6,800-square-foot health spa and fitness center, massage facilities, and Jacuzzi.

Euphoria Beauty Center Salon

Hours: **9:00 A.M. to 700 P.M. (daily)**

Appointments: Required, call (702) 740-6420

Located in New York–New York is a full-service salon and barber shop, staffed by professionally trained hair, nail, and skin specialists. An appointment is required.

Say "Cheese" but don't puke! While riding Manhattan Express, your photo will be taken. As you exit the ride, you'll be able to buy a souvenir photo of yourself traveling at 67 m.p.h.

Casino

New York–New York's 84,000-square-foot casino is designed to make you feel as if you're outside in New York City. It offers classic Las Vegas–style gaming, featuring 72 gaming tables and 2,200 slot machines. Visitors can try their hand at blackjack, craps, roulette, mini-baccarat, progressive Pai Gow poker, Caribbean Stud poker, Let It Ride, Big Six, casino war, and keno, all available in the main casino area. For those who prefer to follow professional sports, the casino also offers a race and sports book.

Shopping

Although New York–New York doesn't offer a mall-like shopping experience, throughout the resort you'll find unusual shops, including:

- Park Avenue Collections—Fashion apparel, shoes, and accessories for men, women, and children plus New York–New York clothing.

For less than $200, couples are invited to renew their wedding vows during a special ceremony that includes the minister, the renewal ceremony itself, a single long stem rose, a souvenir renewal certificate, and prerecorded music. This Relive the Romance package is available on weekends only and offers a memorable way to celebrate an anniversary or simply reaffirm your love.

- I Love New York–New York Signature Store—Here you'll find over two thousand novelty and apparel items, many with a New York theme. This is the place to buy New York–New York merchandise.
- Houdini's Magic Shop—Ongoing demonstrations by skilled magicians make this shop a fun place to browse through, even if you're not looking to make a purchase. Chances are, however, you'll see an illusion or magic trick you want to take home and show your friends and coworkers. Other items available include gags and novelties.
- Soho Village—New York–themed fashions and gifts, plus evening wear, gift baskets, fine cigars, and cigar accessories are among the items offered in this shopping area.
- Vegas Express—This railroad-themed specialty store features children's apparel, toys, collectibles, and gifts for all ages. A large selection of Las Vegas–themed gifts and products are also available.
- The Newsstand—Newspapers, magazines, paperback books, health and beauty aides, snack foods, tobacco products, sundries, and beverages are sold here.
- New York Jewelry & Watch Co.—Browse the large selection of gold and platinum jewelry, including wedding bands and watches.
- Cashman's Photo Magic—Using the latest computer technology, your image will be superimposed onto any one of over two hundred playful scenarios. This is also the place to go for 30-minute photo processing or camera supplies.

Wedding Chapels

Offering a view of "Central Park" (Las Vegas–style), New York–New York's wedding chapels offer both glamour and elegance. The resort's wedding coordinators will help you plan the perfect wedding. Floral arrangements, photography, videography, private bridal rooms, and a variety of other services are available, allowing you to create a wedding ceremony that will be remembered for a lifetime. At least six different wedding packages are available, and the resort itself can accommodate receptions of virtually any size.

Paris Las Vegas

Theme: Paris, France

Room Rate: $$$ / $$$$ ($101+)

Number of Rooms: 2,916 rooms, including 295 suites

Casino: 85,000 square feet, featuring 100 table games, over 2,200 slot and video poker machines, a separate high-limit slots and table game area), and a race and sports book

Dining: Eight Parisian-style restaurants, including a buffet, plus five lounges

Primary Show: *Notre Dame de Paris*

Special Attractions: Replicas of French landmarks, including a 50-story Eiffel Tower, plus Paris-themed wedding packages

Reservations: (888) BON-JOUR

Web Site: *www.paris-lv.com*

Address: 3645 Las Vegas Boulevard South
Las Vegas, NV 89109

Overall Resort Rating Based on Amenities and Rates

Ages Up to 5	Ages 6–15	Ages 16–20	Ages 21 & Up	Senior Citizens
⚀	⚀ ⚁	⚀ ⚁	⚀ ⚁	⚀ ⚁

Name a famous place in the United States or abroad, such as New York, Hollywood, Italy, Monte Carlo, Rio, or Paris, and chances are there's a themed hotel in Las Vegas that re-creates the ambiance of that state of country. Case in point: the Paris Las Vegas, which is one of the newest hotels on the Las Vegas Strip. It opened in September 1999, and is located next to Bally's on Flamingo Road, within walking distance to the Flamingo Hilton, Caesars Palace, Bellagio, and The Mirage. Inside and out, this resort offers the splendor of Paris, including detailed re-creations of some of France's most famous landmarks.

Unlike many of the other new hotels in Las Vegas, this one isn't family oriented. There are no theme park rides, kid-oriented shows, or organized activities for young people. Instead, what you'll find is an array of fine-dining restaurants, a casino where the majority of the table games require high minimum bets, and shops that cater to a sophisticated shopper.

Guest Room Accommodations

European interior design and architecture are what set this resort apart from all others in Las Vegas. Although the guest rooms offer the same basic amenities you'd fine anywhere else on the Strip, the décor is definitely French. For example, rooms contain an armoire that serves as a closet. The bathrooms are done in marble and contain a separate shower and bathtub.

Basic guest rooms are comfortable and offer a variety of sleeping arrangements, from a single king-size bed to two queen-size beds. Smoking and nonsmoking rooms are available (your preferences should be made when making a reservation).

Paris Las Vegas is modeled after the famous Hotel de Ville and features a single 34-story tower that contains all of the guest rooms and suites. As with all Las Vegas hotels, it's necessary to walk directly through the casino and past the shops in order to get to the guest room elevators from the hotel's main entrance.

Whether you stay in a basic room or a luxurious suite at the Paris Las Vegas, you'll enjoy the following amenities:

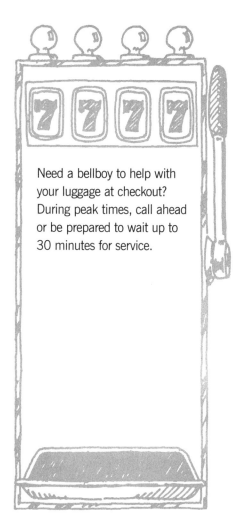

Need a bellboy to help with your luggage at checkout? During peak times, call ahead or be prepared to wait up to 30 minutes for service.

- Pay-per-view movies and On-command videos
- Cable television
- Two-line phones
- Voice mail
- Hair dryer
- Data-port for laptops (no outlets)
- Full-length and makeup mirrors
- Separate shower and bathtub
- Iron and ironing board
- In-room safes
- 24-hour room service

The hotel also offers a business center, lobby concierge, four concierge floors, a salon and barber shop, tour and travel desk, car rentals, complimentary valet parking, European health spa, and a rooftop swimming pool.

Fine Dining

Paris Las Vegas offers dining experiences for almost any budget, however, the focus is on authentic French fine dining. Late-night dining options at this property are limited, although a 24-hour coffee shop is open at Bally's, which is only a short walk away (and connected, so you never have to step outdoors). The one shortcoming: When visiting the real Paris, it's hard to miss the many carts and dining establishments that serve crêpes. Unfortunately, guests of the Paris Las Vegas will be hard pressed to find an authentic dessert crêpe at most of the dining establishments.

The Eiffel Tower Restaurant ($$$)

Reservations: (888) BON-JOUR

This restaurant offers what the management calls their "signature dining experience." The restaurant itself is located 11 stories above the Strip in the resort's 50-story Eiffel Tower replica. While dining, guests are entertained by a live piano player as they choose from a selection of gourmet French dishes that have been tailored for the American palate.

La Rotisserie des Artistes ($$$)

Reservations: (888) BON-JOUR

Classic French cuisine is the specialty of this two-level fine-dining establishment that offers meat, fish, poultry—all slow roasted in rotisserie ovens and served with a choice of marinades and sauces. This restaurant offers an open kitchen as well as an open view of the casino floor.

Mon Ami Gabi ($$ / $$$)

Reservations: (888) BON-JOUR

This is a Parisian-style cafe that offers outdoor seating along the Las Vegas Strip. In fact, if you enjoy people watching, this is the only outdoor cafe that overlooks the Strip. If the weather is too hot for your taste, there's also indoor seating available. Mon Ami Gabi is open for breakfast, lunch, and dinner, plus offers late-night dining. Croissants and pastries, salads, and sandwiches are among the menu items. If you're looking for quality food, especially after attending a late show, this is an excellent choice.

$ = entrees under $10; $$ = under $20; $$$ = over $20

"Everything we do, from food preparation to our service to the décor, will be carried out in the French tradition. After our guests have feasted at one of our restaurants, we want them to reminisce about their experience," says executive chef Eric Scullier.

Le Provencal ($$ / $$$)

Reservations: (888) BON-JOUR

Pizzas, pastas, salads, chicken, and meat dishes are the specialty of this Italian-style, informal restaurant that serves food with a French flair. An extensive wine list is available.

Casual Dining

Le Village Buffet ($ / $$)

The classic Las Vegas all-you-can-eat buffet has a French twist, featuring dishes from five French provinces. Each station in the buffet offers food from a different province. Most entrees, however, are prepared to order, which is something that sets this buffet experience apart from others. Breakfast ($10.95), lunch ($14.95), and dinner ($21.95) are all served on a first-come basis.

Le Cafe ile St. Louis ($$)

Reservations: **No advance reservations accepted. Put your name in at the door, but be prepared for up to a one-hour wait during peak times.**

Although this restaurant is designed to make guests feel as though they're dining outdoors at a French cafe, the entire restaurant is indoors. It's equivalent to an upscale coffee shop and is located near the hotel's casino. Open 24 hours a day, this cafe tends to get crowded during peak times as well as late night, when far fewer restaurants are open. Up to an hour wait is typical after a late-night show. A full menu of American and French dishes are available. One highlight of the menu is its large selection of European coffees.

Jean Jaques' Boulangerie ($$)

No visit to Paris would be complete without tasting fresh pastries. This restaurant is a fully operational French bakery. You'll see the bakers hard at work as you walk past the display cases filled with mouth-watering pastries, breads, and other items made on-premises and fresh out of the

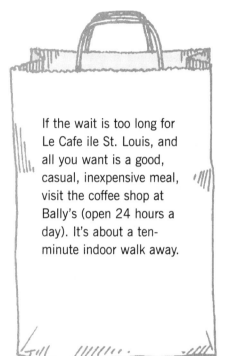

If the wait is too long for Le Cafe ile St. Louis, and all you want is a good, casual, inexpensive meal, visit the coffee shop at Bally's (open 24 hours a day). It's about a ten-minute indoor walk away.

$ = entrees under $10; $$ = under $20; $$$ = over $20

oven. Sandwiches, salads, soups, pastries, and croissants with assorted fillings complete the menu. The French bread baked here is also delivered twice daily to the resort's other restaurants.

Le Cafe du Parc ($$)

Reservations: Not accepted

Located near the hotel's rooftop swimming pool, this cafe is open seasonally and offers French-style pizzas, salads, sandwiches, and a large selection of alcoholic and nonalcoholic beverages.

Lounges

- Napoleon's—Live entertainment, plus a pipe and cigar lounge are available. The full-service bar offers hot and cold appetizers, French wines, beers, and a large selection of imported microbrews.
- Le Central—With an elevated view of the casino floor, this lounge is located in the main lobby area and offers a menu that changes throughout the day. In addition to a full-service bar, continental tea service is offered, along with French-style snacks, freshly baked rolls, and croissants.
- Le Bar du Sport—Located near the resort's popular race and sports book, this sports bar offers big screen televisions (showing sporting events) and a full-service bar. French-inspired appetizers and snacks are served throughout the day and evening. The lounge also serves as a walk-up bar for casino customers.
- Gustav's Casino Bar—You'll find this lounge inside the main lobby area of the hotel, near the southeastern leg of the Eiffel Tower. Video poker and slot machines are built into some of the seating. Full bar service is available to stool-seated patrons.
- Le Cabaret—Singers and bands perform throughout the afternoon and evening at this lounge, which offers a full-service bar and table service. Table service is available in what's been designed to look like an elegant outdoor atmosphere inside the resort. This is an excellent place for adults to relax, enjoy some music, and have a drink.

$ = entrees under $10; $$ = under $20; $$$ = over $20

Special Attractions

In addition to replicas of famous French landmarks, plus several unique shops, Paris Las Vegas features the musical *Notre Dame de Paris*.

Notre Dame de Paris

Show Times: 7:30 and 10:30 P.M. (Tuesday through Saturday)

Ticket Price: $69.50

Every evening, the Paris Las Vegas Theater features a specially designed English-speaking adaptation of the French musical *Notre Dame de Paris*. This is a full-scale, twenty-first century pop/rock adaptation of Victor Hugo's *Hunchback of Notre Dame*. With its powerful musical score and vibrant acrobatic choreography, *Notre Dame de Paris* has become the most successful musical in French history, selling out shows in Europe and Canada and selling 7 million albums and singles in France, Belgium, Switzerland, and Canada alone. This production made its debut at Paris Las Vegas in January 2000, several months after the resort's grand opening.

Notre Dame de Paris

Ages Up to 5	Ages 6–15	Ages 16–20	Ages 21 & Up	Senior Citizens
Not Suitable	⚀	⚀ ⚁ ⚂	⚁ ⚂ ⚃	⚀ ⚁ ⚂

The Eiffel Tower

Hours: 9:00 A.M. to 1:00 A.M. (daily)

Admission: $8

Paris Las Vegas has no theme park rides, but it does offer a 50-story replica of the Eiffel Tower that provides a great view of the Las Vegas Strip and valley from its observation deck. The reproductions of the French landmarks throughout the resort also make for excellent photo opportunities, although these aren't interactive attractions.

Eiffel Tower

Ages Up to 5	Ages 6–15	Ages 16–20	Ages 21 & Up	Senior Citizens
Not Suitable	⚀ ⚁	⚀ ⚁	⚀ ⚁	⚀ ⚁

Health Club, European Spa, and Salon

Appointments: (702) 946-4366

Spa Hours: 7:00 A.M. to 8:00 P.M. (daily)

Salon: 9:00 A.M. to 7:00 P.M. (daily)

Fitness Center: 6:00 A.M. to 8:00 P.M. (daily)

A wide range of spa services, including several types of massages are available at this 25,000-square-foot spa (separate charges apply for these services). There's also a health club featuring exercise and workout equipment available to hotel guests. There is a daily $22 fee to use the fitness center. This fee is waived when you pay for any spa or salon service, such as a massage.

Casino

The casino at Paris Las Vegas is definitely the resort's centerpiece. The casino, which is smaller than many other Las Vegas casinos, offers a re-creation of the streets of Paris. You'll feel as though you're on an evening stroll outdoors, when in reality you're inside, walking through a casino. Winding cobblestone pathways, French wrought iron street lamps, period architecture, and the River Seine all add to the ambiance.

The casino itself features more than one hundred gaming tables and over two thousand slot machines. Many of the table games require a $25 minimum wager. Thus, the few tables with a $10 minimum tend to be crowded, especially at night.

Shopping

Although there is no shopping mall within Paris Las Vegas, it does contain a large selection of upscale shops, including:

- Ré the Galerie/Atelier of Paris Las Vegas—Vintage reproductions of artwork are displayed and sold here.
- Le Voyage—This travel service can help you better plan your stay in the Las Vegas area by helping you select and book a wide range of tours.

The Eiffel Tower Wedding Package ($2,500) accommodates 20 guests and offers the opportunity to get married at the top of the resort's 50-story Eiffel Tower. The resort's videographer will capture the entire experience, from the time the wedding party enters the glass elevator to the end of the ceremony. Still photographs of the event are also included.

- La Boutique by Yokohama de Paris—Coach-brand purses, wallets, and other accessories.
- La Paradis—Fine jewelry and crystal items.
- Paris Liné—Women's designer apparel and fashion accessories.
- Cartier Lunettes—Eyewear and accessories.
- L'Oasis—Forget your swimsuit? Looking for a related accessory before spending time at the resort's rooftop pool? You'll find what you need here.
- Lenotre—Freshly baked croissants, baked breads, pastries, and chocolates are served here. Walk-up service only is available. Cookbooks, packaged gourmet foods, and other kitchen items are on sale at the gift shop area of this bakery. Pastries cost $4 to $5 each.
- Eiffel Tour—In addition to offering inexpensive Eiffel Tower souvenirs, tickets for the Eiffel Tower's observation deck can be purchased here.
- Eiffel Tour Deux—Paris Las Vegas souvenirs, sundries, film, and other basic necessities are available here.
- Le Journal—Looking for a Paris Las Vegas sweatshirt ($44.95 and up) or T-shirt ($22.95 and up), along with other souvenirs and trinkets from Paris Las Vegas? You'll find these items here, along with a selection of sodas and drinks, magazines, books, cigarettes, inexpensive gifts, and cigars. Le Journal is located near the hotel's elevators and open 24 hours.
- Presse—Magazines, books and newspapers, postcards, tobacco products, and other inexpensive items are available from this shop, located directly opposite Le Journal.
- Les Memoires—This gift shop offers an assortment of gifts from the Dominique Gault line as well as small-scale replicas of Parisian buildings.
- Les Elementes—Home and garden gifts, including fresh and dried flowers, live and artificial topiaries, statues, pottery, and French linens are available here.
- La Vogue—A selection of French lingerie, ladies' intimates, and perfumes are available from this small boutique.

To help you travel between hotels along the Las Vegas Strip, Paris Las Vegas provides access to the Bally's/MGM monorail system. Paris Las Vegas is also connected to Bally's, allowing guests to walk freely between the two hotels, without going outdoors.

- Le Theatre des Arts—Located near the Paris Las Vegas Theater, this shop features a unique selection of items, including the soundtrack to *Notre Dame de Paris.*
- L'Art de Paris—This museum-type store features replicas of famous French artwork. The works on display change regularly. Limited edition gallery pieces, sculpture replicas, and artist-designed jewelry are sold here.
- Les Enfants—For the perfect gift for a young child, visit this shop which offers a selection of French toys and games as well as a line of private label children's clothing.
- La Cave—Any wine connoisseur will be right at home here. The resort's wine cellar offers private label and premium French wines and a daily wine tasting. Cheeses and gourmet foods, along with gift baskets, are also sold here. If you're planning a romantic evening in your room, your first stop should be La Cave. If you're looking to expand your wine collection, items purchased here can be shipped home.

Banquet, Function, and Convention Services

Even if you're not planning a wedding, Paris Las Vegas can accommodate almost any type of party, special event, meeting, or conference within its 140,000 square feet of pillarless function space, which includes one of the largest ballrooms in Las Vegas.

The Paris Ballroom (87,000 square feet) can hold 8,000 people for a reception. Theater–style seating in this ballroom can also be arranged. This space can be divided into nine separate function rooms. In addition, this resort offers several other ballrooms, including the Champagne Ballroom (17,385 square feet) and the Versailles Ballroom (7,685 square feet).

The meeting planners, sales department, and convention services/catering department of Paris Las Vegas and Bally's are combined, offering one of the largest and most experienced staffs in Las Vegas.

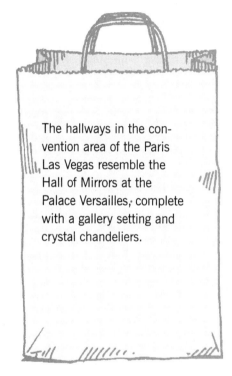

The hallways in the convention area of the Paris Las Vegas resemble the Hall of Mirrors at the Palace Versailles, complete with a gallery setting and crystal chandeliers.

Business Center

Hours: 6:00 A.M. to 7:00 P.M. (weekdays)
          6:00 A.M. to 5:00 P.M. (weekends)

Located near the shops that lead to Bally's, the Paris Las Vegas Business Center offers six PCs available for rental, copiers, fax machines, and full shipping services. The hotel boasts spending $80,000 on a computerized shipping system that allows guests to ship packages worldwide via any major courier. Although there is an extra charge for every service offered at the Business Center, no rates are posted, so be sure to ask about charges beforehand.

If you need to send or receive a fax when the Business Center isn't open, contact the front desk or concierge.

Wedding Chapels

Planning on getting married, but can't afford to take the trip across the Atlantic Ocean to tie the knot in Paris? The Paris Las Vegas offers two wedding chapels and an Eiffel Tower wedding package. A basic wedding package (the Tour De Romance Package) starts at $399 and includes a ceremony complete with music and ministerial services, twelve 4-by-6-inch photos, a bridal bouquet, and a matching groom's boutonniere. Four other, more elaborate, wedding packages are available, ranging in price from $499 to $2,500. A professional wedding coordinator as well as full catering and reception facilities are available.

RIO

Rio

Theme:	Rio de Janeiro
Room Rate:	$$$ ($101–$250)
Number of Rooms:	More than 2,500 suites (this is an all-suite resort)
Casino:	120,000 square feet, featuring over 2,500 slot and video poker machines, over 100 table games, a race and sports book, and a keno lounge, all in an upscale setting.
Dining:	Five fine-dining restaurants and ten casual restaurants, including a buffet
Primary Show:	*David Cassidy at the Copa*
Special Attractions:	Show in the Sky, *Titanic: The Exhibition,* Spa, a golf course, Club Rio nightclub, and Masquerade Village shopping
Reservations:	(888) PLAY-RIO
Web Site:	*www.playrio.com*
Address:	3700 W. Flamingo Road Las Vegas, NV 89103

Overall Resort Rating Based on Amenities and Rates

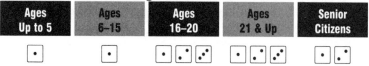

Ages Up to 5	Ages 6–15	Ages 16–20	Ages 21 & Up	Senior Citizens
⚀	⚀	⚀ ⚁ ⚃	⚀ ⚁ ⚃	⚀ ⚁

Every resort along the Strip has its own attitude. Some properties, like the Bellagio or Venetian, attract an upscale, older, and more sophisticated crowd, while places like MGM Grand cater more to business travelers, vacationers in general, and families. Rio definitely caters to a Generation X clientele, offering luxurious accommodations with a party atmosphere. Rio's nightclub, for example, is one of the hottest nightspots in Las Vegas.

As you travel along the Strip, you won't see Rio next to the other mega-resorts. Instead, this property is located a few blocks off of the Strip. A free shuttle bus to and from the Strip is offered throughout the day and night. The taxi fare is also inexpensive to get from Rio to any of the other resorts and attractions along the Strip, so while this property is a bit out of the way, it's not too much of an inconvenience.

If you're in college, a honeymooning couple, or young adult (in your 20s or 30s) visiting Las Vegas to relax, enjoy the casino, hang out by the pool and beach area, or you plan on trying the various activities the resort offers, chances are you won't have to leave Rio's property too often, since this resort offers a wide range of amenities and topnotch facilities, plus restaurants, lounges, entertainment, and comfortable guest rooms at a reasonable price.

Rio does not cater to children. It is targeted to an upscale crowd in their 20s and 30s who are looking for a party atmosphere, complete with casino, entertainment, and nightclub.

Guest Room Accommodations

Rio has more than 2,500 suites (this is an all-suite resort), each providing spectacular views of Las Vegas. Every suite offers more than 600 square feet of living area, with amenities that include a separate dressing area, couch, table with chairs, coffee maker, hair dryer, in-suite refrigerator, iron, ironing board, and an in-suite safe. A range of suite configurations are available, including multiple bedrooms and bedrooms with one king-size or two queen-size beds.

While Rio certainly isn't the cheapest place to stay in Las Vegas, it is by far not the most expensive either. What you receive, however, are excellent accommodations at a fair price. As with all of the hotels, resorts, and mega-resorts, room rates vary greatly, based on season and what conventions are taking place in the Las Vegas area.

Fine Dining

Rio's fine-dining establishments offer the perfect atmosphere for a romantic dinner, business meeting, or formal dinner with friends, associates, or family members. Reservations are recommended for the fine-dining restaurants.

Antonio's Italian Ristorante ($$$)

Reservations: Recommended, call (702) 252-7777

Fine Italian cuisine in an elegant old-world atmosphere is offered.

$ = entrees under $10; $$ = under $20; $$$ = over $20

Buzio's Seafood Restaurant ($$$)

Reservations: Recommended, call (702) 252-7777

Oyster and seafood specialties are highlights at this restaurant. The dining room features an exhibition–style kitchen, so you can watch the expert chefs prepare each meal.

Fiore Rotisserie & Grille ($$ / $$$)

Reservations: Recommended, call (702) 252-7777

Gourmet rotisserie-grilled steaks, seafood, and poultry are the main selections at this restaurant.

Fortunes ($$ / $$$)

Reservations: Recommended, call (702) 252-7777

Fortunes is a meeting ground of East and West. Ancient recipes and rarities from the Orient are combined by master chef Chi Kwon Choi and served in an authentic Chinese dining atmosphere.

Napa Restaurant ($$ / $$$)

Reservations: Recommended, call (702) 252-7777

Country French gourmet cuisine is prepared by renowned chef Jean-Louis Palladin. In addition to offering a selection of French-inspired entrees, the wine list contains more than six hundred selections.

The Wine Cellar

While not a formal restaurant, the Wine Cellar at Rio features a wine tasting room and an inventory of over 45,000 bottles of the world's finest and rarest wines.

Open daily, the Wine Cellar offers something extraordinarily memorable for every nose, palate, and spirit to enjoy. Valued at more than $6 million, the collection includes renown centerpieces, such as the $1 million Chateau d'Yequem collection, with a bottle from every vintage produced between 1855 and 1990, and a bottle of 1800 Madeira that was once owned by President Thomas Jefferson.

$ = entrees under $10; $$ = under $20; $$$ = over $20

For the true wine connoisseur or collector, this will probably be one of the most exciting places to experience during your Las Vegas trip.

Casual Dining

If you're looking for a faster, less expensive, and less formal dining experience, consider one of these restaurants in Rio.

All-American Bar & Grille ($$)

Serving steak and seafood entrees, this restaurant also features a collection of American-made beers and wines.

Bamboleo ($$)

Traditional south-of-the-border cuisine is the house specialty.

Mama Marie's Cucina ($$)

If you're in the mood for Italian, visit this restaurant for its traditional and contemporary Italian specialties.

Mask ($$)

Features cuisine from the Far East.

Toscano's Deli & Market ($ / $$)

This New York–style deli and bakery is the perfect place for lunch or a snack.

Carnival World Buffet ($ / $$)

From the Orient to Italy to Brazil, this all-you-can-eat buffet has 11 distinct dining experiences from around the world. It's also one of the best dining deals at the resort, so bring your appetite. Seating is on a first-come basis. This is one of the best buffets in Las Vegas, so be prepared for a wait. Open for breakfast (8:00 to 10:30 A.M., $7.95); lunch (11:00 A.M. to 3:30 P.M., $9.95); dinner (3:30 to 11:00 P.M., $12.95); and weekend brunch ($12.95).

$ = entrees under $10; $$ = under $20; $$$ = over $20

The mastermind behind the Wine Cellar collection is the president of the International Court of Master Sommeliers, Barrie Larvin, who created the collection for Rio in 1996. Since then, he and his wine staff have pursued their mission to provide everyone (from the novice to the connoisseur) with the opportunity to truly experience and understand the beauty of fine wines.

Village Seafood Buffet ($ / $$)

This all-you-can-eat seafood buffet is one of the best in Las Vegas.

The VooDoo Cafe & Lounge ($$)

Serving the best of the Bayou, the dining room and lounge are located on the 52nd floor and offers an awesome view of Las Vegas. The lounge's juggling bartenders keep things afire with performances throughout the day and night. It's these bartenders who set this cafe and lounge apart and make the dining and drinking experience much more entertaining. Currently, musician Jimmy Hopper entertains audiences with hits from the past and present, from 9:00 P.M. to 2:30 A.M. (Friday through Tuesday).

Sao Paulo Cafe ($ / $$)

Open 24 hours, this cafe offers a large menu of continental dining options.

Star Deli and Bakery ($ / $$)

This "kosher-style" deli features sandwiches and old-time favorites like matzo ball soup and fresh bagels with assorted cream cheese spreads.

Lounges

In addition to the VooDoo Cafe and Lounge, Rio Bamba is another popular lounge at the resort. Live music is presented Wednesday through Sunday, starting at 9:00 P.M.

Special Attractions
David Cassidy at the Copa

Show Times: 7:00 and 9:30 P.M. (Wednesday and Saturday)
7:30 P.M. other days (except Monday, when there are no performances)

Ticket Price: $58

Reservations: (800) PLAY-RIO or TicketMaster

This musical, suitable for adult audiences, follows a love affair spanning decades. David Cassidy stars in this high-energy

$ = entrees under $10; $$ = under $20; $$$ = over $20

Banquet, Function, and Convention Services

Rio boasts 110,000 square feet of the most advanced meeting and special events space in Las Vegas. Rio Pavilion utilizes state-of-the-art technology and design to create a space adaptable to meet any entertainment, meeting, special event, or convention need.

The center's design maximizes user-friendly features, which include built-in registration, office space, dedicated specialty kitchens, multimedia event information display, full theatrical staging, and an adjoining business center. Additionally, the center's hall space is completely adaptable, dividing into as many as 28 rooms, all on one level.

extravaganza with Grammy Award–winning Sheena Easton as the femme fatale.

David Cassidy at the Copa

Ages Up to 5	Ages 6–15	Ages 16–20	Ages 21 & Up	Senior Citizens
Not Suitable	Not Suitable	⚀⚁	⚀⚁⚂	⚀⚁⚂

Club Rio

The Copa Showroom really heats up with Club Rio, which features live entertainment and dancing (featuring performances by top dance bands). Club Rio opens at 10:30 P.M. on Thursday and Friday nights, and at 11:30 P.M. on Wednesday and Saturday nights. When it comes to Las Vegas's after-dark scene, this is one of the hottest nightclubs. The crowd tends to be younger (under 40).

Show in the Sky

Show Times: Noon to 10:00 P.M. (Sunday through Tuesday)
1:00 to 11:00 P.M. (Thursday through Saturday, no Shows on Wednesday)

This unusual indoor show features state-of-the-art floats that suspend from the ceiling and travel above the casino floor. Five themed parades are performed throughout the day: Mardi Gras in New Orleans, Carnivale in Venice, Carnivale in Rio, Village Street Party, and the Disco Swing Party. Guests can take part in the parade by riding floats and wearing costumes unique to each parade. This is a free show that children, teens, and adults alike will enjoy. The balcony on the second level is definitely the best place for viewing this show.

Show in the Sky

Ages Up to 5	Ages 6–15	Ages 16–20	Ages 21 & Up	Senior Citizens
Not Suitable	⚀⚁	⚀⚁	⚀⚁	⚀⚁

Titanic: The Exhibition

Show Times: Ongoing (10:00 A.M. to 10:00 P.M. daily)

Ticket Prices: $15.95 (adults), $14.95 (seniors), $9.95 (children)

Box Office: (702) 252-0493

www.playrio.com/titanic/index.htm

The *Titanic* was the grandest, most luxurious moving object ever built during its time. And decades later, no other story in history has captured our hearts and imaginations like hers. Until recently, it lay undisturbed in the darkness of the North Atlantic, some two-and-a-half miles below the surface.

This museum-quality exhibit features over three hundred authentic artifacts recovered from *Titanic*'s wreck site. The exhibit combines artifacts with pictures, video, and a detailed audio tour that takes visitors through the building of the *Titanic* up until 11:40 P.M. on April 14, 1912, when the mighty ship crashed into an iceberg and sank.

Already seen by over 4 million people when it traveled to museums throughout the world, *Titanic:* The Exhibition will be at Rio at least through 2001. Adults will find this exhibit both emotional and educational, while children and teens may be bored by the lack of special effects and drama they might have already seen in the motion picture *Titanic.*

Titanic: The Exhibition

Ages Up to 5	Ages 6–15	Ages 16–20	Ages 21 & Up	Senior Citizens
Not Suitable	Not Suitable	⚀ ⚁	⚀ ⚁ ⚂	⚀ ⚁ ⚂

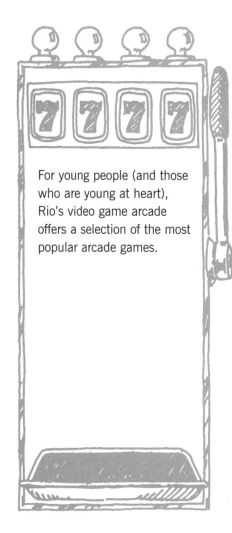

For young people (and those who are young at heart), Rio's video game arcade offers a selection of the most popular arcade games.

Pool Area

In addition to its four heated swimming pools and five Jacuzzi-style spas, Rio offers a complete tropical paradise in the form of Ipanema Beach. Guests can lounge on real sand beaches at the edge of a tropical lagoon. The landscaping includes cascading waterfalls. Additional services offered in this area include personal massages, food and drink (in the Cococabana), plus private cabana rentals.

Golf Course

Information: (888) TO-SECCO

www.butchharmongolfschools.com

Rio is the only Las Vegas resort to offer its own nearby golf course. Set among the rolling foothills of the Black Mountain Range in Las Vegas, Rio Secco Golf Club provides a world-class golf experience. This is an 18-hole, championship course designed primarily for the guests of Rio. It's located 12 minutes (by car) south of the resort.

Designed by Rees Jones, *Golf World* magazine's 1995 Golf Architect of the Year and mastermind behind over one hundred of the world's most fabulous courses, Rio Secco provides both stunning scenery and challenging play.

The unmatched expertise of Butch Harmon, coach to Tiger Woods and past instructor to such PGA notables as Greg Norman and Davis Love III, is available to Rio Secco Golf Club players at his state-of-the-art golf school located on the premises. Players of all skill levels can benefit from the one-on-one training and high-tech analysis and evaluation that Butch and his school provide.

Spa, Health Club, and Salon

Hours:	**Spa: 6:00 A.M. to 7:00 P.M. (daily)**
Salon:	**9:00 A.M. to 6:00 P.M. (daily)**
Fitness Center:	**6:00 A.M. to 7:00 P.M. (daily)**

Appointments and Information: (702) 252-7779

The recently remodeled Rio Spa is a luxurious full-service facility featuring five different types of massage, whirlpools, steam rooms, saunas, lounge, body wraps, complete vanity amenities, private showers, lockers, and complimentary fruit and juice.

Michael's Salon offers a full range of services from haircuts and styles to facials and manicures. Everything from aromatherapy to cleansing facial treatments is available.

The resort's fitness area is a complete facility featuring CYBEX weight training equipment, free weights, treadmills, stationary bikes, and Stairmasters overlooking the beach and pool area.

Casino

Rio's 120,000-square-foot casino contains over 2,500 slot and video poker machines, more than 100 table games (featuring all of the popular favorites—baccarat, blackjack, Big Six, craps, mini-baccarat, Let It Ride, roulette, Pai Gow, and Caribbean Stud poker), as well as a race and sports book and keno lounge. This is certainly one of the nicer, more upscale casinos in the Las Vegas area.

Shopping

Rio's Masquerade Village offers a combination of live entertainment, food, and shopping. The $200-million Masquerade Village area features a carnival atmosphere and the Masquerade Show in the Sky, which is a free, indoor attraction.

In Masquerade Village, you will find designer fashions from Armani, Versace, Speedo, Gucci, Rolex, Torras, and others. Shops include:

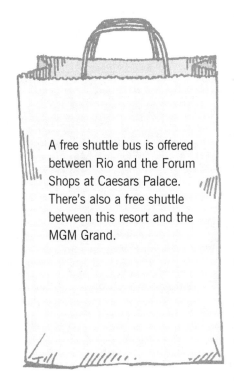

A free shuttle bus is offered between Rio and the Forum Shops at Caesars Palace. There's also a free shuttle between this resort and the MGM Grand.

- Alegre—Men's apparel.
- Bernard K. Passman Gallery—A "wearable art gallery" featuring black coral jewelry.
- Cashman's Photo Magic—Photographic images superimposed onto one of more than two hundred different scenarios.
- Cole Haan Shoes—Specialty shoes and accessories for both men and women.
- Mardi Gras Cigars—A wide selection of handrolled cigars and high-end cigarettes.
- Davante—Eyewear.
- Diamonds International—This shop is staffed by experts in custom diamond jewelry.
- Elegant Pretenders—A selection of the finest in faux jewelry design is sold here.
- Gary's Island/Dick's Last Resort—A complete line of resort wear for both men and women.
- Field of Dreams—Sports and entertainment memorabilia and collectibles.
- Houdini's Magic Shop—Magic tricks, novelties, and gags are sold here. Live magic demonstrations are offered.

- Kid Vegas—Children's specialty clothing and toy store.
- Money Magnetz—A gigantic collection of refrigerator magnets, plus a line of clothing and gifts with a money motif.
- Ben & Jerry's Ice Cream—A great place for a cool snack.
- Wetzel's Pretzels—Homemade pretzels and soft drinks.
- The Pearl Factory—Custom jewelry using cultured pearls.
- Rio Sundries—Souvenirs, Rio merchandise, and other necessities.
- Rio Gift & Logo Shop—Souvenirs, Rio merchandise, and other necessities.
- Roland's Boutique—Evening wear, bridal wear, and accessories.
- Silk Fashions Galleries—Offers the finest in silk fashion wear. Every garment is made with 100-percent pure silk.
- Simple Pleasures—Featuring lingerie, bath and body products, perfumes, gifts for the home, women's fashions, antiques from Paris, and much more.
- Speedo Authentic Fitness—Nevada's first outlet with a complete line of Speedo fitness wear.
- Watch Zone—High-end fashion watches and accessories.

Wedding Chapels

An entire floor of Rio's 51-story tower is dedicated to weddings and honeymoon couples. The resort's wedding facilities include three elegantly decorated chapels and an elaborate Hollywood-theme honeymoon suite. A variety of wedding packages are available, with prices starting at $375.

All wedding packages include wedding consultation with an expert Rio wedding coordinator, minister's fees, photography, fresh-cut bridal bouquet and matching groom boutonniere, wedding music, and a Rio-monogrammed keepsake marriage certificate holder.

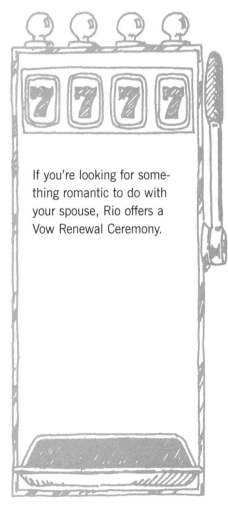

If you're looking for something romantic to do with your spouse, Rio offers a Vow Renewal Ceremony.

Riviera Hotel & Casino

Theme: Classic Las Vegas

Room Rate: $$ ($51–$100)

Number of Rooms: 2,075 rooms, including 78 suites and 78 petite suites in five main towers

Casino: 125,000 square feet, featuring 1,400 slot machines and video poker machines, and a wide range of table games, plus a race and sports book

Dining: Seven restaurants, including the World's Fare Buffet and Kristofer's Steakhouse

Primary Shows: *Splash, Crazy Girls,* and *An Evening at La Cage*

Special Attractions: The Riviera Comedy Club and tennis courts

Reservations: (800) 794-9451

Web Site: *www.theriviera.com*

Address: 2901 Las Vegas Boulevard South
Las Vegas, NV 89109

Overall Resort Rating Based on Amenities and Rates

Ages Up to 5	Ages 6–15	Ages 16–20	Ages 21 & Up	Senior Citizens
⚀	⚀⚀	⚀⚀	⚀⚀	⚀⚀

The Riviera Hotel and Casino has a long history in Las Vegas. Since opening in 1955, when Liberace was the biggest name on the Strip, the hotel has undergone extensive expansion and refurbishment. Through the 1960s, '70s, and '80s, the Riviera continued to attract some of the biggest names in entertainment. Unfortunately, in the 1990s, when mega-resorts like MGM Grand, the Luxor, the Venetian, and New York–New York opened along the Strip, the Riviera couldn't keep up.

Instead, this hotel has focused on providing a classic Las Vegas experience, mainly with its casino and traditional Las Vegas–style shows (complete with showgirls). These days, instead of trying to showcase the biggest names in entertainment, the Riviera offers four highly entertaining productions that appeal to a broad adult audience.

As for guest room accommodations, the Riviera falls in the middle in terms of price. It isn't one of the cheapest places to stay on the Strip, nor is it the most expensive by far. The rooms have recently been refurbished, and in 1988, the Monaco Tower was built, which doubled the size of the hotel. In 1990, the casino was expanded to 125,000 square feet, making it one of the largest on the Strip.

The Riviera will appeal mainly to adult travelers looking for a moderately priced hotel that doesn't have the frills of a mega-resort, but does offer comfortable rooms, a choice of restaurants, several shows, and a large casino.

Guest Room Accommodations

With its multiple towers, the Riviera has over 2,100 rooms, including basic guest rooms, full suites, and petite suites. Each tower has two floors set aside for nonsmoking rooms. If you're interested in reserving one of these rooms, be sure to request it when making your reservation. The Riviera is less expensive than other hotels but does charge $20 for each extra person (beyond two) staying in the room.

Here's a rundown on what each tower offers:

- The Monaco Tower—Located next to the hotel's convention center, restaurants, shops, and parking, the 24-story Monaco Tower features 942 deluxe guest rooms. Each contains amenities such as refrigerators and hair dryers. All rooms contain floor safes. The 42 petite suites also include an alcove study and wet bar. For the ultimate in accommodations, the two-story penthouse suites feature Jacuzzis, entertainment centers, and lovely panoramic views of Las Vegas.
- The Monte Carlo Tower—This 15-story tower features 229 deluxe rooms with refrigerators, hair dryers, floor safes, and window sitting areas. Wet bars and sofas come with the 14 spacious petite suites while the two floors of penthouse suites boast oversized living and dining rooms, full-service bars, Jacuzzis, and balconies.
- The Mediterranean Tower—With 502 deluxe rooms, this 11-story tower was the Riviera's original nine-story wing. It contains 21 suites, 18 petite suites, and one honeymoon suite. It's located directly above the casino.
- The San Remo Tower—Located poolside, the San Remo Tower features 244 deluxe rooms and six suites. The garden-style suites feature a full bar with refrigerator, a four-person dining area, and a patio with quick access to the pool.

Fine Dining

When it comes to dining at the Riviera, guests and visitors alike have a handful of choices, including a restaurant serving Chinese cuisine, a traditional Italian restaurant, a steak house, and a buffet. Reservations are accepted but not required at the fancier restaurants.

Ristorante Italiano ($$)

Hours: 5:30 to 11:00 P.M. (Friday through Tuesday)

Ristorante Italiano presents the earthy cooking of Tuscany and the northern Italian countryside, splashed with a dose of Milanese class. La Stanza Bella, located inside Ristorante Italiano, is a private dining area available for groups up to twenty-four.

Kristofer's Steak House ($$ / $$$)

Hours: 5:30 to 11:00 P.M. nightly

This classic steakhouse features a Mediterranean atmosphere and serves fine steaks, fresh seafood, Midwestern prime rib, and double-rib spring lamb chops. The daily "blackboard" specials include a selection of fixed-price dinners.

Casual Dining

For breakfast, lunch (brunch), dinner, or a midday or midnight snack, the Riviera offers several inexpensive dining options, most of which are suitable for the entire family.

Rik'Shaw ($$)

Causal dining with a Far Eastern ambiance is the best way to describe this restaurant. It brings the mystery of the Orient to the Riviera with elegant, affordable Chinese dining.

Kady's Coffee Shop ($)

Overlooking the pool, Kady's is a full-service restaurant serving breakfast, lunch, and dinner entrees, 24 hours a day.

$ = entrees under $10; $$ = under $20; $$$ = over $20

World's Fare Buffet ($)

A prime rib carving station and a variety of international foods are among the offerings at this all-you-can-eat buffet. It's open daily for breakfast, lunch, and dinner, and offers a champagne brunch on Saturday and Sunday.

The Mardi Gras Food Court ($)

If you're in the mood for something fast and inexpensive, the food court offers a handful of franchise favorites, including Burger King, Kabalen, Taco Riko, Panda Express, Pizza Hut, TCBY, Riksson Cafe Express, and Dragon Sushi.

Hound Doggies ($)

Located in the casino's Nickel Town area, this fast-food establishment offers a selection of snack foods.

Lounges

- Le Bistro Bar & Lounge—Designed to be a throwback to the New York nightclubs of the 1930s, Le Bistro Bar and Lounge overlooks the main casino. Entertainers perform nightly, including a "Tribute to Elvis" from 4:00 to 7:30 P.M. There is no cover charge; however, there is a one-drink minimum.
- Kristofer's Bar—This lounge overlooks the pool and garden area. It's the perfect getaway for special encounters.
- Splash Bar—Located next to Rik'Shaw Restaurant, this lounge offers a full-service bar.
- The Flying R Bar—Located in the casino's Nickel Town area, this is a nice place to take a break and have a drink.

Special Attractions

Comedy, showgirls, music, big production numbers, celebrity impersonators, water ballet, and much more can be enjoyed at the Riviera's popular shows. These shows are primarily suitable for an adult (over 18) audience. The Riviera's box office can be reached by calling (702) 794-9433.

$ = entrees under $10; $$ = under $20; $$$ = over $20

Splash

Show Times:	7:30 and 10:30 P.M. (nightly)
Ticket Prices:	$39.50 (reserved seating)
	$49.50 (VIP reserved seating)
Box Office:	(702) 794-9433

For years, *Splash* was a water show, but it was recently overhauled—and frozen! It now features on-stage ice skating, dance numbers, and singing (mostly lip-synced), plus a few special effects. The updated show includes all-new specialty acts and production numbers, featuring showgirls in glamorous costumes (although they're topless), world-class ice skaters, motorcycle daredevils, and a handful of entertaining specialty acts. The jugglers are the best part of the show.

Splash

Ages Up to 5	Ages 6–17	Ages 18–20	Ages 21 & Up	Senior Citizens
Not Suitable	Not Suitable	•	•	•

Crazy Girls

Show Times:	8:30 and 10:30 P.M. (nightly, except Thursday)
Ticket Price:	$19.25 (includes one drink)
	(Add $7 extra for dinner at the World's Fare Buffet)
Box Office:	(702) 794-9433

For adults only, this topless show is described by the Riviera as Las Vegas's "Sexiest Topless Revue." Two performances are presented nightly (except Thursday) with an added midnight show on Saturday in the Mardi Gras Pavilion. The show features comedy, music, and dance, in addition to a cast of sexy showgirls. This show caters primarily to a mature male audience.

Crazy Girls

Ages Up to 5	Ages 6–17	Ages 18–20	Ages 21 & Up	Senior Citizens
Not Suitable	Not Suitable	• •	• •	•

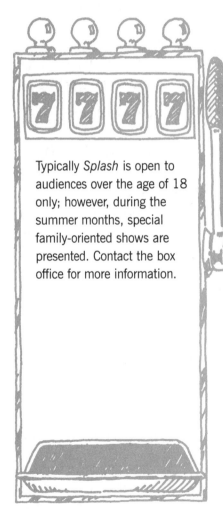

Typically *Splash* is open to audiences over the age of 18 only; however, during the summer months, special family-oriented shows are presented. Contact the box office for more information.

According to Frank Marino, wardrobe is the most essential part of his act. He changes about twenty times during the hour-and-a-half production. His closet contains over two thousand costumes, costing between $1,000 and $5,000 each. A wardrobe coordinator maintains the costumes and assists Marino in his many quick-as-lightning changes. Check out his Web site for more information: *www.frankmarino.com.*

An Evening at La Cage

Show Times:	7:30 and 9:30 P.M.
	(nightly, except Tuesday, when there is no show)
	7:30, 9:30, and 11:15 P.M. (Wednesday)
Ticket Prices:	$22.25 (includes one drink)
	$29.75 for VIP seating and line pass
	(Add $7 extra for dinner at the World's Fare Buffet)
Box Office:	(702) 794-9433

An exciting re-creation of its famous namesakes in New York and Los Angeles, *La Cage* features the most accomplished female impersonators in the world, highlighted by Frank Marino as a memorable Joan Rivers (plus other well known personalities).

Keeping in mind that this entirely male cast impersonates some of the world's best-known female entertainers, *An Evening at La Cage* is fun-filled, funny, and highly entertaining. It's well worth the ticket price. This is definitely the best show at the Riviera.

An Evening at La Cage

Ages Up to 5	Ages 6–17	Ages 18–20	Ages 21 & Up	Senior Citizens
Not Suitable	Not Suitable	⚀ ⚁	⚀ ⚁ ⚂	⚀ ⚁ ⚂

The Riviera Comedy Club

Show Times:	8:00 and 10:00 p.m. (nightly)
	8:00, 10:00, and 11:45 p.m. (Friday and Saturday)
Ticket Price:	$11.25 (includes one drink)
	$22.75 (for VIP seating and line pass)
	(Add $7 extra for dinner at the World's Fare Buffet)
Box Office:	(702) 794-9433

Some of America's hottest comedians take center stage in this intimate comedy club that's reminiscent of a Manhattan nightclub, complete with neon-studded walls and canopied entrance. In addition to headliner comedians, the Riviera Comedy Club features specialty performers such as ventriloquists, hypnotists, "shock" comedians, and more. Contact the hotel's box office for a performance schedule.

Spa, Health Club, and Salon

The Riviera contains a full-service health club, which offers massage, face cleansings, body salt loofahs, and seaweed wraps. The facility includes a sauna and steam room. There's also a 2,000-square-foot gym available to hotel guests.

For athletic activities, the hotel also offers two lighted tennis courts and an Olympic-sized swimming pool with a pool deck lounge and courtyard.

Casino

As one of the largest casinos on the Strip, you can bet (literally) that the Riviera offers the games you're looking for. Table games include craps, roulette, baccarat, Pai Gow, Sic Bo, Caribbean Stud poker, blackjack, and Let It Ride. There are also over 1,400 slot and video poker machines. A keno lounge and race and sports book round out the casino's offerings.

If you're new to gambling, check out the Riviera's Web site for free online tutorials on each game offered in the casino.

Shopping

Some of the shops and boutiques you'll find at the Riviera include:

- Amazing Pictures—Put a photo of your face on the body of (other) famous and beautiful people.
- Candlemania—Handmade, one-of-a-kind candles are available here, plus a selection of current and retired Beanie Babies.
- Chocolate Heaven—A wide variety of chocolates and other confectionery delights to satisfy anyone's sweet tooth.
- Doc James—Cigars and golf accessories, magazines, and gift items.

- Dorinna International Folk Arts—Authentic Russian folk art.
- Hotel Gift Shop—Liquors, newspapers, sundries, gifts, and souvenirs are among the offerings. (Located in the Monaco Tower arcade.)
- International Pearl—Pearl jewelry is created with pearls harvested directly from oysters on the premises.
- Logo Shop—Choose from an assortment of Riviera- and Las Vegas–themed apparel and merchandise. This is a great place to purchase souvenirs.
- Marshall Rousso—Upscale women's wear.
- Shoes by Norman Kaplan at the Riviera—Women's shoes, handbags, and accessories are among the offerings.
- Signed, Sealed & Delivered I—Sports and celebrity autographs and memorabilia plus other collectibles.
- The Magic Shop—Close-up and stage magic tricks are sold here. This is a fun place to visit, because free lessons and demonstrations are offered on an ongoing basis.
- Thunderbird Jewels Boutique—Fun jewelry, designer watches, and accessories.
- Toni Cats & Company—Assorted gifts and novelties featuring cats are offered at this purr-fectly unusual shop. (Sorry, no dogs allowed.)
- Rainbow Letter Art—Hawaiian original letter art is created before your eyes. These pieces of artwork make an unusual souvenir, especially for young people.
- Vegas Leisure Magnets—A huge selection of magnets, key chains, super balls, and playing cards.
- Welcome to Las Vegas—Glitzy women's casual and sports wear.
- Wine Street—Fine wines and champagnes are offered. Labels can be personalized in 30 minutes.

Banquet, Function, and Convention Services

Information: (702) 794-9410

The Riviera has a convention center on site that offers 150,000 square feet of meeting and convention space, featuring the Grande Ballroom, Royale Pavilion, the penthouse Top of the Riviera Ballroom, plus many smaller

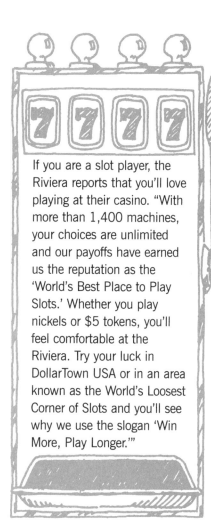

If you are a slot player, the Riviera reports that you'll love playing at their casino. "With more than 1,400 machines, your choices are unlimited and our payoffs have earned us the reputation as the 'World's Best Place to Play Slots.' Whether you play nickels or $5 tokens, you'll feel comfortable at the Riviera. Try your luck in DollarTown USA or in an area known as the World's Loosest Corner of Slots and you'll see why we use the slogan 'Win More, Play Longer.'"

meeting rooms. Special services available include ice carvings, flowers, musicians, dance floors, video screens, special lighting equipment, projectors, and a wide selection of menu options (contact the catering department).

Business Center

Hours: 8:00 A.M. to 6:00 P.M. (Monday through Friday)
9:00 A.M. to 5:00 P.M. (Saturday and Sunday)

Information: (702) 794-9500

If you're visiting Las Vegas on business, the Riviera's business center will help you stay in contact with your office and get your work done more efficiently. The following services are available. (Separate fees apply for many of these services.)

- Fax, copying, and computer services
- Equipment rental: cellular phones, pagers, and luggage carts
- Secretarial services
- Notary service
- Other services: office supplies, printing, temporary support personnel, and interpreters
- Shipping and receiving services

For the hotel's younger guests, an arcade/entertainment area is available that features the latest video games, pinball machines, skee ball, and an electronic shooting gallery. There's also a pool and tennis courts to keep younger people entertained.

Wedding Chapel

Hours: 9:00 A.M. to 10:00 P.M. (Monday through Saturday)
9:00 A.M. to 7:00 P.M. (Sunday)

Information: (702) 794-9494

www.las-vegas-wedding.com

If you're planning to tie the knot in Las Vegas, the Riviera offers a lovely wedding chapel facility plus a variety of wedding packages to accommodate anyone's wishes (and budget). Advanced planning, however, is strongly advised.

Sahara Hotel & Casino

Theme:	Moroccan
Room Rate:	$ / $$ (under $50–$100)
Number of Rooms:	1,720 guest rooms and suites
Casino:	85,000 square feet, featuring all of the popular table games (50 tables), slot machines, video poker machines, keno, and a race and sports book
Dining:	Six restaurants, including a newly renovated buffet
Primary Show:	World-class magician Steve Wyrick
Special Attractions:	Sahara Speedworld (featuring virtual reality rides and games), the NASCAR Cafe, and a roller coaster
Reservations:	(888) 696-2121
Web Site:	*www.saharahotelandcasino.com*
Address:	2535 Las Vegas Boulevard South Las Vegas, NV 89109

Overall Resort Rating Based on Amenities and Rates

Ages Up to 5	Ages 6–15	Ages 16–20	Ages 21 & Up	Senior Citizens
⚀	⚀ ⚁	⚀ ⚁	⚀ ⚁	⚀ ⚁

The Sahara Hotel and Casino has a long history in Las Vegas, beginning in the 1950s—an era when Elvis Presley and the famed Rat Pack were the entertainment icons of the city. In its day, long before the mega-resorts like MGM Grand, Bellagio, the Luxor, and the Venetian were ever conceived, the Sahara Hotel and Casino was a trendy hangout for many Hollywood stars.

Hundreds of big-name performers, including Mae West, Tony Bennett, Marlene Dietrich, Don Rickles, and even the Beatles, performed in the hotel's famed Congo Room and Casbar Lounge.

Despite its ongoing evolution, the Sahara wasn't able to maintain the reputation and notoriety it once had. In 1995, the property was sold to William G. Bennett who immediately began a $100-million renovation project that was finally completed in early 2000. The now modernized Sahara Hotel and Casino features a new theater—The Sahara Theater—new restaurants (including the NASCAR Cafe), a race car–themed entertainment complex (called Sahara Speedworld), and a roller coaster.

The Sahara Hotel and Casino is one of the oldest hotels on the Strip as well as one of the least expensive. During nonpeak times, basic room rates start as low as $49 per night. Plenty of free parking is available.

Located next door to the Wet 'n Wild theme park (a water park that appeals mainly to children and teens), the Sahara Hotel and Casino offers basic amenities at a low price, which makes it popular for people traveling on a budget who want to stay on the Strip.

Guest Room Accommodations

Now that the property's renovations are complete, the Sahara Hotel and Casino offers over 1,700 guest rooms and suites that are decorated in a Moroccan motif. Basic rooms offer one king-size bed or two queen-size beds, while suites are available in one-, two-, or three-bed-room configurations.

Other Hotel Amenities

- Beauty salon and barber
- Car rental desk
- Video game arcade

Fine Dining

The Sahara has six restaurants, including the NASCAR Cafe, plus room service (but only between 9:00 A.M. and midnight). The Sahara Steak House, however, offers the most formal dining experience on the property.

The Sahara Steak House ($$$)

Reservations: Recommended, call (702) 737-2111

Timeless favorites, such as New York steak, Australian lobster tail, rib-eye served on the bone, and filet medallions (prepared tableside), are the house specialties at this steakhouse. All entrees come with a choice of soup or salad and a baked potato or rice. The menu also includes a variety of appetizers and side dishes. The restaurant is open nightly for dinner, from 5:00 to 10:00 P.M.

$ = entrees under $10; $$ = under $20; $$$ = over $20

Casual Dining

The Sahara offers a selection of competitively priced dining options providing casual atmospheres, including some restaurants that are extremely family oriented.

Paco's Hideaway ($$)

This authentic Mexican restaurant is open nightly from 5:00 to 10:00 P.M. Traditional Mexican dishes are featured on the menu and the full-service bar offers a wide selection of specialty and exotic drinks, including its own version of the classic margarita.

The NASCAR Cafe ($$)

Featuring an all-American menu, the NASCAR Cafe is a family-oriented theme restaurant based on the incredibly popular NASCAR racing. The dining room is equipped with giant projection screen televisions that feature NASCAR racing, driver profiles, and the latest NASCAR news. Throughout the restaurant, NASCAR memorabilia is on display, including authentic NASCAR Winston Cup cars. Just as the Hard Rock Cafe appeals to people who love music and Planet Hollywood appeals to movie buffs, the NASCAR Cafe has become a preferred restaurant among racing fans of all ages. In conjunction with this cafe, Sahara Speedworld offers one-of-a-kind, intense virtual driving games.

Caravan Coffee Shop ($ / $$)

Open 24 hours a day, this coffee shop offers an extensive menu that features popular American dishes. Nightly dinner specials and Night Owl specials are served from 6:00 to 11:00 P.M.

Sahara Buffet ($)

This newly renovated, all-you-can-eat buffet is open daily for brunch (7:00 A.M. to 3:00 P.M.) and dinner (4:00 to 10:00 P.M.). It's located on the north side of the casino. Brunch is priced at a mere $4.99 per person, while dinner is priced at only $5.99, making it one of the least expensive dining options on the entire Strip. On Sunday, a special champagne brunch is served from 8:00 A.M. to 3:00 P.M.

$ = entrees under $10; $$ = under $20; $$$ = over $20

Shopping

The Sahara has several shops and boutiques on-property, but is also a short distance from the Forum Shops at Caesars Palace and the Fashion Show Mall (at 3200 Las Vegas Blvd. South).

Lounges

- Thirsty Camel Bar—Located in the main casino area, beer, wine, cocktails, and frozen drinks are available at this full-service bar.
- Bogie's Bar—Located next to the Sahara Steak House, full bar service is offered.
- Casbar Lounge—In 1954, this lounge began showcasing high profile entertainers in an intimate, 120-seat setting. The lounge continues to offer live music nightly, as well as full bar service.

Special Attractions

If you're a NASCAR fan, whether or not you choose to stay at the Sahara Hotel and Casino, you'll want to visit the NASCAR Cafe as well as the newly renovated Sahara Speedworld.

Sahara Speedworld

Prices: **$8 a ride for Indy cars; $3 entry to the 3-D theaters**
Information: **(702) 737-2750**

Featuring virtual reality attractions such as 3-D theaters, motion simulator rides, and arcade games, this is the ideal entertainment complex for racing fans. Sahara Speedworld is open daily, from 10:00 A.M. to 11:00 P.M., and on Friday and Saturday until midnight. Since the opening of the NASCAR Cafe in March 2000, Sahara Speedworld has been adapted to more of a NASCAR theme. A roller coaster is also being built on-property, allowing guests to experience thrills at speeds up to 70 m.p.h.

Magician Steve Wyrick

In the newly renovated Sahara Theater, magician/illusionist Steve Wyrick performs nightly in a multimillion dollar show with tickets that are competitively priced. (At the time this book was being written, the show was still in development and hadn't yet opened.)

The Congo Showroom

Box Office: **(702) 737-2515**

The Congo Showroom features a variety of performers from comedians to musicians. Call the box office for a show lineup.

Banquet, Function, and Convention Services

The Sahara offers catering services for weddings, birthdays, receptions, and other special events. Contact the hotel directly for more information.

Pool

The Sahara offers a 5,000-square-foot heated swimming pool with plenty of deck area for tanning. Hours of operation vary by season (typically 8:00 A.M. to 8:00 P.M. in the summer). Thirteen private cabanas are also available for daily rental. There's also a gazebo-covered spa and a nearby snack bar. The spa is open year-round from 9:00 A.M. to 5:00 P.M.

Casino

The Sahara started off as a bingo parlor and evolved into a casino. Over the years, the casino has stayed up with the times, and continues to offer gamblers plenty of table games, slots, video poker machines, plus keno and a race and sports book.

Recently, the casino began offering "21st Century Blackjack," a game where jokers are wild and hands don't bust. There are two objectives in 21st Century Blackjack: to build a hand that totals 21 and to beat the dealer. The game is played with six decks of cards with the jokers included in each deck. Jokers are wild and total a hard 21 when combined with any other card. Two jokers beat any hand, and if the dealer and player both have totals that exceed 21, the hand is a push (the player does not win or lose). This game has become one of the most popular live table games at the Sahara.

The casino also offers over fifty table games, including all of the popular games, like craps, roulette, Caribbean Stud, Let It Ride, Pai Gow, and Spanish 21.

By joining the Sahara's Slot Club, players can begin receiving benefits and rewards after earning as few as 200 points. Membership to the club is free. The more slots you play, the more points you earn. Points can then be redeemed for cash and comps.

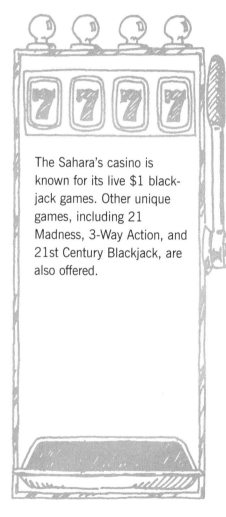

The Sahara's casino is known for its live $1 blackjack games. Other unique games, including 21 Madness, 3-Way Action, and 21st Century Blackjack, are also offered.

Stratosphere Tower Hotel & Casino

Theme: The tallest free-standing observation tower in America

Room Rate: $$ ($51–$100)

Number of Rooms: 1,500 rooms and suites

Casino: 100,000 square feet, featuring 1,600 slot machines, 49 table games, a keno lounge, a poker room, and a race and sports book

Dining: An assortment of fine-dining and casual restaurants, many featuring an incredible view of the Strip and the surrounding valley. The mall, located in the tower, features several fast-food options.

Primary Show: *Viva Las Vegas* and *American Superstars*

Special Attractions: The indoor/outdoor observation desk (1,149 feet high), the Big Shot thrill ride, and the High Roller coaster

Reservations: (800) 99-TOWER

Web Site: *www.stratlv.com*

Address: 2000 Las Vegas Boulevard
Las Vegas, NV 89104

Overall Resort Rating Based on Amenities and Rates

Ages Up to 5	Ages 6–15	Ages 16–20	Ages 21 & Up	Senior Citizens
•	• ••	• ••	• ••	• ••

Stratosphere Tower instantly became a Las Vegas Strip landmark when it opened in 1996. The tower itself can be seen from virtually anywhere in the Las Vegas area, and its observations decks provide an incredible view. This is definitely one of the less expensive hotels and casinos along the Strip. It caters to a wide range of clientele, with a focus on families and those traveling on a budget.

Even if you're staying at another hotel along the Strip, it's worth taking a taxi ride to Stratosphere Tower to check out the observation decks and,

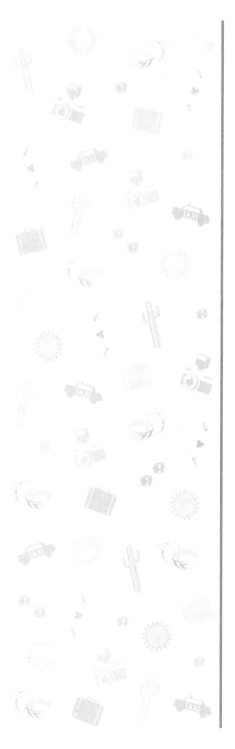

if you're daring enough, to experience the thrill rides at the top of the tower itself. If you have a rental car, plenty of free parking is available.

Guest Room Accommodations

The Stratosphere has 1,500 rooms and suites that are competitively priced for a Las Vegas Strip hotel and resort. Unfortunately, the hotel is at the extreme far end of the Strip, making it necessary to take a car, taxi, or shuttle bus to any other locations along the Strip.

Guest room accommodations feature either one king-size bed or two queen-size beds. Rooms are equipped with a variety of amenities, such as in-room safes and hair dryers. If you're willing to spend a bit more money, the Stratosphere offers 120 suites with first-class comfort and amenities. Nonsmoking rooms are available upon request.

Fine Dining

Stratosphere certainly is not a low-budget hotel, but it's not a five-star resort either. Understanding that Stratosphere is a competitively priced resort, it offers one fine-dining restaurant plus a variety of lower priced restaurants that cater more to travelers on a budget and families.

Top of the World Restaurant and Lounge ($$ / $$$)

Reservations: Strongly recommended, call (702) 380-7711

Offering one of the most spectacular views in Las Vegas, the Top of the World Restaurant and Lounge features a revolving dining room that rotates 360 degrees each hour, giving diners views of the Strip and the surrounding valley. The menu features an assortment of entrees from around the world, including New Zealand rack of lamb and Chilean sea bass.

The restaurant is open for dinner from 5:00 to 11:00 P.M. Sunday through Thursday and from 5:00 P.M. to midnight on Friday and Saturday. Advanced reservations are strongly recommended, since dining room seating it limited to 360. There's a $15 per person minimum.

$ = entrees under $10; $$ = under $20; $$$ = over $20

Casual Dining

As a family-oriented resort and casino, Stratosphere offers a range of less expensive dining options. These restaurants do not require reservations, and the dress is always casual. During peak times, guests can expect a wait to be seated.

Roxy's Diner ($$)

This 1950s-style diner offers burgers and fries, along with a soda fountain. Shakes, sandwiches, salads, and meatloaf are among the menu options. Roxy's is open daily for breakfast, lunch, and dinner from 5:00 A.M. to 8:00 P.M. Sunday through Thursday, and from 5:00 A.M. to 11:00 P.M. Friday and Saturday. Not only does this restaurant offer an excellent dining value, it also incorporates some entertainment. The wait staff wears 1950s uniforms, and a juke box plays nonstop hits from the era.

Montana Cafe & Grille ($$)

Salads, sandwiches, steaks, pasta, prime rib, and the catch of the day are among the popular menu items at this cafe that is open 24 hours a day on weekends, and from 11:00 A.M. to 5:00 A.M. the rest of the week. A full breakfast menu is also always available, although some dinner entrees are only available after 5:00 P.M.

Stratosphere Buffet ($ / $$)

What would a Las Vegas resort and casino be without an all-you-can-eat buffet? The Stratosphere's buffet offers a wide range of entrees from around the world, so chances are you'll find plenty to quench your appetite. The carving station, for example, features prime rib, roast beef, or turkey. Every Friday and Saturday evening, the Stratosphere Buffet offers the Seafood Fantasy Buffet from 4:00 to 9:00 P.M.

The price of this all-you-can-eat extravaganza is $11.25 per person. The buffet is open for breakfast from 8:00 to 11:00 A.M.; lunch is from 11:00 A.M. to 4:00 P.M.; and dinner is from 4:00 to 9:00 P.M. As with any buffet on the Strip, expect to wait for a seat during peak periods, since buffets tend to be popular with families.

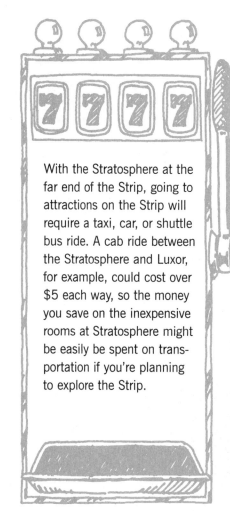

With the Stratosphere at the far end of the Strip, going to attractions on the Strip will require a taxi, car, or shuttle bus ride. A cab ride between the Stratosphere and Luxor, for example, could cost over $5 each way, so the money you save on the inexpensive rooms at Stratosphere might be easily be spent on transportation if you're planning to explore the Strip.

$ = entrees under $10; $$ = under $20; $$$ = over $20

Fellini's Tower of Pasta ($$)

This Italian restaurant offers a selection of pastas, veal, chicken, and seafood, plus an extensive wine list, homemade Italian desserts, and specialty coffees. It's a great place for a meal or a late-night snack. Fellini's Tower of Pasta is open nightly for dinner only, from 5:00 to 11:00 P.M. (Sunday through Thursday) and from 5:00 P.M. to midnight on weekends. Reservations are accepted here.

Triple Crown Deli ($ / $$)

If you're in the mood for a sandwich and fast service, check out the Triple Crown Deli. This New York–style deli offers sandwiches, salads, and pizza by the slice. It's open Monday through Thursday from 9:00 A.M. to 900 P.M., and 9:00 A.M. to 11:00 P.M. Friday through Sunday.

Lounges

Top of the World Lounge

Located directly above the Top of the World Restaurant is the 220-seat Top of the World Lounge. In addition to offering a full-service bar, the lounge offers a wide selection of cigars, spirits, beers, and fine wines from around the world. The lounge is open Thursday through Sunday from 10:00 A.M. to 1:00 A.M., and until 2:00 A.M. on Friday and Saturday. The lounge also offers a full lunch menu from 11:00 A.M. to 4:00 P.M. Live pop, R&B, and jazz music is presented every evening from 8:00 P.M. to 1:00 A.M.

Images Cabaret

Located on the casino level, this lounge offers full bar service and live entertainment every Tuesday, Wednesday, Thursday, and Sunday from 8:00 P.M. to 1:30 A.M., and Friday and Saturday evenings from 9:00 P.M. to 2:30 A.M.

Special Attractions

The Stratosphere offers a handful of entertaining ways to enjoy your time in Las Vegas, from taking spectacular pictures from the observation decks,

After dinner, be sure to try the Chocolate Stratosphere Tower for dessert! It's a chocolate replica of the tower . . . delicious!

$ = entrees under $10; $$ = under $20; $$$ = over $20

riding one of the two thrill rides at the very top of the tower, or experiencing family-oriented shows.

The Pepsi Cola Indoor/Outdoor Observation Deck

Visitors to Stratosphere can enjoy a 360-degree panoramic view of Las Vegas from the climate-controlled indoor observation deck. This is the place to visit for anyone who is afraid of heights, yet wants a spectacular view. Located 857 feet above ground, the indoor observation deck features two gift shops, a snack bar, and the loading area for the resort's two thrill rides—the Big Shot and the High Roller.

Located a bit higher, on level 109 (869 feet above the ground), the outdoor observation deck allows you to experience the incredible view while also enjoying fresh air in a somewhat open environment. The only way to travel higher up the Stratosphere Tower is on its thrill rides. No matter the observation deck, don't forget your camera!

High Roller and the Big Shot

Several Las Vegas Strip hotels and resorts now offer theme parks or thrill rides. At New York–New York, for example, a roller coaster whips around the perimeter of the resort. Stratosphere's claim to fame is its two thrill rides that have been built at the very top of the tower, so the rides themselves are over 100 stories above the ground.

High Roller is the world's highest roller coaster. The ride follows an 865-foot track that circles the outside of the tower at speeds up to 30 m.p.h. The scariest part of this ride is its height. It's not particularly fast, and there are no sharp dips, just a few sharp turns. What riders can expect is an awesome view, since the entire ride is located outside. One ride includes two trips around the track.

If you're looking for something a bit scarier and don't mind high-speed drops, the Big Shot offers an exciting new twist on the freefall ride now found at many amusement parks. Sixteen passengers at a time are launched 160 feet (in 2.5 seconds), along the 228-foot mast extending like a needle from the very top of the Stratosphere Tower. Riders are then dropped, allowing them to fall at speeds over 45 m.p.h.

Both rides usually operate from 10:00 A.M. to 1:00 A.M. Sunday through Thursday, and 10:00 A.M. to 2:00 A.M. Friday and Saturday. (Hours vary, however, based on weather and season.) The price to ride High Roller is $5, and the price for each Big Shot ride is $6. Package deals are available that allow visitors to experience both rides at a discount, or to visit the observation decks and experience the rides. For example, observation tower admission plus one ride on High Roller costs $9, while observation tower admission combined with a ride on Big Shot is priced at $10. A package offering both rides and admission to the observation tower is priced at $14 a person.

There is a 48-inch minimum height requirement for both rides. During peak times, expect a wait.

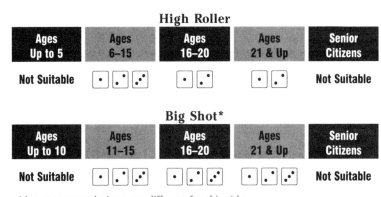

High Roller

Ages Up to 5	Ages 6–15	Ages 16–20	Ages 21 & Up	Senior Citizens
Not Suitable	⚀ ⚁ ⚂	⚀ ⚁	⚀ ⚁	Not Suitable

Big Shot*

Ages Up to 10	Ages 11–15	Ages 16–20	Ages 21 & Up	Senior Citizens
Not Suitable	⚀ ⚁ ⚂	⚀ ⚁ ⚂	⚀ ⚁ ⚂	Not Suitable

Age recommendations are different for this ride

Shows

Shows in Las Vegas have changed a lot over the years, as high-budget shows have replaced traditional variety shows and lounge acts. Many resorts and casinos have built state-of-the-art, fully customized theaters to be the permanent homes to Broadway productions or other unique shows. *Cirque du Soleil 'O',* for example, is presented in Bellagio's $100 million, custom-built theater. With these high-budget productions come high ticket prices, some reaching $100 a seat.

Stratosphere Tower Hotel and Casino, however, offers live shows that are reminiscent of traditional Las Vegas–style variety shows and musicals. These aren't high-budget productions, yet they are thoroughly entertaining and offer low ticket prices, making them excellent values.

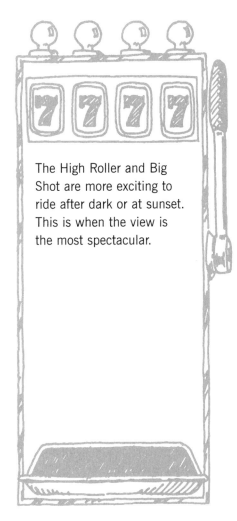

The High Roller and Big Shot are more exciting to ride after dark or at sunset. This is when the view is the most spectacular.

American Superstars

Ticket Prices: $22.95 (adults) / $16.95 (children)

Box Office: (702) 380-7711 or (800) 99-TOWER

The chances of running into Gloria Estefan, the Spice Girls, Will Smith, and the Temptations during your trip to Las Vegas are pretty slim; however, *American Superstars* offers a tribute to these and many other well known entertainers.

This high-energy show is presented in the Broadway Showroom every Sunday, Monday, and Tuesday at 7:00 P.M., and Wednesday, Friday, and Saturday at 7:00 and 10:00 P.M.

The fun-filled musical performance features talented impersonators and is suitable for the entire family. For the price, this show offers an excellent value, although it doesn't compare to shows like *Siegfried & Roy* or one of the *Cirque du Soleil* shows, where ticket prices are over $75 each. Children and teens in particular will like *American Superstars*. After the show, the cast meets audience members in the theater lobby.

American Superstars

Ages Up to 5	Ages 6–15	Ages 16–20	Ages 21 & Up	Senior Citizens
Not Suitable	⚀⚁	⚀⚁	⚀⚁	⚀⚁

Viva Las Vegas

Ticket Price: $10

Box Office: (702) 380-7711 or (800) 99-TOWER

Experience *Viva Las Vegas* and travel back to the golden years of Las Vegas, when variety shows were popular. The fun-filled and highly entertaining show combines comedy acts with singing, dancing, and several different specialty acts. Suitable for the entire family, this show is presented afternoons only, at 2:00 and 4:00 P.M. (daily, except Sunday), and features traditional Las Vegas–style showgirls.

Viva Las Vegas

Ages Up to 5	Ages 6–15	Ages 16–20	Ages 21 & Up	Senior Citizens
Not Suitable	⚀⚁	⚀⚁	⚀⚁	⚀⚁

If you're hooked on the Las Vegas slot machines, visit *CJ's Casino Emporium*, (702) 380-1220, which sells used slot machines (both modern and antique). Prices range from several hundred dollars to several thousand; however, they're all actual slot machines once used in the major casinos. In some states (such as Alabama, Hawaii, Indiana, Nebraska, and South Carolina), owning any type of real slot machine is prohibited. In other states, it's legal to own a slot machine manufactured before certain years (i.e., pre-1984 in Colorado and pre-1941 in New York), while some states have minimum age requirements to buy the machines.

Casino

Stratosphere's 100,000-square-foot casino features 1,600 slot machines along with 49 table games, plus a keno lounge, poker room, and a race and sports book. Some of the table games offer low minimum bets, which make them ideal for casual gamblers.

Shopping

Stratosphere Tower offers a mall just above the main casino, near the tower entrance, that contains 35 stores and 11 retail kiosks that cater primarily to tourists. You'll find a combination of clothing stores (such as Victoria's Secret and Bernini Sport), plus several inexpensive (fast-food) dining options, including McDonald's, Nathan's, and Mama Llardo's Pizzeria. Many of these stores offer less expensive items than the Forum Shops at Caesars Palace or the Fashion Show Mall near Treasure Island.

In addition to specialty shops in the mall area of Stratosphere Tower, there are several cart-based businesses that sell unique products and souvenirs. One popular cart offers pendants, bracelets, and key chains with a custom-made locket containing a piece of rice with a personalized name or message written on it.

Banquet, Function, and Convention Services

The Stratosphere Tower offers an array of function rooms and a wedding chapel, plus a staff trained to help you plan any type of meeting or function.

Other Resort Services

Although the Stratosphere Tower Hotel and Casino isn't considered lavish, it does offer an array of amenities and a good value overall. Some of the other guest services and amenities you'll find here include a car rental desk, video arcade, swimming pool, spa, and a tour/show desk.

If you'll be attending a convention at the Las Vegas Convention Center, you should know that the Stratosphere is 1.3 miles from the convention center itself.

Treasure Island at The Mirage

Theme: An 18th century pirate village—Buccaneer Bay

Room Rate: $$ / $$$ ($51–$250)

Number of Rooms: 2,891 guest rooms, including 212 suites in three 36-story towers

Casino: 75,000 square feet, featuring over 2,000 slot and video poker machines, a keno lounge, a race and sports book, plus a wide range of table games

Dining: Four fine-dining restaurants, plus five casual-dining options

Primary Show: *Cirque du Soleil Mystére*

Special Attractions: An elaborate (outdoor) re-creation of a sea battle between the pirate ship *Hispaniola* and a British frigate presented nightly in front of the hotel (in Buccaneer Bay, overlooking the Strip); monorail service between Treasure Island and The Mirage

Reservations: (800) 944-7444 or (800) 288-7206

Web Site: *www.treasureisland.com*

Address: 3300 Las Vegas Boulevard South
Las Vegas, NV 89109

Overall Resort Rating Based on Amenities and Rates

Ages Up to 5	Ages 6–15	Ages 16–20	Ages 21 & Up	Senior Citizens
2	2	3	3	2

Located next to the famous Mirage resort and operated by Mirage Resorts, Inc. (which also operates the Golden Nugget Las Vegas and Bellagio), Treasure Island shares over 100 acres of property with The Mirage along the Strip. Treasure Island, however, is somewhat less expensive than its sister properties, yet offers similar accommodations and services, although slightly less posh.

Treasure Island, which opened in October 1993, is an excellent choice for families traveling with children and teens, in part because of the pirate motif. (In terms of kid-oriented activities, resorts like the MGM Grand, Circus Circus, and Excalibur offer a bit more selection for people not old enough to drink or gamble.) A free monorail service connects Treasure Island with The Mirage.

All public areas of Treasure Island maintain the theme of an elegant Caribbean hideaway, based loosely on a village created by Robert Louis Stevenson in his novel *Treasure Island*. Surrounding the front of the resort is Buccaneer Bay Village, a replica of a thriving Old World village. The large cove area in front of the resort is where a sea battle between the British naval officers on their ship HMS *Britannia* and the pirates, aboard the *Hispaniola*, re-create a theatrical battle on the high seas, complete with special effects and pyrotechnics.

Guest Room Accommodations

All of the basic guest rooms in Treasure Island have recently undergone a $60-million redesign. European fabrics and custom-woven carpeting provide an elegant background upon which traditional wood furnishings are set. Each room features floor-to-ceiling windows with an excellent view of the mountains, the Strip, or the resort's lovely pool area. The color scheme features soft earth tones. Guest rooms contain a single king-size bed or two queen-size beds, a desk, color television, bureau, and small table with two chairs.

In addition to 2,891 guest rooms, Treasure Island features several different types of suites.

The official Treasure Island Web site (*www. treasureisland.com*) features special discount offers and promotional deals on the resort's suites for Sundays through Thursdays. These offers aren't available by calling the toll-free number.

- Petite Suites—These suites are larger than basic guest rooms. Like the regular guest rooms, the suites are elegantly styled with traditional furnishings and custom fabrics. Each of these suites features a king-size bed and an intimate sitting area as well as his and her bathrooms.
- Executive Suites—Each of these suites features a king-size bed and comfortable sitting area plus luxurious his and her bathrooms. They're a bit larger than the Petite Suites.
- Tower Suites—The Tower Suites offer the ideal combination of elegance and comfort in spacious surroundings. Each suite features a king-size bed, a large sitting and dining area, as well as elaborate his and her bathrooms and walk-in closets.
- Luxury Suites—The Luxury Suites offer a large bedroom with a king-size bed and also a separate living room and dining area. Each

Luxury Suite features his and her bathrooms, a whirlpool bathtub, and a variety of in-room amenities, including a wet bar.

- Premier Suites—The Premier Suites are Treasure Island's most spacious and exclusive suites. They offer top-of-the-line amenities and facilities. Located on the top floors of the towers, they offer panoramic views of the city and the resort's theatrical ship battle, and include a full entertainment center, wet bar, Jacuzzi, and walk-in closet. Elegant his and her bathrooms feature gold-plated fixtures and boast fine amenities.

Fine Dining

Treasure Island's fine-dining establishments have a "dressy casual" dress code and do not allow children under the age of five. Thus, these restaurants aren't designed for families with young children.

The Plank ($$$)

Reservations: **Strongly recommended, call (702) 894-7111 or (702) 894-7223**

Steak and mesquite-grilled seafood, plus broiled lobster, shrimp scampi, and grilled scallops are among the offerings at this restaurant that has an intimate library feel. The walls are lined with bookcases containing old books and artifacts. Dinner is served nightly from 5:30 to 11:00 P.M.

The Buccaneer Bay Club ($$$)

Reservations: **Strongly recommended, call (702) 894-7111 or (702) 894-7223**

Located on the second level of the resort and overlooking Buccaneer Bay, this restaurant gives diners an excellent view of the Strip and the nightly pirate show. Indulge in such entrees as Cornish game hen, sautéed Chilean sea bass, or shrimp scampi sauté. Dinner is served nightly from 5:00 to 10:30 P.M. Like all of the fine-dining establishments at Treasure Island, this one is perfect for an intimate dinner, a business dinner, or to celebrate a special occasion such as an anniversary.

$ = entrees under $10; $$ = under $20; $$$ = over $20

Banquet, Function, and Convention Services

Information: (800) 944-7711 or (702) 894-7711

Like other resorts along the Strip, Treasure Island offers an abundance of meeting and banquet space, convention and meeting facilities, and a staff of highly trained event planners who are available to assist you in coordinating your function for up to 1,000 people. Over 18,000 square feet of meeting space is available at Treasure Island.

Wedding Chapels

Information:
(800) 866-4768
or (702) 894-7700

Decorated in the European tradition, Treasure Island features two wedding chapels. One chapel seats 30 people, while the other seats 60. A range of wedding services are available, including wedding planning, videotaping and photography, dressing rooms, bouquets, and champagne glasses. A special wedding package can also be arranged aboard the HMS *Britannia*, a replica of a British naval frigate. The Crown Jewel wedding package includes a ceremony aboard the ship (located in front of the resort), with the ceremony performed by the British captain. Hours are 8:00 A.M. to 6:00 P.M. daily.

Madame Ching's ($$$)

**Reservations: Strongly recommended, call (702) 894-7111
or (702) 894-7223**

In case you're not up-to-date on your pirate history, Madame Ching was one of the most famous female pirates. This restaurant offers Szechuan and Cantonese cuisine that is reminiscent of Old World China. Grandfather chicken, steamed salmon filet, and Macadamia beef are among the entree offerings. Madame Ching's is located next to the Treasure Island Buffet. Dinner is served Wednesday through Sunday from 5:30 to 11:00 P.M.

Francesco's ($$$)

**Reservations: Strongly recommended, call (702) 894-7111
or (702) 894-7223**

This restaurant offers a wide selection of Italian specialties, such as fresh pasta, antipasti, and Mediterranean-style seafood. The restaurant itself is decorated with original artwork created by celebrities such as Tony Bennett and Phyllis Diller. It also has an open kitchen, so you can see the chefs at work as they prepare your meal. Dinner is served nightly from 5:30 to 11:00 P.M.

Casual Dining

Let's face it, it's probably not within your budget to experience each meal at one of Treasure Island's fine-dining restaurants. Even if money isn't an issue, perhaps you'd rather spend your evenings seeing a show or playing at a casino as opposed to experiencing a multicourse meal. Whether you're looking for something faster, less expensive, or more casual, Treasure Island also offers several casual dining alternatives that are suitable for the entire family. Reservations are not required for any of these cafes or restaurants.

The Lookout Cafe ($ / $$)

Open 24 hours, this cafe overlooks the casino and offers a wide assortment of menu items, including salads, sandwiches, and breakfast

$ = entrees under $10; $$ = under $20; $$$ = over $20

foods as well as lunch and dinner entrees. Even if you're looking for dessert or a snack, chances are you'll find it at the Lookout Cafe, which offers full table service. For those late-night food cravings, you could order room service or, instead, dine at the Lookout Cafe and enjoy the hustle and bustle of the casino atmosphere (while playing keno from your table).

The Black Spot Grille ($$)

Designed to look like a sidewalk cafe, you'll find this grille in the heart of Treasure Island's shopping promenade. This is an Italian bistro that offers pizza, pasta dishes, burgers, and a variety of salads. There's also a low-fat menu available for health-conscious diners. The Black Spot Grille is open Sunday through Thursday from 11:00 A.M. to 11:00 PM, as well as on Friday and Saturday from 11:00 A.M. to 12:30 A.M.

The Treasure Island Buffet ($)

Open daily for breakfast, lunch, and dinner, this all-you-can-eat buffet offers a wide selection of foods at one flat rate. The menu changes throughout the day, and daily specials are always offered. Like all buffets at the Las Vegas resorts, this one offers an excellent value. Guests are seated and served on a first-come basis, so be prepared to wait to get in, especially during peak times. At a price of under $10 per person, this remains one of the best buffet deals along the Strip.

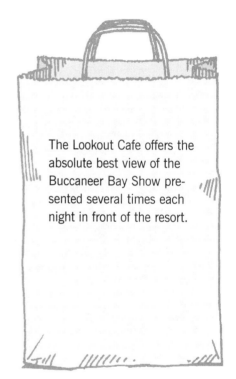

The Lookout Cafe offers the absolute best view of the Buccaneer Bay Show presented several times each night in front of the resort.

The Delicatessen ($ / $$)

For a quick and inexpensive snack or New York–style deli sandwich, drop by the Delicatessen. Soups and an assortment of desserts are also offered. Open 11:00 A.M. to midnight, Monday through Friday, and 9:00 A.M. to midnight on Saturday and Sunday.

Sweet Revenge ($)

This ice cream parlor offers soft-serve ice cream, frozen yogurt, sundaes, and other dessert items, plus a small menu of snack foods, such as sandwiches, hot dogs, and muffins. Sweet Revenge is the perfect place to stop for dessert or if you're traveling with children and you're looking for a quick and affordable place to eat.

$ = entrees under $10; $$ = under $20; $$$ = over $20

Starbucks Coffee ($)

The coffee you love from the Starbucks in your hometown is available at Treasure Island. Whether it's for that morning dose of caffeine to get you moving, or you need to take some time to relax during the day or evening, drop by Starbucks Coffee for coffee, cappuccino, espresso, Frappuccino, and fresh pastries.

Lounges

The bars and lounges within Treasure Island are open to anyone over the age of 21, and include:

Additional Hotel Services

- 24-hour room service
- Car rentals
- Self-parking and valet parking available
- No child care service

- The Battle Bar—Located next to Treasure Island's race and sports book, the Battle Bar is a great place to share the excitement of major sporting events with other fans and friends. From the outdoor patio, experience the ambiance of Buccaneer Bay or the thrill of the Buccaneer Bay Show. Full bar service is offered.
- Swashbuckler's—In addition to offering traditional bar service, a menu of Treasure Island's "specialty concoctions" are offered at this 24-hour lounge. You'll find Swashbuckler's in the heart of the casino.
- The Gold Bar—Working up a thirst while playing the casino's slot machines or table games is common. If you want to stay in the casino area, yet take a break from the gambling action, drop into the Gold Bar, a full-service bar located close to the casino floor.
- Hideaway Lounge—Looking for the ideal place to meet some friends or business associates for drinks? Do you want to spend some quality time with a loved one after dinner or before (or after) a show? Enjoy topnotch musical combos performing the sounds of today and yesterday in a comfortable lounge atmosphere. Full bar service is offered.

Special Attractions

Entertainment in Treasure Island is limited to *Cirque du Soleil Mystére*, the Buccaneer Bay Show, spending time at the casino, dining at a restaurant,

$ = entrees under $10; $$ = under $20; $$$ = over $20

or spending time at one of the resort's bars or lounges, several of which offer live entertainment.

Cirque du Soleil Mystére

Show Times:	7:30 and 10:30 P.M. (Wednesday through Sunday)
Ticket Price:	$75 each (price includes tax)
Box Office:	(800) 392-1999 or (702) 796-9999

Cirque du Soleil is a Montreal-based circus troupe that has been in existence since 1984. This isn't your typical circus, however. Designed for adults but suitable for teens, Cirque du Soleil has several traveling tour groups and a permanent U.S. home at Treasure Island and Bellagio, as well as at Pleasure Island at Disney World in Orlando, Florida.

Cirque du Soleil's show *Mystére* is presented exclusively at Treasure Island and features 72 acrobats, comedians, actors, singers, dancers, and musicians from 18 countries. In addition to the incredible performances, the live music, sets, and costumes are absolutely incredible.

Mystére is performed twice nightly (except Monday and Tuesday) in a 1,500-seat theater designed exclusively for the show. Tickets should be purchased in advance from the box office, since performances typically sell out.

If you've never seen a Cirque du Soleil show, this one offers a night's worth of topnotch entertainment that's well worth the price of admission. Located down the Strip at the Bellagio, Cirque du Soleil presents another show, called '*O,*' an unusual show that mostly takes place in water.

Mystére is revamped every few months as new specialty acts are added and others are changed. The show is considerably better now than it was a few years ago when it first premiered in Las Vegas. It'll definitely appeal to a more mainstream audience than *Cirque du Soleil 'O.'*

Acclaimed by a worldwide audience of over 18 million, with numerous prizes and distinctions to its credit, Cirque du Soleil is a unique organization that is responsible for reinventing and revolutionizing the circus arts.

Cirque du Soleil has been pleasing the public with a novel show concept that is as original as it is nontraditional. Each show is an astonishing theatrical blend of circus arts and street performance, wrapped up in spectacular costumes and fairyland sets, and staged to spellbinding music and magical lighting. There are no animals in a Cirque du Soleil production.

For more information about Cirque du Soleil, visit their official Web site at *www.cirquedusoleil.com*.

Cirque du Soleil Mystére

Ages Up to 5	Ages 6–15	Ages 16–20	Ages 21 & Up	Senior Citizens
⚀	⚀⚁	⚀⚁⚂	⚀⚁⚂	⚀⚁⚂

The Buccaneer Bay Show

Show Times: 4:00, 5:30, 7:00, 8:30, 10:00, and 11:30 P.M.
(nightly, weather permitting)

This free show is suitable for people of all ages. It features a simulated ship-to-ship battle, complete with special effects and pyrotechnics. Children who are afraid of traditional fireworks might also find the loud explosions in this simulated battle frightening. The best viewing area is in the front of the resort, standing on the risers near the center of the cove area. This show has taken place more than 8,000 times to date, using more than one-half million pyrotechnic devices, and it has been witnessed by more than 16 million people. To see a live action video preview of this show, visit the Treasure Island Web site at *www.treasureisland.com*.

The Buccaneer Bay Show

Ages Up to 5	Ages 6–15	Ages 16–20	Ages 21 & Up	Senior Citizens
⚀	⚀⚁	⚀⚁	⚀⚁	⚀⚁

For $99 to $250 (or more) a day, you can sign up for a spa and beauty salon package, which might include a massage, manicure, facial, or aromatherapy bath, for example. Appointments should be made in advance.

Pool

The pool at Treasure Island is accented with shady awnings, brightly colored flowers, and dozens of varieties of leafy palms. Complimentary towels and lounge chairs are provided to all guests. Cabana rentals are available for full and half days and include bottled water, juices, sodas, television with cable, telephone, rafts, and changing room. Sundries, including suntan lotion, dive masks, and sunglasses, are available for sale. A cocktail and snack bar is conveniently located poolside. This is an outdoor pool, so it's open seasonally.

Spa, Health Club, and Salon

Hours: 9:00 A.M. to 7:00 P.M. (daily)

Appointments: (702) 894-7472

The Spa at Treasure Island is available only to hotel guests. Amenities offered include men's and women's locker room facilities, complete with saunas, whirlpools, and steam baths. Workout attire, robes, and sandals are available. There is a daily admission fee to use the spa facilities that can be billed directly to your room. Additional services offered within the spa are also billed separately.

The exercise room within the spa offers stationary bicycles, treadmills, stair climbers, CYBEX weight training machines, and free weights. There's also a full-service juice bar and complete vanity amenities available.

In conjunction with the health club facility, you can also pamper yourself at the resort's full-service spa and beauty salon. A full complement of services are available from the salon, including hairstyling, pedicures, manicures, and facials. Additional spa services include:

- Aromatherapy
- Paraffin body masks
- Seaweed body wraps
- Back treatments
- Facials and makeup, from alpha hydroxy treatments to lash and brow tinting
- Body exfoliation
- Hair styling, from cuts to coloring
- Nail treatments, from paraffin to nail artwork

Casino

Continuing the old Caribbean hideaway theme, Treasure Island's casino is decorated in gold and white-washed tones and features artifacts from around the world. As for gaming, the casino offers over 2,000 slot and video poker machines, along with an assortment of gaming tables (including blackjack, roulette, Caribbean Stud, Pai Gow, Let It Ride, Big Six, craps, mini-baccarat, Spanish 21, and baccarat). There's also a large race and sports book, plus keno.

Shopping

In addition to the shops and boutiques located inside Treasure Island, the resort is a short walk from the Fashion Show Mall, a rather large, indoor mall located along the Strip. It's also a short walk (or cab ride) from the Forum Shops, which features dozens of upscale shops and theme restaurants.

Within Treasure Island, you'll find these shops:

- Damsels—A collection of contemporary women's sportswear and accessories is available.
- D. Fine—Men's designer label clothing can be found here.
- Captain Kids—A selection of Treasure Island merchandise, plus toys and plush animals are sold here.
- The Watch Shop—Looking for a new watch? The Watch Stop offers a wide selection of watches and fine jewelry. You might also want to visit the various watch stores and jewelers located at the Forum Shops, which are connected to Caesars Palace (a short walk away).
- Treasure Island Store—Calvin Klein fashion apparel, along with souvenirs and sundries, is available.
- The Candy Reef—Chocolates, candies, and a selection of other sweets are sold here. If you have a sweet tooth, you're sure to find something to satisfy your cravings.
- Treasure Island Collections—Men's apparel and nautical-themed gifts are sold in this boutique.
- The Buccaneer Bay Shoppe—Treasure Island merchandise, including clothing and other souvenirs, is sold here.
- Mutiny Bay Shop—Located near the resort's arcade, this shop sells snacks and toys.
- The Crow's Nest—Treasure Island merchandise, plus a selection of Cirque du Soleil items, is sold here.
- *Mystére* Store—This boutique offers official Cirque du Soleil merchandise and gifts not available elsewhere (except from the Cirque du Soleil main order catalog). The soundtrack from *Mystére* and other Cirque du Soleil shows can be purchased here, along with clothing items and other unique gifts.
- Island Provisions—Poolside supplies and sundries, such as suntan lotion, are available here.

For information about the Treasure Island Slot Club, call (800) 688-4777 or (702) 894-7573.

Tropicana Resort & Casino

Theme:	A Caribbean village
Room Rate:	$$ ($51–$100)
Number of Rooms:	1,800 guest rooms and suites
Casino:	Features table games, including baccarat, blackjack, Big Six, craps, mini-baccarat, Let It Ride, roulette, Pai Gow, and Caribbean Stud poker, keno, plus slot and video poker machines
Dining:	Four fine-dining restaurants and a classic Las Vegas–style buffet
Primary Shows:	*Illusionary Magic of Rick Thomas* and *Best of The Follies Bergere . . . Sexier Than Ever*
Special Attractions:	The Casino Legends Hall of Fame (exhibit), The Comedy Stop (comedy club), three swimming pools (including an indoor pool), and the Island Water Park.
Reservations:	(888) 826-TROP or (888) 826-8767
Web Site:	*www.tropicanalv.com*
Address:	3801 Las Vegas Boulevard South Las Vegas, NV 89109

Overall Resort Rating Based on Amenities and Rates

Ages Up to 5	Ages 6–15	Ages 16–20	Ages 21 & Up	Senior Citizens
⚀	⚀ ⚁	⚀ ⚁	⚀ ⚁	⚀ ⚁

The Tropicana Resort and Casino was one of the first casinos to be built on the now famous Las Vegas Strip. In 1995, the entire resort underwent a total renovation and refurbishment; however, this resort property continues to offer the nostalgia of Las Vegas's golden era and incorporates 1970s-style décor.

One of the most stunning features of this resort is the outside landscaping, which features palm trees, weeping willows, exotic flowers, waterfalls, and koi ponds. This tropical theme is continued indoors. The majority of the public areas feature pastel coloring, which is also used in many of the guest rooms.

Aside from the video arcade and the water park, the Tropicana primarily caters to an adult clientele, offering classic Las Vegas–style shows, yet relatively inexpensive rooms for a resort property on the Strip. Overall, the property offers comfort and quality accommodations, but nothing overly luxurious or fancy.

Guest Room Accommodations

Most of the guest rooms at the Tropicana are located in two different towers—the Paradise Tower and the Island Tower. There are also Garden Rooms, located in a series of smaller, three-story buildings.

Paradise Tower offers what the resort's management calls "premium rooms," which are located closest to the casino. Each of these rooms contains a refrigerator, iron, ironing board, in-room safe, hair dryer, and TV (with pay-per-view movies). The rooms face north and south of the Strip and contain either one king-size bed or two queen-size beds.

Rooms in the Island Tower are considered "deluxe accommodations" and are located closer to the pool and convention area of the resort. These rooms contain many of the same amenities as rooms in the Paradise Tower and have one king-size bed (with a pullout sofa) or two queen-size beds.

The Garden Rooms are in smaller, three-story buildings located close to the casino and parking lot. Many of these rooms are close to the pool area, and some offer balconies with views of Tropicana's lovely landscaping.

Fine Dining

In addition to 24-hour room service, the Tropicana offers the following fine-dining restaurants. For reservations, call (702) 739-2222.

Pietro's ($$ / $$$)

Reservations: (702) 739-2222

Open Wednesday through Sunday evenings for dinner only (5:00 to 11:00 P.M.), Pietro's offers a wide selection of entrees, prepared tableside in an intimate setting. Appetizers include Nova Scotia smoked salmon, a

$ = entrees under $10; $$ = under $20; $$$ = over $20

seafood medley, and a Gulf shrimp cocktail. Prior to the main course, a selection of soups and salads are available. Main entrees include chicken, roasted duckling, double cut lamb chops, charbroiled New York steak, filet mignon, and roasted rack of lamb.

Savanna ($$$)

Reservations: (702) 739-2222

Serving steak, pasta, seafood, and chicken dishes from around the world, Savanna is open Tuesday through Saturday for dinner only (5:00 to 11:00 P.M.). Appetizers include lobster cocktail and fresh oysters or clams on the half shell. Soups and salads are also available. Main entrees include angel hair pasta and scampi rock shrimp, tequila chicken breast, basil pesto-crusted roasted rack of lamb, prime New York steak, grilled dry-aged prime rib eye steak, filet mignon and lobster tail, grilled swordfish, and jerk shrimp on a skewer. In addition to offering a large selection of desserts, the menu of specialty drinks, gourmet coffees, fine wines, and cognacs is also impressive.

Mizuno's Japanese Steakhouse ($$ / $$$)

Reservations: (702) 739-2222

This traditional Japanese steakhouse offers a full sushi bar as well as steak, chicken, and seafood dishes prepared and served at your table by highly trained chefs. All entrees include soup, salad, teppanyaki vegetables, steamed rice, shrimp, and ice cream or sherbet for dessert. Mizuno's Japanese Steakhouse is somewhat expensive (meals range in price from $24 to $50); however, people of all ages will enjoy the lively atmosphere, the show that the chefs perform as they prepare the food, and the food itself. An assortment of Japanese beers and other exotic drinks are available (including sake). Open for dinner every night, from 5:00 to 10:45 P.M.

Golden Dynasty ($$)

Reservations: (702) 739-2222

In Las Vegas, most hotels and resorts have a Chinese or Asian restaurant, and the Tropicana is no exception. Golden Dynasty offers a wide selection of traditional Cantonese, Mandarin, and Szechuan entrees as well as

$ = entrees under $10; $$ = under $20; $$$ = over $20

other specialties served in an authentic Chinese atmosphere. Golden Dynasty is located on the casino level of the resort and is open Sunday through Tuesday evenings from 5:00 to 11:00 P.M., as well as Friday and Saturday nights from 5:00 P.M. to midnight.

Casual Dining
Island Buffet ($ / $$)

This classic, Las Vegas–style, all-you-can-eat buffet serves brunch (7:30 A.M. to 1:30 P.M.) and dinner (4:30 to 10:00 P.M.) throughout the week. The dining room overlooks the resort's five-acre garden and pool area. This buffet is known for its all-you-can-eat prime rib and shrimp. No reservations are accepted, so be prepared to wait to be seated during peak meal times.

Coffee Shop ($ / $$)

Open 24 hours a day, the Coffee Shop offers a wide selection of foods, so guests can enjoy a meal or snack, anytime day or night.

Lounges

- The Celebration Lounge & Casino—This newly renovated lounge is located near the front of the casino. It offers a full bar service and ongoing live entertainment.
- The Harbor Bar—Home of the Harbor Bar's Three Tenders, a group of singing bartenders who perform an ongoing set of tunes ranging from country favorites to Frank Sinatra's greatest hits. The Harbor Bar, of course, also offers a full bar service. Margaritas are the house specialty.

Special Attractions

The Tropicana presents a selection of unique shows and attractions, many intended for a mature audience. The Casino Legends Hall of Fame, for

$ = entrees under $10; $$ = under $20; $$$ = over $20

example, gives visitors a detailed look at the history of Las Vegas, while the *Best of The Follies Bergere . . . Sexier Than Ever* show displays classic, Las Vegas–style entertainment, complete with showgirls.

Illusionary Magic of Rick Thomas

Show Times: 2:00 and 4:00 P.M. (except Friday)

Ticket Price: $15.95 per person for a table
$20.95 per person for a booth

Box Office: (702) 739-2411

This magic act, suitable for most ages, features grand illusions, such as showgirls and tigers disappearing before the audience's eyes.

Illusionary Magic of Rick Thomas

Ages Up to 5	Ages 6–15	Ages 16–20	Ages 21 & Up	Senior Citizens
Not Suitable	⚀⚁	⚀⚁	⚀⚁	⚀⚁

Best of The Follies Bergere . . . Sexier Than Ever

Show Times: 8:00 and 10:30 P.M. (except Thursday)

Ticket Prices: $49.75 per person for a table
$59.75 per person for a booth

Las Vegas's longest running show now features big production and dance numbers from past Follies shows, plus new production numbers that the producers boast are "sexier than ever." This is a colorful, upbeat, and fun-filled show, suitable for adults only. It's a traditional Las Vegas–style show, complete with showgirls. People under the age of 16 are not admitted to the show.

Best of The Follies Bergere . . . Sexier Than Ever

Ages Up to 5	Ages 6–15	Ages 16–20	Ages 21 & Up	Senior Citizens
Not Suitable	Not Suitable	⚀⚁	⚀⚁	⚀⚁

The Tropicana's indoor pool features the world's first swim-up blackjack tables. The tables have a special water-proof layout and the drop boxes are heated to dry paper money. Towels are used to keep players' hands and coins dry. There's also a separate swim-up bar that accommo-dates up to 25 people.

The Casino Legends Hall of Fame

Admission: $4 per person ($3 for seniors)

The Tropicana is the home to the largest collection of casino memorabilia ever assembled. The exhibit also pays homage to those who made Las Vegas the gaming and entertainment capital of the world. It traces the evolution of Nevada gaming from its legalized inception in 1931 through present day. Every year, the Casino Legends Hall of Fame honors a new group of individuals whose significant contributions in their respective careers have made an impact on the gaming and entertainment industries of Las Vegas.

Visitors will see exhibits and artifacts from casinos that have been closed for decades, plus get a taste of the newest and most extravagant mega-resorts being built in Las Vegas today. More than seven hundred casinos are represented in the museum. The collection includes hundreds of photographs, audio and video footage, rare antiques, plus 10,000 other items.

The Casino Legends Hall of Fame is open to everyone, but adults who enjoy gambling or who have been coming to Las Vegas over the past few decades will particularly enjoy the displays.

Island Water Park

The Tropicana boasts over five acres of tropically landscaped grounds, pools, lagoons, waterfalls, ponds (containing exotic fish), and exotic birds. Within this area are three swimming pools (the largest of which is 295 feet long and 75 feet wide). There's also a heated indoor pool. The weather determines the months of operation for the outdoor pools.

In the indoor area of the gardens, over twenty-five exotic birds, including flamingos, white swans, black swans, macaws, toucans, and Brazilian parrots, make their home. The overall garden area features over sixty varieties of trees, ground cover, foliage, and flowers.

The Comedy Stop

Show Times: 8:00 and 10:30 P.M. nightly

Ticket Price: Varies

Every night at least two comedians perform at the Comedy Stop. Call (702) 739-2411 for a current lineup.

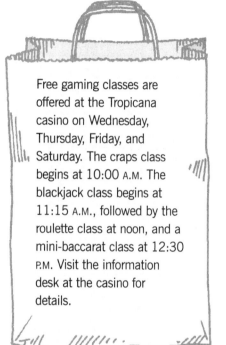

Free gaming classes are offered at the Tropicana casino on Wednesday, Thursday, Friday, and Saturday. The craps class begins at 10:00 A.M. The blackjack class begins at 11:15 A.M., followed by the roulette class at noon, and a mini-baccarat class at 12:30 P.M. Visit the information desk at the casino for details.

Spa, Health Club, and Salon

Although the Tropicana's spa, health club, and salon facilities aren't as fancy as what you'll find at the Luxor, Venetian, or Bellagio, for example, the spa and salon here do offer a full selection of services, and the health club is fully equipped with exercise equipment.

Casino

Tropicana's casino is fully equipped with slot and video poker machines, keno, a race and sports book, plus all of the popular table games. Both high and low limit slots and table games are available, making this casino suitable for all types of gamblers.

Shopping

The Tropicana offers a small selection of shops on-property, however, the resort is located close to the Forum Shops in Caesars Palace as well as plenty of other shopping areas. Located just outside of the main building (in the resort's courtyard area) is a kiosk containing an oxygen bar. This is a unique experience and something you'd typically find in a trendy city like Los Angeles.

Banquet, Function, and Convention Services

Information: (888) 826-8767

The Tropicana offers full banquet, function, and convention facilities as well as an enchanting wedding chapel and an outdoor gazebo where wedding ceremonies are also held. The gazebo weddings are suitable for up to 30 guests, and a variety of different wedding packages are offered.

The Venetian

Theme:	Venice, Italy
Room Rate:	$$$$ ($250+)
Number of Rooms:	Over 6,000 suites
Casino:	120,000 square feet, featuring 122 table games, 2,500 slot and video poker machines, keno, plus a race and sports book, all in a casino that resembles a Venetian palace
Dining:	Twelve upscale restaurants, plus casual dining spots, including Warner Bros. Stage 16 Restaurant
Special Attractions:	The Canyon Ranch SpaClub, Grand Canal Shoppes, and Madame Tussaud's Celebrity Encounter wax museum
Reservations:	(888) 2-VENICE or (702) 414-1000
Web Site:	*www.venetian.com*
Address:	3355 Las Vegas Boulevard South Las Vegas, NV 89109

Overall Resort Rating Based on Amenities and Rates

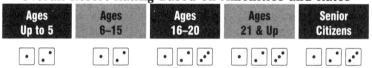

Ages Up to 5	Ages 6–15	Ages 16–20	Ages 21 & Up	Senior Citizens
⚀⚁	⚀⚁	⚀⚁⚂	⚀⚁⚂	⚀⚁⚃

Located on the site of the old Sands Hotel (which was imploded on November 26, 1996), the $1.5-billion Venetian Resort complex is one of the most luxurious, prestigious, and state-of-the-art resorts in Las Vegas. Catering to an upscale (and older) clientele, this is one of the newest resorts on the Strip (it opened May 3, 1999). This resort alone contains more hotel rooms (luxury suites) than the entire island of Bermuda. Upon stepping into the Venetian's main lobby for the first time, the experience can only be described as breathtaking, and the experience gets better from there!

According to the Venetian's management, "The resort appeals to world travelers, business professionals, conventioneers and families—people who enjoy going far beyond the simple 'must see' attractions to experience a 'must see, stay, dine, shop, and enjoy' resort destination."

The Venetian expertly mixes business and pleasure in grand style and luxury, combining the world's largest private convention center with the world's largest hotel, retail, and casino complex—all dedicated to honor the beauty, romance, and visionary spirit of Venice, Italy. Best of all, if you're traveling to Las Vegas from within the United States, no passport is required and everyone speaks English.

To ensure the entire resort retains its truly Italian flair, two historians are on retainer by the hotel, making sure that the famous landmarks that have been re-created throughout the resort maintain their authenticity. St. Mark's Square, Campanile Tower, Ca'd'Oro, Doge's Palace, the Grand Canal, and the Rialto Bridge are among the re-creations.

Guest Room Accommodations

The Venetian is the first Las Vegas resort to offer suites exclusively. Guests enjoy spacious 700-square-foot suites with finely appointed accommodations that include a plush private bed chamber (featuring draped canopies), an oversized 130-square-foot bathroom (finished in Italian marble), and a sunken living room area that includes a convertible sofa, two upholstered chairs, a desk, and a game table. Additionally, the standard suites offer an in-room safe, a fully stocked mini-bar, a dedicated fax machine that doubles as a copier and computer printer, three telephones (with dual lines and data port access), and two 27-inch televisions (with pay-per-view movies and cable programming).

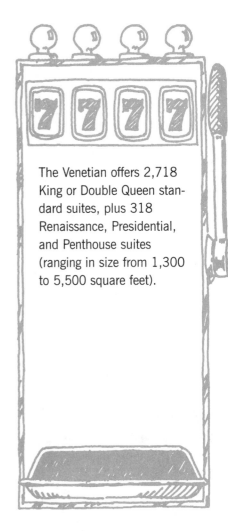

The Venetian offers 2,718 King or Double Queen standard suites, plus 318 Renaissance, Presidential, and Penthouse suites (ranging in size from 1,300 to 5,500 square feet).

These suites are almost double the size of the most luxurious deluxe rooms and basic guest rooms at other resorts and hotels along the Strip.

Yes, you're going to pay more to stay at the Venetian. It's definitely one of the more pricey resorts in Las Vegas, but in this case, the high room rates are worth it.

Fine Dining

The Venetian epitomizes true elegance in terms of accommodations and amenities, so it should come as no surprise that the resort also offers an assortment of fine-dining establishments. Whether strolling through a re-created sixteenth-century streetscape or dining along the replicated Grand Canal, visitors to the Venetian have a passport to a world of culinary delights. Reservations are recommended for these restaurants.

Postrio ($$ / $$$)

Reservations: Not required

This San Francisco bistro created by world-renowned chef Wolfgang Puck offers California cuisine with Asian and Mediterranean influences. Postrio is open daily for lunch and dinner.

Star Canyon ($$ / $$$)

Reservations: Recommended, call (702) 414-3772

Award-winning Texas cuisine is served at this restaurant created by Chef Stephan Pyles, who has been called "an absolute genius in the kitchen" by the *New York Times*. Open daily for lunch from 11:30 A.M. to 2:30 P.M.

Taqueria Canonita ($$ / $$$)

Reservations: Recommended, call (702) 414-3773

This Stephan Pyles restaurant specializes in Mexican cuisine. It is open from 11:00 A.M. to 11:00 P.M. Sunday through Thursday, and 11:00 A.M. to midnight on Friday and Saturday.

Delmonico Steakhouse ($$ / $$$)

Reservations: Recommended, call (702) 414-3737

Guests of this restaurant will enjoy a classic American steak-house menu inspired by Chef Emeril Lagasse. Open daily for lunch and dinner.

Canaletto ($$ / $$$)

Reservations: Recommended, call (702) 733-0070

From the creators of Il Fornaio comes this fine-dining restaurant that serves authentic Northern Italian cuisine from the Veneto region. Open Sunday through Thursday from 11:00 A.M. to midnight, and Friday and Saturday from 11:00 A.M. to 1:00 A.M.

$ = entrees under $10; $$ = under $20; $$$ = over $20

Lutèce ($$ / $$$)

Reservations: Not required

This upscale restaurant specializes in traditional French cuisine. Open daily for lunch and dinner and located on the casino level of the resort, Lutèce offers both indoor and outdoor seating.

Pinot Brasserie ($$ / $$$)

Reservations: Recommended, call (702) 414-8888

Modeled after the famed Los Angeles eatery created by Joachim Splichal, this bistro offers an assortment of Italian and French dishes, plus a large wine menu. Open for lunch and dinner.

Royal Star ($$ / $$$)

Reservations: Not required

Master Hong Kong chefs combine ancient traditions with modern creativity to offer California Chinese cuisine at its best. Located along Restaurant Row on the casino level, the Royal Star is open daily from 9:00 A.M. to midnight.

Valentino ($$ / $$$)

Reservations: Recommended, call (702) 414-3000

This restaurant is modeled after Piero Selvaggio's famed Italian restaurant known for its regional dishes, Valentino's Los Angeles, named one of the best Italian restaurants in America. Located along Restaurant Row on the casino level. The Wine Bar & Grill is open from 11:30 A.M. to 11:00 P.M. daily.

Zeffirino ($$ / $$$)

Reservations: Recommended, call (702) 414-3500

Fine Italian cuisine, presented by chef-to-the-stars Paolo "Zeffirino" Belloni is served here. House specialties include seafood with an Italian flair, such as filet of sole Piccola, lobster tail, and grilled fish. Located canalside at the Grand Canal Shoppes.

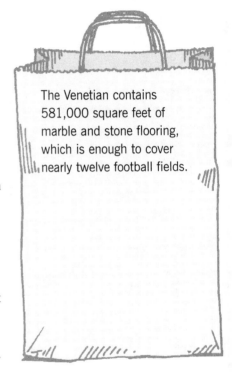

The Venetian contains 581,000 square feet of marble and stone flooring, which is enough to cover nearly twelve football fields.

$ = entrees under $10; $$ = under $20; $$$ = over $20

Casual Dining

Grand Lux Cafe ($)

The Grand Lux Cafe (from the creators of The Cheesecake Factory) offers relaxed dining, good service, and large portions. With over 150 menu items, the cafe is open 24 hours a day and is located at the Grand Canal Shoppes casino level.

Pronto! ($)

If you get hungry while gambling, be sure to stop at Pronto!, a snack shop located next to the race and sports book.

Warner Bros. Stage 16 Restaurant ($ / $$)

Take a step away from Venice and enjoy the excitement of family-oriented dining combined with a touch of movie magic. This restaurant re-creates the atmosphere of the original Warner Bros. movie studio lot, built in 1926. Each area of the restaurant features a different movie theme, from pictures such as *We're in the Money* (1933), *Casablanca* (1943), and *Batman* (1989). The menu offers a blend of Mediterranean, Asian, European, and American dishes. Open daily from 11:00 A.M. to 1:00 A.M.; reservations are not required.

La Strada Food Court ($)

Included in this food court area are San Gennaro Grill, Pizzeria Enzo, Santa Lucia Cafe, Häagen-Dazs, Vico's Burritos, Panda, and Rialto Deli.

Lounges

- Rialto Bar—Open from 11:00 A.M. to 2:00 A.M., this bar presents live piano music every evening.
- La Scena—Live nightly entertainment is provided at this full-service bar, which is open 24 hours a day.
- High-Limit Lounge—Open 24 hours a day, this lounge is located in the High Limits area of the casino.
- Occulus—Open 24 hours a day, this lounge is located in the center of the casino.

$ = entrees under $10; $$ = under $20; $$$ = over $20

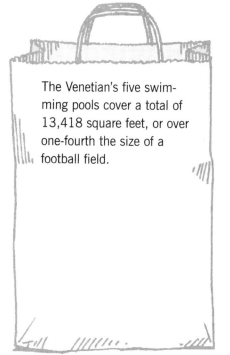

The Venetian's five swimming pools cover a total of 13,418 square feet, or over one-fourth the size of a football field.

Special Attractions

Madame Tussaud's Celebrity Encounter

Hours :   10:00 A.M. to 10:00 P.M.

Tickets: $12.50 per adult, $10.75 for senior citizens, and $10 for children (under 12)

One of London's top visitor attractions has crossed the Atlantic. Madame Tussaud's Celebrity Encounter spans over 28,000 square feet and features over 100 masterfully crafted wax figures portraying many of the all-time great stars who have performed in Las Vegas. Film, television, and sports celebrities, plus Las Vegas icons are all part of this exhibit, which is suitable for people of all ages. All of the clothing worn by the wax figures belonged to the actual celebrity counterparts, which adds to the incredible lifelike appearance of the figures.

The first figure you'll see as you enter this attraction is talk show host Jerry Springer. Visitors are encouraged to touch, photograph, and examine each of the life-size figures closely as they make their way through this attraction at their own pace.

Not only does this attraction feature wax figures of celebrities, it attracts real-life celebrities as well. During one January afternoon, both weatherman Al Roker and Dr. Ruth were spotted walking around.

Madame Tussaud's Celebrity Encounter

Ages Up to 5	Ages 6–15	Ages 16–20	Ages 21 & Up	Senior Citizens
⚀	⚀ ⚁	⚀ ⚁	⚀ ⚁	⚀ ⚁ ⚂

C2K

Tickets and Information: (702) 948-3007

www.clubC2K.com

C2K is a state-of-the-art theater and dance club that features nightly entertainment by singing impressionist Andre-Philippe Gagnon. After midnight, C2K transforms into one of Las Vegas's hottest dance clubs. There is a cigar bar on the mezzanine level as well as a sushi bar.

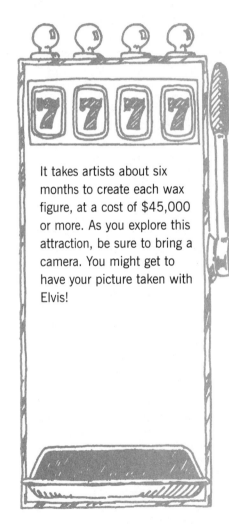

It takes artists about six months to create each wax figure, at a cost of $45,000 or more. As you explore this attraction, be sure to bring a camera. You might get to have your picture taken with Elvis!

One activity offered at SpaClub that you won't find at other Las Vegas–area spas is rock wall climbing. Individuals or groups up to three may enjoy safe, private instruction on the facility's indoor 40-foot wall (limit one person on the wall at any given time). The current rate is $45 for 30 minutes or $85 for 60 minutes, which includes expert instruction.

• • •

Tipping at the ClubSpa is not necessary. Gratuities are included in the price of all services, with the exception of Canyon Ranch Salon services and the Canyon Ranch Cafe.

Theaters of Sensation

Tickets: $7 to $9 per person

Enjoy a variety of adventures when you experience one of these simulator rides that operate throughout the day and evening. Three 3-D shows are presented each hour.

Gondola Rides

Tickets: $10 per adult, $5 per child

Why just walk or dine along the re-created Grand Canal when you can experience an authentic (and extremely romantic) gondola ride. Same-day reservations are required. Visit the loading dock in St. Mark's Square as early in the day as possible to ensure your ride. This is a great way for honeymooners or those celebrating an anniversary or engagement to end a lovely evening after enjoying one of the resort's restaurants.

Canyon Ranch SpaClub

Hours: 5:30 A.M. to 10:00 P.M.

Appointments and information: (702) 414-3600 or (877) 220-2688

www.canyonranch.com

When it comes to world-class spas, several are found in Las Vegas, including the spas at the Luxor and Bellagio. The newest addition to this list is definitely the Canyon Ranch SpaClub at the Venetian.

This 65,000 square-foot-facility is a full-service spa and fitness club located near the five-acre pool deck. The facility offers over one hundred services, including massage and therapeutic bodywork, hydro massage, aloe glaze, herbal wraps, mud, salt, and seaweed treatments, and Watsu.

The SpaClub also offers a complete fitness facility with classes, a wellness center staffed by physicians, nutritionists, and educators, a full-service salon, a retail store, and the Canyon Ranch Cafe (open for breakfast, lunch, and dinner).

The SpaClub is open to anyone over 16; however, resort guests receive priority in appointments for spa treatments and services. All SpaClub cancellations must be received at least 24 hours prior to appointment time or the fee is charged.

A $25 daily pass is available to use the facilities. You'll have access to fitness classes, a body composition analysis, plus use of the fitness center, cold dip, steam room, whirlpool, sauna, and locker rooms for an entire day. Robes, slippers, and complimentary beverages in the spa reception area are provided. Special multi-day or multi-service package deals are also available. Personal fitness training, which covers cardiovascular exercise, strengthening, and stretching, is also offered for $85 for a 50-minute session and $45 for a 25-minute followup session.

Aside from the spa and fitness center, full salon services are also available. All appointments should be made as far in advance as possible.

Casino

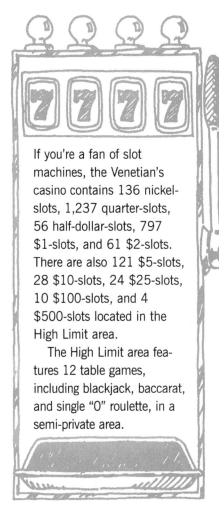

Inside the replicated facade of the Doge's Palace is a 120,000 square foot casino. The 122 table games include craps, blackjack, roulette, Let It Ride, Caribbean Stud poker, Pai Gow poker, mini-baccarat, Pai Gow tile, and a Big Six wheel. A race and sports book, keno lounge, and single-zero roulette are also offered. The casino also offers 2,500 slot machines, including the multi-property, linked progressive games. Special slots unique to the Venetian include "Treasures of Venice," Venetian Dollars, and Gallileo's Gold Dollars.

Like all of the popular casinos in Las Vegas, the Venetian offers a slot club that allows guests to earn points by using their membership card when playing the casino's slot machines. Members can earn complimentary meals, show tickets, discounted room rates, and other prizes.

If you're a fan of slot machines, the Venetian's casino contains 136 nickel-slots, 1,237 quarter-slots, 56 half-dollar-slots, 797 $1-slots, and 61 $2-slots. There are also 121 $5-slots, 28 $10-slots, 24 $25-slots, 10 $100-slots, and 4 $500-slots located in the High Limit area.

The High Limit area features 12 table games, including blackjack, baccarat, and single "0" roulette, in a semi-private area.

Grand Canal Shoppes

Hours: **10 A.M. to 11:00 P.M. (Sunday through Thursday)**
               10 A.M. to midnight (Friday and Saturday)

Sure, you'll find more than 65 elegant boutiques and unique merchandise in the Venetian's Grand Canal Shoppes, but that's only the beginning. Serenading gondoliers and Venetian glassblowers are also

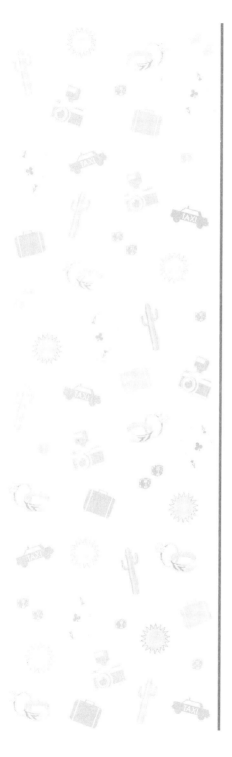

on-hand to lend added authenticity to your shopping experience. This classy indoor mall combines Venetian cobblestone walkways, arched bridges, and winding canals with a mix of unique and beautiful shops. Highlights include:

- BCBG Max Azria—Contemporary women's fashions. With critically acclaimed, award-winning collections, and a loyal following of Hollywood's top celebrities, this fashion powerhouse has evolved into one of the hottest names in the fashion industry today.

- Bernard Passman Gallery—Black coral gallery. For more information about the artistry of Bernard K. Passman, check out the Passman Web site at *www.passman.com.*

- Ca'd'Oro—When the Venetian Hotel was first conceived, Ca'd'Oro signed on to become the pre-eminent jewelry store in Las Vegas, helping set the tone for other stores at the Grand Canal Shoppes.

- Canyon Ranch Living Essentials—A wide variety of beauty products, spa accessories, and sportswear from Canyon Ranch SpaClub.

- Davante—An upscale eyewear shop catering to the fashion conscience.

- Davidoff—One of the world's tonier tobacconists, Davidoff of Geneva has modernized the old-style men's smoking club.

- Erwin Pearl—Tailored to glamorous jewelry, including gold, silver, pearls, Austrian crystal, hand enameling, and glass beading.

- Qualitá Fine Art—This world-class retail fine art gallery presents classical, contemporary, and modern art to the new and seasoned collector.

- Houdini's Magic—Dedicated to preserving Houdini's name and magical artistry for all generations. Items available include Houdini memorabilia such as the handcuffs used in escapes, magic tricks, gags, pranks, and novelties.

- Il Prato—This shop is a respected source of collectible masks and fine paper goods.

- Jimmy Choo—Malaysian-born Jimmy Choo was undoubtedly Princess Diana's preferred shoemaker, thanks to his handmade satin, strappy sandals. When she needed shoes to match a particular outfit, the Princess would call Choo at his office and he would drive to Kensington Palace. Armed with samples of shapes, colors, and fabrics, they would sit together on the floor to make final choices.

- Lladro—The works of the Lladro brothers are considered to be the finest porcelain art of the second half of the twentieth century.

- Mikimoto—The originator of cultured pearls since 1893, Mikimoto specializes in the finest Akoya cultured pearl and South Sea pearl jewelry collections.

- Regis Galerie—Art and antique lovers will discover an ambiance of centuries gone by at Regis Galerie, which specializes in nineteenth century French antiques, period art glass, nineteenth and twentieth century bronzes, oil paintings, chandeliers, and palatial objects of art.

- Tolstoys—A unique store offering fine contemporary and vintage writing instruments, quality time pieces, timeless collectibles, and related accessories for home and office.

Banquet, Function, and Convention Services

Still known as the Sands Expo, this conference center and exposition hall has been expanded to 1.7 million square feet (configurable into up to 110 meeting rooms), making it one of the most modern convention, meeting, and exhibit facilities in Las Vegas. Even before this new expo center was built, over 250 shows and events were booked five years in advance.

In addition to the Sands Expo center, the Venetian also offers the Venetian Ballroom (85,000 square feet) and the Palazzo Ballroom (13,500 square feet). The Venetian contains a wedding chapel and a selection of elegant wedding packages.

CHAPTER FIVE

Smaller Hotels and Resorts in or near Las Vegas

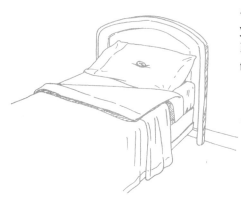

The Las Vegas Strip is always reinventing itself. Mega-resorts now dominate the scene, but several smaller or older hotels and casinos on the Strip deserve mention. This chapter covers those properties as well as resorts under construction. In addition, if you visit Las Vegas, you may want to consider staying in one of the many hotels in the greater Las Vegas area. They're not as convenient as properties on the Strip, but they are sometimes less expensive and less busy.

Aladdin

3667 Las Vegas Boulevard South
Las Vegas, NV 89109
(800) 634-3424
www.aladdincasino.com

Theme:	Arabian Nights
Room Rate:	$$$ / $$$$ ($101+)
Number of Rooms:	2,567 rooms and suites
Casino:	100,000 square feet, featuring over 2,800 slot and video poker machines, 87 gaming tables, and a race and sports book. There is a separate gaming area for high-stakes players, the London Club, a European-style gaming salon.
Dining:	Twenty-one fine-dining and casual restaurants are located in the main resort area and Desert Passage shopping area, including Lombardi's (Italian), Commander's Palace (Creole food), the Blue Note Jazz Club, Bice (Italian), the Macanudo Steakhouse & Club (American-style), and the Beluga Bar (seafood).
Primary Show:	A new musical show will debut in late 2000 or early 2001
Special Attractions:	An all-new mega-resort with a complete array of amenities, activities, and features. Street performers are on-hand to entertain guests throughout the property. The Desert Passage shopping area features

over 130 shops and boutiques. A full spa and health club is available, as well as an outdoor pool located six stories above the Strip.

Overall Resort Rating Based on Amenities and Rates

Ages Up to 5	Ages 6–15	Ages 16–20	Ages 21 & Up	Senior Citizens

According to ancient legend, the mythical Phoenix ruled the skies for 500 years before ending its life in a blaze of glory, only to arise anew from the ashes. On April 27, 1998, with a little help from television star Joan Lunden and 860 charges of dynamite, the historic Aladdin Resort and Casino was reduced to rubble. And like the Phoenix, a newer, stronger Aladdin has risen from the ashes. Designed by the Los Angeles office of RTKL/ID8 and BBGM Interiors of New York, the new Aladdin Resort and Casino features larger-than-life elements taken from the legendary *1,001 Arabian Nights*.

At a cost of over $1.4 billion, the new Aladdin resort was built on the same site as its predecessor, which was totally demolished to make way for this state-of-the-art resort. The resort has 1,878 standard (but spacious) rooms, 466 parlor rooms, and 223 suites. Each room has a marble bathroom, separate shower and bathtub, private toilets, and two phone lines, plus a handful of other amenities.

The Aladdin is one of the only hotels in Las Vegas with a separate hotel lobby, so guests don't have to walk through the casino to get to and from their room. Furthermore, the elevators are positioned so guests never have to walk more than seven doors from the elevator to their room.

The Aladdin also offers a full-service health spa and fitness center, a swimming pool, and a 500,000-square-foot shopping area called the Desert Passage. The resort was created to cater to a wide range of visitors, from business travelers to vacationers, families, and honeymooners. In terms of its offerings it is up-to-par with its neighbors: MGM Grand, New York–New York, the Monte Carlo, Bellagio and Paris Las Vegas.

Barbary Coast

3595 Las Vegas Boulevard South
Las Vegas, NV 89109
(888) 227-2279
www.barbarycoastcasino.com

Theme:	None
Room Rate:	$ / $$ (under $50–$100)
Number of Rooms:	200
Casino:	30,000 square feet, featuring all of the popular table games, a race and sports book, slot and video poker machines, and keno
Dining:	Two fine-dining restaurants and one casual restaurant
Primary Show:	Three bars and a lounge, some offering live musical entertainment
Special Attractions:	The casino and above-average room accommodations at low prices are what attract gamblers and business travelers to this property.

Overall Hotel Rating Based on Amenities and Rates

Ages Up to 5	Ages 6–15	Ages 16–20	Ages 21 & Up	Senior Citizens
Not Suitable	•	•	• •	• •

Although Barbary Coast certainly isn't the largest or most luxurious mega-resort on the Strip, its rooms are extremely spacious and nice, offering a "home-away-from-home" atmosphere. Single and double rooms are available (along with suites), all of which are comfortable and nicely decorated in a Victorian style. The overall property itself, however, is somewhat outdated. It lacks many of the features and amenities commonly found at other hotels and resorts along the Strip.

Barbary Coast caters to adults interested in gambling. It also offers some nice restaurants, including Michael's (open nightly, with seatings at 6:30 and 9:30 P.M.), where the specialties of the house include fresh Dover sole, rack of lamb, Chateaubriand for two, and lamb or veal chops. Reservations are necessary. Call (702) 737-7111.

This hotel is walking distance from Bally's, Caesars Palace, Bellagio, Flamingo Hilton, and other mega-resorts, so guests have plenty of dining, shopping, and entertainment options nearby. What makes this property attractive are its low room rates and location on the Strip.

Casino Royale

3419 Las Vegas Boulevard South
Las Vegas, NV 89109
(800) 854-7666

Theme:	None
Room Rate:	$ / $$ (under $50–$100)
Number of Rooms:	152
Casino:	30,000 square feet, featuring table games, slot and video poker machines, and a sports book
Dining:	Two casual restaurants—Trilussa and Denny's (the ultimate in fast-food establishments)
Primary Show:	None
Special Attractions:	Swimming pool

Overall Hotel Rating Based on Amenities and Rates

Ages Up to 5	Ages 6–15	Ages 16–20	Ages 21 & Up	Senior Citizens
⚀	⚀	⚀	⚀ ⚁	⚀ ⚁

Offering low room rates, Casino Royale is a small, older hotel that is located in the heart of the Strip, which makes it convenient for getting to and from other resort properties and Las Vegas area attractions. Aside from two fast-food restaurants and a bar, and the rather small casino, this property offers little in the way of entertainment. If you have your heart set on staying at a hotel or resort on the Strip, and the mega-resorts are booked solid, Casino Royale is a good alternative for gamblers and budget travelers.

Holiday Inn Boardwalk Casino

3750 Las Vegas Boulevard South
Las Vegas, NV 89109
(800) 635-4581 or (800) HOLIDAY

Theme:	Coney Island midway/carnival
Room Rate:	$ / $$ (under $50–$100)
Number of Rooms:	653
Casino:	33,000 square feet, featuring 650 slots, 20 table games, and a race and sports book
Dining:	Two casual restaurants, and a deli buffet
Primary Show:	*The Dream King Starring Trent Carlini*
Special Attractions:	Outdoor swimming pool

Overall Hotel Rating Based on Amenities and Rates

Ages Up to 5	Ages 6–15	Ages 16–20	Ages 21 & Up	Senior Citizens
⚀	⚀⚁	⚀⚁	⚀⚁	⚀⚁

The Holiday Inn Boardwalk Casino is one of the least expensive hotels on the Strip. Near the Monte Carlo, it is little more than a typical Holiday Inn hotel (as opposed to a resort or mega-resort). The hotel itself offers few amenities other than clean, ordinary rooms, and a small and not at all fancy casino. There are no fine-dining restaurants here.

The good news is that it's possible to get a room for $39 to $59 at the Holiday Inn Boardwalk and the room will be clean. When booking your reservation and checking in, however, insist on a room in what's considered "the new tower." (Also, ask for a room with a view of the Strip. One of the best things about this hotel is that, if your room is facing the right direction, you'll get an awesome view of virtually the entire Strip.)

The hotel's casino is small and offers very low minimum bets ($3) on virtually all of the table games (which include blackjack, poker, Caribbean Stud poker, craps, Let It Ride, "21" Madness, and roulette.

As for the restaurants and buffet (open 24 hours), the prices are very low, but in this case, let's just say you get what you pay for. Basically, if you're looking for an inexpensive but clean place to stay that's conveniently located directly on the Strip, consider the Holiday Inn Boardwalk Casino. At the time this book was written, plans were underway to tear down this hotel (and neighboring shops) to build an all-new mega-resort sometime in the not so distant future.

There's a gift shop in the lobby that sells souvenirs and drinks. Across the street, you'll find a McDonald's, Blimpie, Fat Burger, Pizza Hut, and a Walgreens (open 24 hours). If you're looking for a good, fairly priced meal, consider walking next door to the Monte Carlo and eating at the Cafe, which offers a far better selection than what you'll find at any of the Holiday Inn Boardwalk's dining establishments.

Elvis fans won't want to miss *The Dream King Starring Trent Carlini* show presented nightly in the casino's lounge area. While this one-man show is extremely low budget, Trent Carlini is an extremely talented Elvis impersonator who takes his audience through a musical retrospective of Elvis's career. At $24.95, the ticket price for the show is reasonable. The show is presented nightly at 8:30 P.M.

The Dream King Starring Trent Carlini

Ages Up to 5	Ages 6–15	Ages 16–20	Ages 21 & Up	Senior Citizens
Not Suitable	Not Suitable	⚁ ⚂	⚀ ⚁ ⚃	⚁ ⚂ ⚄

The Frontier

3120 Las Vegas Boulevard South
Las Vegas, NV 89109
(800) 694-6966

Theme:	The Wild West
Room Rate:	$$ ($51–$100)
Number of Rooms:	986
Casino:	41,000 square feet, featuring all of the popular table games, keno, a race and sports book, and slot and video poker machines
Dining:	Three casual-dining restaurants

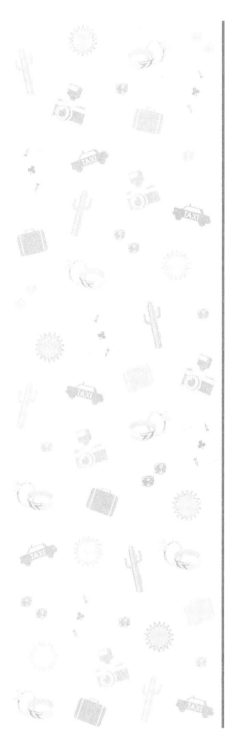

Primary Show: Live country music performed at Gilley's Dancehall and Saloon

Special Attractions: Classic Las Vegas casino, swimming pool, and tennis courts

Overall Hotel Rating Based on Amenities and Rates

Ages Up to 5	Ages 6–15	Ages 16–20	Ages 21 & Up	Senior Citizens
Not Suitable	Not Suitable	⚀	⚀ ⚁	⚀ ⚁

The Frontier was the second casino or gambling hall to open on the Strip, back in 1942. (El Rancho was the first.) Since then, little has been done to stay in touch with the times, although it's been rebuilt three times over the years. This continues to be a classic casino, catering to a clientele that comes to Las Vegas to gamble—not see shows, shop, or experience theme park attractions. The casino is known for offering single-deck blackjack and $3 to $5 minimum bet tables. There's also a bingo room.

Aside from the casino, the property offers a swimming pool and tennis courts, along with three casual restaurants, but no health club, fitness center, or business center. The guest room accommodations are nothing fancy, but adequate.

Stardust

3000 Las Vegas Boulevard South
Las Vegas, NV 89109
(800) 824-6033

Theme:	None
Room Rate:	$$$ ($101–$250)
Number of Rooms:	2,431
Casino:	80,000 square feet, featuring 1,950 slot and video poker machines, gaming tables, a race and sports book, and a keno lounge
Dining:	Five restaurants
Primary Show:	Wayne Newton

Special Attractions: Two swimming pools, a fitness center, and shopping area

Overall Resort Rating Based on Amenities and Rates

Ages Up to 5	Ages 6–15	Ages 16–20	Ages 21 & Up	Senior Citizens
⚀	⚀	⚀	⚀ ⚁	⚀ ⚁

Built in the late 1950s, the Stardust is one of the oldest and most recognizable resorts and casinos on the Strip. With its neon exterior, it's hard to miss this rather large complex, especially at night. While the property has undergone renovations over the years, it continues to maintain itself as a classic Las Vegas–style casino that caters primarily to adults looking to gamble.

The resort has kept a low profile over the past decade or so. When Stardust decided to add a new show, the resort gave Las Vegas legend Wayne Newton a 10-year deal worth an estimated $25 million each year. As a result of this unprecedented deal that kicked off in January 2000, Newton performs exclusively at Stardust for 40 weeks a year in a 920-seat theater that has been remodeled and renamed the Wayne Newton Theater.

In recent years, Stardust has built four new restaurants, a shopping mall, and a 32-story, 1,550-room tower. And in early 2000, plans were underway for a new meeting and convention facility to be built where the resort's original rooms and suites from the 1950s once were.

If you're looking for a classic Las Vegas experience reminiscent of what the Strip was like in "the early years," and your primary interest is in gambling, Stardust offers comfortable accommodations at a reasonable rate.

Other Las Vegas Area Hotels, Motels, and Resorts

In addition to the dozens of well known hotels, motels, and resorts on or near the Strip (or the downtown area), there are hundreds of smaller, often less expensive properties where visitors to the city can stay. Virtually every U.S. hotel chain has a property somewhere in the Las Vegas area.

The following is a sampling of some of the off-Strip hotels, motels, inns, and spas you may want to consider in order to save money, to get better accommodations for your money, or if the resorts along the Strip are totally booked. To learn more about any of these properties, contact them directly, speak with a travel agent, or contact a hotel reservation service.

Alexis Park Resort & Spa	(800) 582-2228	Club De Soleil	(702) 221-0400
Alexis Park Resort	(702) 796-3300	Comfort Inn (5 Las Vegas area locations)	(800) 228-5151
Algiers Hotel	(800) 732-3361	Comfort Inn	(702) 399-1500
Arizona Charlie's Hotel & Casino	(702) 258-5111	Continental Hotel & Casino	(702) 732-8538
Best Inn & Suites	(702) 632-0229	Crowne Plaza Hotel	(800) 227-6963
Best Western Heritage Inn	(702) 798-7736	Days Inn	(702) 731-2111
Best Western Main Street Inn	(702) 382-3455	Del Mar Resort Motel	(702) 384-5775
Best Western Mardi Gras Inn	(702) 731-2020	Econo Lodge	(800) 553-2666
Best Western McCarran Inn	(702) 798-5530	Economy Inn	(702) 384-7540
Best Western	(800) 634-2020	Extended Stay America	(800) 398-7829
Beverly Palms Hotel	(702) 382-7797	Four Points Hotel (Sheraton)	(800) 325-3535
Binion's Horseshoe Hotel & Casino	(702) 382-1600	Four Seasons Hotel	(702) 632-5000
Blaire House	(702) 792-2222	Gold Coast	(888) 402-6278
Boulevard Hotel	(702) 320-2000	Gold Spike Hotel & Casino	(702) 384-8444
Bourbon Street Hotel & Casino	(702) 737-7200	Gold Strike Hotel & Gambling Hall	(702) 477-5000
Budget Suites of America (Boulder Hwy.)	(702) 454-4625	Hacienda Hotel & Casino	(702) 293-5000
Budget Suites of America (Paradise Rd.)	(702) 699-7000	Hampton Inn	(800) 426-7866
Budget Suites of America (Stardust Rd.)	(702) 732-1500	Hampton Inn	(877) 584-6835
Budget Suites of America (W. Tropicana Ave.)	(702) 739-1000	Hawthorn Inn & Suites	(800) 528-1234
Buffalo Bill's Resort & Casino	(702) 679-5160	Holiday Inn	(800) 465-4329
California Hotel–Casino & RV Park	(702) 385-1222	Homestead Guest Studios	(888) 782-9473
Clarion	(800) 252-7466	Howard Johnson Inn	(800) 634-6439

Hyatt Hotels & Resorts	(800) 233-1234	Showboat Hotel, Casino & Bowling Center	(702) 385-9123
La Quinta Inn	(800) 687-6667	Silverton Hotel & Casino	(800) 588-7711
Main Street Station	(702) 387-1896	St. Tropez All Suites Hotel	(800) 666-5400
Marriott Courtyard	(800) 244-3364	Super 8 Motel	(800) 800-8000
Marriott Residence Inn	(800) 244-3364	The New Frontier	(800) 794-8200
Marriott Suites Las Vegas	(800) 244-3364	The Orleans	(800) ORLEANS
Maxim Hotel & Casino	(800) 634-6987	The Reserve Hotel Casino	(702) 558-7000
Nevada Landing Hotel & Casino	(702) 387-5000	ThriftLodge	(800) 525-9055
Polo Towers	(800) 935-2233	Travelodge Las Vegas Strip	(800) 578-7878
Quality Inn	(800) 228-5151	Vacation Village Hotel & Casino	(800) 658-5000
Ramada Inn	(800) 731-6100	Villager Lodge	(800) 429-1074
Sheraton Hotels & Resorts	(800) 325-3535	Westward-Ho Casino	(702) 731-2900
		World Trade Center Hotel	(702) 369-5750

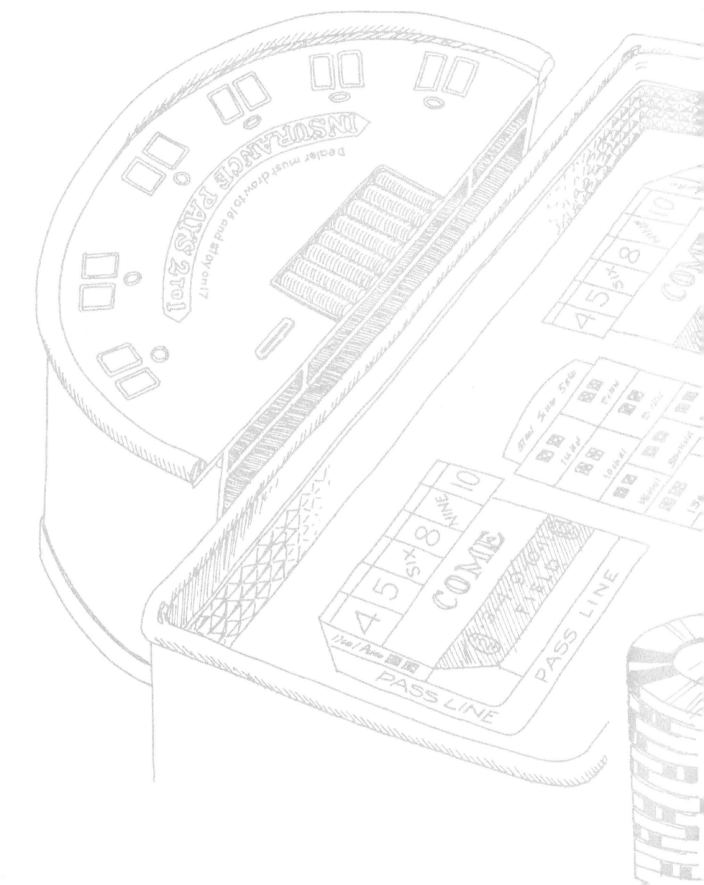

CHAPTER SIX

More Attractions
and Activities

No matter where you're staying in Las Vegas, virtually all of these attractions, shops, activities, and restaurants are a short drive away. Taxi service is available from all of the hotels, resorts, and casinos. As a general rule, taxi drivers should be tipped $1 to $2 for fares under $10 and 15 to 20 percent for higher fares. That is, of course, if you're provided with friendly service. Many of the taxi drivers in Las Vegas are extremely knowledgeable about things to see and do in and around the city, so don't hesitate to ask for their recommendations.

The resorts and hotels on the Las Vegas Strip certainly offer a wide range of activities, attractions, shopping experiences, and restaurants. Nevertheless, as one of the country's top tourist and convention destinations, the Las Vegas area has plenty of other exciting attractions.

Here are a handful of the things to see and do in and around Las Vegas, whether you're traveling alone on business, celebrating a honeymoon or anniversary, or you're on vacation with your children.

Attractions
M&M World

Showcase Mall (next to the MGM Grand)

Ticket Price: $3 per person

Hours: 10:00 A.M. to midnight (Sunday through Thursday)
**   10:00 A.M. to 1:00 A.M. (Friday and Saturday)**

(702) 740-2525

M&M plain chocolate candies have been around since 1941, but only recently have these candies taken on a life of their own—in 3-D computer generated animation, just like their popular TV commercials. Every 20 minutes, visitors can experience a comical 3-D movie starring the popular M&M candies. Visitors take a light-hearted tour of M&M Academy. While this attraction is a glorified commercial for M&M candies, it is thoroughly entertaining as visitors become an "M'bassador of fun." After the movie, guests will find themselves in a colorful M&M store that sells all sorts of unique M&M merchandise and candies.

M&M World

Ages Up to 5	Ages 6–15	Ages 16–20	Ages 21 & Up	Senior Citizens
⚀	⚀ ⚁ ⚄	⚀ ⚁ ⚃	⚀ ⚁	⚀ ⚁

Sega GameWorks

Showcase Mall (next to the MGM Grand)

Hours: 10:00 A.M. to 2:00 A.M. (Sunday through Thursday)

10:00 A.M. to 4:00 A.M. (Friday & Saturday)

(702) 432-4263

www.gameworks.com

Sega GameWorks is a family-oriented, high-tech entertainment complex containing over 300 video games, Internet services, restaurants, pool tables, and the world's tallest free-standing rock climbing structure. Sega GameWorks is a joint-venture between DreamWorks, Sega, and Universal Studios.

The best time to visit this complex is during a weekday afternoon. Video games, pinball machines, and attractions cost $.50 to $3. However, a special card can be purchased offering unlimited play on all video games for a flat fee of $20.

Sega GameWorks is a great place to celebrate a child's birthday party or for teenagers and young adults to spend several hours having fun, eating, and drinking (if they're of legal age). The biggest drawback to this state-of-the-art arcade is the price. It's expensive! Yet, if you want to check out the latest video game arcade machines and virtual reality simulators, chances are you'll find them at Sega GameWorks first.

Ages Up to 6	Ages 6–15	Ages 16–20	Ages 21 & Up	Senior Citizens
⚀	⚀ ⚁ ⚂	⚀ ⚁ ⚂	⚀ ⚁	⚀

Activities

Many people who visit Las Vegas are content relaxing and being low-key. For everyone else, the city offers an incredible selection of thrilling, interactive activities. Sure, some of the activities listed in this section can be a bit intense and aren't for everyone, but if you're looking for something exciting to do (like bungy jump, skydive, or drive a racing car), you'll find it in Las Vegas.

As you'd probably guess, many of these activities aren't suitable for young children and senior citizens.

SkyDiveLasVegas.com

(800) U-SKYDIV or (702) 293-1860

Take a 20-minute lesson and then jump freefall tandem from an airplane flying 120 to 200 m.p.h. Originates from the Boulder City Airport (20 minutes from Las Vegas Strip). Shuttle service to the airport is available. This is an actual skydiving experience, and recommended for people with a daredevil streak within them.

SkyDiveLasVegas.com

Ages Up to 5	Ages 6–15	Ages 16–20	Ages 21 & Up	Senior Citizens
Not Suitable	Not Suitable	⚀ ⚁ ⚂	⚀ ⚁ ⚂	Not Suitable

AJ Hackett Bungy Las Vegas

810 Circus Circus Drive
(702) 385-4321
www.ajhackett.com.au/index.html

Located near Circus Circus, the operators of this bungy jumping facility call it "the safest gamble in town." Participants must be over the age of 13 and weigh at least 90 pounds. Anyone with enough guts to travel to the top of the 171-foot platform (17 stories), is given prejump instructions and fitted with a harness. The actual jump lasts just four seconds, but for most people, that's more thrill than they have experienced in a lifetime. No reservations are required. The company often runs special promotions and coupons, offering $5 off a first jump or a discounted second jump. Ask for details.

AJ Hackett Bungy Las Vegas

Ages Up to 5	Ages 6–15	Ages 16–20	Ages 21 & Up	Senior Citizens
Not Suitable	Not Suitable	⚀ ⚁ ⚂	⚀ ⚁ ⚂	Not Suitable

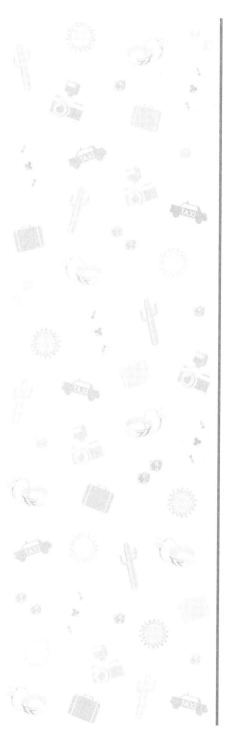

Wet 'n Wild

Hours:	Open daily starting at 10:00 A.M.
	Closing time varies based on season
	(6:00 to 10:00 P.M.)

2601 Las Vegas Boulevard South
Las Vegas, NV 89109
(702) 871-7811
www.wetnwild.com/las-vegas

Wet 'n Wild is one of America's most exhilarating water parks. The Las Vegas location is along the Las Vegas Strip. Wet 'n Wild has more than a dozen ways to beat the heat, from thrilling water slides to other more relaxing rides for swimmers of all ages. Las Vegas visitors can cool off in Wet 'n Wild's nearly 1.5 million gallons of fresh water, maintained at comfortable temperatures and circulated through a state-of-the-art filtering system.

Admission is $25.95 per person for people over age 10 ($19.95 for children). A season pass is available for $95. When the temperature gets hot in the summer months, Wet 'n Wild offers a perfect family destination where everyone can cool down.

Wet 'n Wild				
Ages Up to 5	**Ages 6–15**	**Ages 16–20**	**Ages 21 & Up**	**Senior Citizens**
⚀	⚀ ⚁ ⚂	⚀ ⚁ ⚂	⚀ ⚁	⚀

CART Driving 101 "The Official Driving Experience of CART"

6915 Speedway Boulevard
Las Vegas, NV 89115
(877) CART-101
www.driving101.com

Ever dream of speeding around a race track? CART Driving 101 offers you the opportunity to ride in or drive an open wheel, full-size 550 horsepower Champ Car. Top speeds reach 140 to 170 m.p.h. Prices for this experience range from $199 (which allows participants to ride six miles as a passenger with a professional instructor in a specially designed two-seat purpose-built Champ Car) to over $3,000 (for a two-day driving program

The following weight restrictions apply to anyone interested in indoor skydiving: For males over 6 feet tall, the maximum weight is 230 pounds. For males under 6 feet, the maximum weight is 220 pounds. For females over 6 feet tall, the maximum weight is 200 pounds. For women 5 feet 6 inches to 6 feet, the maximum weight is 180 pounds. For women under 5 feet 6 inches, the maximum weight is 160 pounds.

that includes 120 miles on the track, concentrating on more advanced racing techniques and highlighted by an individual, on-track session with an instructor). Just pick a date on your calendar and sign up in advance.

CART Driving 101

Ages Up to 5	Ages 6–15	Ages 16–20	Ages 21 & Up	Senior Citizens
Not Suitable	Not Suitable	⚀ ⚁ ⚂	⚀ ⚁ ⚂	Not Suitable

FlyAway Indoor Skydiving

Hours: 10:00 A.M. to 7:00 P.M. (Monday through Saturday)
10:00 A.M. to 5:00 P.M. (Sunday)

200 Convention Center Drive
Las Vegas, NV 89109
(702) 731-4768
www.FlyAwayIndoorSkydiving.com

Experience the thrill of skydiving indoors for $35 per person. This includes a 20-minute training class, all of the necessary equipment and a 15-minute flight session shared by five flyers. The actual flying time for each person is about 3 minutes.

Located near the Las Vegas Convention Center, this complex allows people to experience the thrill of "Tunnel Flying" (a.k.a. indoor skydiving) for a relatively low cost. All necessary equipment is provided, and the overall experience (including training) takes about one hour. For an additional $15, a videotape of your experience can be purchased.

Indoor skydiving is designed to create the feeling of regular skydiving without much of the risk. The facility uses a large electric motor and propeller that can create wind speeds up to 120 miles per hour. The skills needed to fly the tunnel are basically the same skills needed to skydive.

Training classes are scheduled every 30 minutes, so advanced reservations aren't required during most times. If you have limited time, however, it's best to schedule your visit in advance.

FlyAway Indoor Skydiving

Ages Up to 5	Ages 6–15	Ages 16–20	Ages 21 & Up	Senior Citizens
Not Suitable	⚀ ⚁	⚀ ⚁ ⚂	⚀ ⚁ ⚂	Not Suitable

United Artists / Showcase Movie Theaters

Showcase Mall (next to the MGM Grand)
(702) 225-4828

You'll find many of the latest box office hits playing at this eight-screen theater. Ticket prices are $7.50 (adults) or $4 (children and matinees). All theaters are equipped with THX sound. Movies typically begin around 10:30 A.M. and run throughout the day and night. Midnight movies are shown nightly.

World of Coca-Cola

Showcase Mall (next to the MGM Grand)

Hours: 10:00 A.M. to midnight (Sunday through Thursday)
10 A.M. to 1:00 A.M. (Friday and Saturday)

Ticket Price: $3.50
(800) 720-COKE or (702) 270-5953

This is an interactive exhibit featuring everything that's Coca-Cola. You'll see memorabilia and clips of classic commercials, see how Coca-Cola is made (and bottled), and have the chance to taste different flavored sodas made by Coca-Cola and sold throughout the world. This is an attraction suitable for people of all ages, but it will be of particular interest to children and teens. Yes, this is basically a hands-on commercial for Coca-Cola, but anyone who enjoys drinking the soda will probably find this self-guided exhibit interesting. Learn the history of the world's most popular soft drink, which was created back in 1886 and is currently available in over two hundred countries.

World of Coca-Cola

Ages Up to 5	Ages 6–15	Ages 16–20	Ages 21 & Up	Senior Citizens
Not Suitable	⚁	⚁	⚁	⚀

Cowboy Trail Rides (horseback riding)

(702) 387-2457

Horseback riding tours, sunset rides, and western barbecue packages are available. Ground transportation to and from major Las Vegas area hotels is provided. Call for details and pricing.

Cowboy Trail Rides

Ages Up to 5	Ages 6–15	Ages 16–20	Ages 21 & Up	Senior Citizens
Not Suitable	⚀ ⚁ ⚂	⚀ ⚁ ⚂	⚀ ⚁ ⚂	⚀

The Desert Inn Golf Club enjoys the unique distinction of being the only golf course on the Las Vegas Strip, as well as the sole resort course in the world to have annually hosted PGA, LPGA, and Senior PGA tour events (the PGA's Las Vegas Invitational, the Senior PGA's Las Vegas Senior Classic, and the LPGA PageNet Tour Championship).

Bowling Alleys (Las Vegas Area)

Gold Coast

4000 W. Flamingo
(702) 367-4700

The Orleans

4500 W. Tropicana Avenue
(702) 365-7400

Sam's Town

5111 Boulder Highway
(702) 454-8022

Santa Fe

4949 Rancho Drive North
(702) 658-4995

Showboat

2800 Fremont Street
(702) 385-9153

Las Vegas Area Golf Clubs/Courses

Angel Park Golf Club

100 S. Rampart Boulevard
(702) 254-4653

Black Mountain Country Club

500 Greenway Road
(702) 565-7933

Callaway Golf Center

Las Vegas Boulevard at Sunset Road
(702) 896-4100

Desert Inn Golf Club
Located behind the former Desert Inn
(702) 733-4290

Desert Rose Golf Course
5483 Clubhouse Drive
(702) 431-4653

Las Vegas Municipal Golf Course
4300 Washington Boulevard
(702) 646-3003

Las Vegas National
1911 E. Desert Inn Road
(702) 734-1796

Las Vegas Paiute Golf Course
10325 Nu-wav Kaiv Boulevard
(702) 658-1400

The Legacy
130 Par Excellence Drive
(702) 897-2187

Los Prados Country Club
150 Los Prados
(702) 645-5696

Painted Desert Golf Club
5555 Painted Mirage Way
(702) 645-2570

Palm Valley
9201 Del Webb Boulevard
(702) 363-4373

Reflection Bay Golf Club at Lake Las Vegas Resort
1605 Lake Las Vegas Parkway
(702) 740-GOLF

Rhodes Ranch Country Club
20 S. Rhodes Ranch Parkway
(702) 740-4114

Shopping

For people who were born to shop, Las Vegas is a veritable mecca of exciting stores and boutiques. The one mall that's a must-see Las Vegas destination is the Forum Shops at Caesars Palace. This mall offers unique shops combined with one-of-a-kind attractions, plus a wide range of restaurants. No matter what you're shopping for, however, chances are you'll find it at one or more of the following shopping malls.

Beltz Factory Outlet World

7400 Las Vegas Boulevard South
(702) 896-5599

Hours: 10:00 A.M. to 9:00 P.M. (Monday through Saturday)
                10:00 A.M. to 6:00 P.M. (Sunday)

This indoor mall is several miles from the Las Vegas Strip. It offers 155 outlet stores under one roof, including Levi's, Jones New York, Calvin Klein, Reebok, and Esprit. Save up to 75 percent off suggested retail prices. This outlet mall is no different than one you'd find in any other city, which means it is nothing fancy.

The Fashion Show Mall

Spring Mountain Road (across from Treasure Island)
(702) 369-0704
www.thefashionshow.com

Hours: 10:00 A.M. to 9:00 P.M. (weekdays)
                10:00 A.M. to 7:00 P.M. (Saturday)
                Noon to 6:00 P.M. (Sunday)

This upscale mall is located on the Las Vegas Strip and is walking distance from several popular resorts. The indoor mall features over 145 specialty shops and restaurants, plus Saks Fifth Avenue, Neiman Marcus, Macy's, Dillard's, and Robinsons–May.

The Forum Shops at Caesars

3500 Las Vegas Boulevard South
(702) 893-4800

Hours: 10:00 A.M. to 11:00 P.M. (Sunday through Thursday)
                10:00 A.M. to midnight (Friday and Saturday)

This is one of the most popular malls in the world (not to mention one of the most beautiful). Visitors can easily spend an entire afternoon and/or evening exploring this mall, with over one hundred upscale stores and restaurants, plus a handful of popular chain stores and other attractions (such as the IMAX motion simulator/movie experience, *Race to Atlantis*). A complete description of the Forum Shops at Caesars can be found in Chapter 4.

Fashion Outlet Las Vegas

(702) 847-1400

Hours: 10:00 A.M. to 9:00 P.M. (Monday through Saturday)
                10:00 A.M. to 8:00 P.M. (Sunday)

You'll find over one hundred world-class designer outlets in one location, approximately 30 minutes south of Las Vegas (on I-15). A shuttle service is available from the New York–New York hotel and casino. Save 20 to 70 percent every day. Designers include Bally, Banana Republic, Gap, J. Crew, Kenneth Cole, Timberland, Versace, and Williams Sonoma.

Theme Dining

Many Las Vegas resorts offer theme-dining experiences on property, such as the WCW-Nitro Grill (Excalibur), Planet Hollywood (the Forum Shops), and the Rainforest Cafe (New York–New York). Located in a stand-alone location, however, is the Harley Davidson Cafe, which is the motorcycle enthusiast's answer to the Hard Rock Cafe.

Like all major cities, Las Vegas offers several clubs and bars that cater to a gay/lesbian clientele, such as the Gipsy, 4605 Paradise Road, (702) 733-9677, or ANGELS/LACE, 4633 Paradise Road, (702) 791-0100. For a more complete listing of these bars and clubs, point your Web browser to:

- *www.gayworldguide. com/lasvegas/bars.htm*
- *www.five-one.com /lvuc/alternative.html*
- *www.gayvegas.com*

Harley-Davidson Cafe ($$)

3725 Las Vegas Boulevard South
Las Vegas, NV 89109
(702) 740-4555

Located near the MGM Grand, New York–New York, and Monte Carlo hotels, the Harley-Davidson Cafe can't be missed from the outside. The building is decorated with a 28-foot-high, 15,000-pound Harley-Davidson Heritage Softail Classic bike. Once you step inside the massive two-story structure, you'll see dozens of Harley-Davidson motorcycles on display, along with hundreds of pictures and pieces of memorabilia.

This restaurant celebrates the heritage of Harley-Davidson's 90-plus year history by offering a festive, family dining atmosphere. There's also a full bar and two Harley-Davidson merchandise shops.

The menu offers a range of appetizers (like the delicious Kellogg's Corn Flakes coated chicken fingers), as well as soups, salads, and a large selection of entrees (ranging in price from $8.95 to $16.95). Burgers, BBQ items, fajitas, sandwiches, and desserts round out the extensive menu. The quality of the food and the service is topnotch.

The Harley-Davidson Cafe offers an excellent value, very much like a Hard Rock Cafe or Planet Hollywood but with a motorcycle theme. If you are interested in motorcycles, this is definitely one place you'll want to dine while visiting Las Vegas. The only other Harley-Davidson Cafe is in New York City.

Dive!

The Fashion Show Mall
(702) 369-3483

Moviemaker Steven Spielberg helped conceive this unique restaurant concept, which takes diners on an undersea voyage. The menu is diverse and full bar service is available. Another excellent family-oriented dining option.

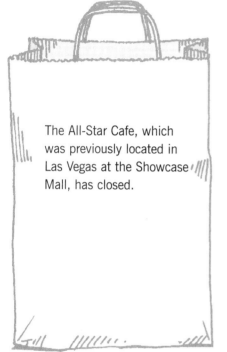

The All-Star Cafe, which was previously located in Las Vegas at the Showcase Mall, has closed.

$ = entrees under $10; $$ = under $20; $$$ = over $20

Museums

Virtually every city in America has museums that promote the city's or state's heritage. Las Vegas is no different. In addition to more traditional museums, however, Las Vegas offers very unique museums, such as the Elvis-A-Rama Museum, Guinness World of Records Museum, King Tut's Tomb & Museum, and Liberace Museum & Foundation. The following is a listing of museums you'll find in the Las Vegas area. Many offer self-paced exhibits or recorded audio tours.

Boulder City / Hoover Dam Museum

1301 Arizona Street
Boulder City
(702) 294-1988
Hours: 10:00 A.M. to 5:00 P.M. (Monday through Saturday)
            Noon to 5:00 P.M. (Sunday)

Clark County Heritage Museum

1830 S. Boulder Highway
(702) 455-7955
Hours: 9:00 A.M. to 4:30 P.M. (daily)

Elvis-A-Rama Museum

3401 Industrial Road
(702) 309-7200
Hours: 11:00 A.M. to 6:00 P.M. (daily)
Admission: $14.95 per person

If you're an Elvis fan, you'll enjoy seeing this $3-million exhibit featuring original Elvis memorabilia. This is an educational, yet entertaining look at the life and career of Elvis Presley (a.k.a. "The King"). A free tribute show starring performer Tim Welch as Elvis is presented daily at noon, 2:00 P.M., 4:00 P.M., and 5:00 P.M.

Guinness World of Records Museum

2780 Las Vegas Boulevard
(702) 792-3766
Hours: 9:00 A.M. to 6:00 P.M. (daily)

King Tut's Tomb & Museum

Luxor Hotel

(702) 626-4000

Hours: 9:00 A.M. to 11:00 P.M. (daily)

Las Vegas Natural History Museum

900 N. Las Vegas Boulevard

(702) 384-3466

Hours: 9:00 A.M. to 4:00 P.M. (daily)

Liberace Museum & Foundation

1775 E. Tropicana

(702) 798-5595

Hours: 10:00 A.M. to 5:00 P.M. (Monday through Saturday)
1:00 to 5:00 P.M. (Sunday)

See the glittering costumes worn by this superstar performer, along with his personal jewelry collection, pianos, exotic cars, and other belongings. This is a must-see attraction for Liberace's fans.

Lied Discovery Children's Museum

833 N. Las Vegas Boulevard

(702) 382-3445

Hours: 10:00 A.M. to 5:00 P.M. (Tuesday through Sunday)

Marjory Barick Museum of Natural History

4505 S. Maryland Parkway at UNLV

(702) 895-3381

Hours: 8:00 A.M. to 4:45 P.M. (Monday through Friday)
10:00 A.M. to 2:00 P.M. (Sunday)

Nevada State Museum

700 Twin Lakes Drive

(702) 486-5205

Hours: 9:00 A.M. to 5:00 P.M. daily

Titanic: The Exhibit

Rio Suite Hotel & Casino

3700 West Flamingo

(702) 252-0493

Hours: 10:00 A.M. to 10:00 P.M. (daily)

This exhibit, which has toured the country, chronicles the sinking of the *Titanic* and showcases over two hundred actual artifacts retrieved from the wreck site. Through 2001, it has found a home at the Rio. The ticket price is $15.95 (adults), $14.95 (seniors), and $9.95 (children). The exhibit, however, may not interest children under sixteen because it is presented in a formal, documentary-style fashion (via an audio tour).

Treasures of Mandalay Bay Museum

3950 Las Vegas Boulevard
(702) 632-6140
Hours: 9:00 A.M. to midnight (daily)

This museum features a $40-million permanent collection of rare gold and silver coins, colorful and unique Old West bank notes, and historic Nevada mining town memorabilia, such as nineteenth-century gold bars and assay receipts. The museum is open daily and is located off Mandalay Bay's casino floor, across from Bali Trading Company. Admission is $6 per person (children under 12 are free). Guests are free to roam throughout the 1,100-square-foot museum area at their leisure. For people who enjoy money—collecting it, saving it, spending it, or simply learning its history—this museum offers an interesting way to spend a few hours.

Sightseeing Tours: Las Vegas, the Grand Canyon, and Hoover Dam

Whether you'd like to travel by car, bus, all-terrain vehicle, helicopter, small plane, or blimp, there are literally dozens of tour companies that provide unique and exciting adventures based in and around the Las Vegas, Hoover Dam, and Grand Canyon areas. In addition to contacting the tour companies listed here, be sure to speak with the concierge at your hotel who should be able to recommend a tour package that meets your interests and budget. The tours listed here are some of the more exotic and exciting sightseeing experiences available.

For additional ideas about what to see and do in Las Vegas, be sure to pick up a complimentary copy of *What's On: The Las Vegas Guide* (*www.ilovelasvegas.com*), *24/7 Magazine* (*www.taxitops.com*), and/or *ShowBiz Weekly* (*www.vegas.com*). These publications are distributed at most of the hotels, motels, and casinos in the Las Vegas area. They list current shows (including special performances, concerts, and limited engagements), plus information and reviews of restaurants located outside of the resorts and casinos.

Papillon Grand Canyon Helicopters

245 E. Tropicana Ave. South, Suite 121
Las Vegas, NV 89109
(888) 635-7272 or (702) 736-7243
www.papillon.com

Since 1995, this tour company has been providing tourists with truly memorable helicopter tours of the Las Vegas, Grand Canyon, and Hoover Dam areas. The company operates over 30 single-engine, turbine-powered helicopters that carry six passengers each and travel at a cruising speed of 110 to 130 m.p.h.

The basic "Las Vegas in a Whole New Light" tour includes a breathtaking aerial trip along the Strip. The entire tour lasts approximately one hour, but the actual flight time is about 15 minutes. (Price: $68 per person—and well worth it!) Other tour packages are available, including an absolutely incredible tour of the Grand Canyon, which will be remembered for a lifetime. All of the tours offered by Papillon are guaranteed to be memorable, exciting, and very safe. If you've never ridden in a helicopter, the Las Vegas area offers some of the best scenery around.

Papillon Helicopter Tours

Ages Up to 5	Ages 6–15	Ages 16–20	Ages 21 & Up	Senior Citizens
Not Suitable	▫▫▫	▫▫▫	▫▫▫	▫▫▫

Las Vegas Helicopters, Inc.

3712 Las Vegas Boulevard South
(702) 736-8954
www.lvhelicopters.com

Beyond its nightly Las Vegas Strip rides and tours of the Grand Canyon, one of the best things about this helicopter tour company is that the helipad is located right on the Strip. Fly over the sea of colored lights and excitement that is Las Vegas at night. Grand Canyon tours cost $299 to $599 per person.

Las Vegas Helicopter Tours

Ages Up to 5	Ages 6–15	Ages 16–20	Ages 21 & Up	Senior Citizens
Not Suitable	⚀⚁⚂	⚀⚁⚂	⚀⚁⚂	⚀⚁⚂

Las Vegas.com Airship (blimp rides)

(877) LV-BLIMP or (702) 646-2888

www.vegas.com

Yes, a helicopter tour is a memorable way to see Las Vegas, but if you want something a bit more unusual . . . take a blimp ride. Flights begin daily at sunset and operate hourly. Blimp rides aren't cheap ($179 per person, Monday through Thursday, and $199 Friday and Saturday), but the experience is well worth it. A special daily sunset cruise is also offered for $229 per person.

Space is limited so advanced reservations are definitely required. The blimp operates from the Vision Air Terminal at the North Las Vegas Airport. A complimentary shuttle service is offered to and from your hotel.

Las Vegas.com Airship Rides

Ages Up to 5	Ages 6–15	Ages 16–20	Ages 21 & Up	Senior Citizens
Not Suitable	⚀⚁⚂	⚀⚁⚂	⚀⚁⚂	⚀⚁⚂

Gray Line Bus Tours

4020 East Lone Mountain Road
North Las Vegas, NV 89031
(800) 634-6579
www.pcap.com/grayline.htm
www.grayline.com

Established in 1910, Gray Line Worldwide is one of the largest sightseeing tour companies in the world. While its bus tours of Las Vegas and other sights in Nevada are informative and an excellent value, due to their

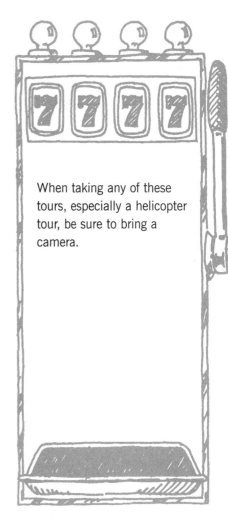

When taking any of these tours, especially a helicopter tour, be sure to bring a camera.

duration, children tend to get bored quickly, so be sure to bring along activities for them to do on the bus. These tours are designed more for adults and seniors.

Gray Line Bus Tours

Ages Up to 5	Ages 6–15	Ages 16–20	Ages 21 & Up	Senior Citizens
Not Suitable	·	· ··	· ·· ···	· ·· ···

The following are three of the eight bus tours currently available from Gray Line:

- Grand Canyon Indian Country Tour (10-hour duration)—Leaves at 7:30 A.M. Your pioneer-attired guide will narrate the history of the Las Vegas Valley and describe the scenic mesas, desert landscapes, and ancient Joshua tree forest. You'll also visit Indian reservation terrain, including the Hualapai Indian Reservations where your Indian guide will take you on a ground tour of his ancient land of the Grand Canyon. A BBQ lunch is served at Guano Point. Prices: $119 (adults), $109 (children), $114 (seniors).

- Hoover Dam Shuttle (transportation only / several hours or all-day duration)—Leaves daily at 8:30 A.M., 10:30 A.M., 12:30 P.M., and 2:30 P.M. The Gray Line driver and guide narrates the ride to Hoover Dam. Last shuttle back to Las Vegas departs at 5:00 P.M. Prices: $19 (adults), $15 (children), and $17 (seniors).

- Neon and Lights Tour (3.5 hour-duration)—Departs nightly at 6:30 P.M. This is a guided tour of Las Vegas after dark. The tour includes seeing the evening roadside shows of mega-resorts and full narration as the bus explores Las Vegas, the Neon City. Riders also get to visit the Fremont Street Experience (light show) in downtown Las Vegas. Plus, you'll see the Tropicana Hotel Legends museum. Prices: $28 (adults), $26 (children), and $26 (seniors).

To save $5 per tour ticket when booking a Gray Line tour, make your reservation with a major credit card on its Web site: *www.pcap.com/ grayline.htm*. Members of AAA or CAA are entitled to a 10-percent discount on any Gray Line tour of one day or less, in the United States. AARP members are also offered a 10-percent discount. Members should present a valid membership card at the time of purchase to the Gray Line office or to a designated AAA travel agent. A maximum of six discounts per purchase for immediate family members are permitted. Other special offers or discounts may not be used in conjunction with the AAA discount.

ATV Action Tours

Reservations (888) 288-5200

www.actiontours.com

ATV Action Tours allows adventurers to see a part of Las Vegas that few choose to experience—the southwestern Nevada desert driving an off-road all-terrain vehicle.

- The Bitter Springs and Valley of Fire State Park Tour is a six-hour excursion that begins daily at 7:00 A.M. It includes a 28-mile off-road trek on the Moapa Indian Reservation. Price: $109 per person.
- The Mt. Charlson Adventure is a three-and-a-half-hour adventure that begins daily at 8:00 A.M. and 1:00 P.M. Price: $65 per person.
- The four-hour Hoover Dam Tour kicks off at 8:00 A.M. and 1:00 P.M. daily. Price: $69 per person.

Several other exciting tours are also offered by ATV Action Tours.

ATV Action Tours

Ages Up to 5	Ages 6–15	Ages 16–20	Ages 21 & Up	Senior Citizens
Not Suitable	⚀ ⚁ ⚂	⚀ ⚁ ⚂	⚀ ⚁ ⚂	⚀ ⚁

If you'd like to experience a white water rafting adventure, ask about their one-, two-, or three-day tours, ranging in price from $369 to $775 per person. There's also a Sand Buggy Adventure and a Waverunner Adventure package available.

Children under five years of age are not permitted on these tours. People under 18 must be accompanied by a parent or guardian.

Everything® **Get Published Book**
$12.95, 1-58062-315-8

Everything® **Get Ready For Baby Book**
$12.95, 1-55850-844-9

Everything® **Golf Book**
$12.95, 1-55850-814-7

Everything® **Guide to New York City**
$12.95, 1-58062-314-X

Everything® **Guide to Walt Disney World®, Universal Studios®, and Greater Orlando**
$12.95, 1-58062-404-9

Everything® **Guide to Washington D.C.**
$12.95, 1-58062-313-1

Everything® **Herbal Remedies Book**
$12.95, 1-58062-331-X

Everything® **Homeselling Book**
$12.95, 1-58062-304-2

Everything® **Homebuying Book**
$12.95, 1-58062-074-4

Everything® **Home Improvement Book**
$12.95, 1-55850-718-3

Everything® **Internet Book**
$12.95, 1-58062-073-6

Everything® **Investing Book**
$12.95, 1-58062-149-X

Everything® **Jewish Wedding Book**
$12.95, 1-55850-801-5

Everything® **Kids' Money Book**
$9.95, 1-58062-322-0

Everything® **Kids' Nature Book**
$9.95, 1-58062-321-2

Everything® **Kids' Puzzle Book**
$9.95, 1-58062-323-9

Everything® **Low-Fat High-Flavor Cookbook**
$12.95, 1-55850-802-3

Everything® **Microsoft® Word 2000 Book**
$12.95, 1-58062-306-9

Everything® **Money Book**
$12.95, 1-58062-145-7

Everything® **One-Pot Cookbook**
$12.95, 1-58062-186-4

Everything® **Online Business Book**
$12.95, 1-58062-320-4

Everything® **Online Investing Book**
$12.95, 1-58062-338-7

Everything® **Pasta Book**
$12.95, 1-55850-719-1

Everything® **Pregnancy Book**
$12.95, 1-58062-146-5

Everything® **Pregnancy Organizer**
$15.00, 1-55850-336-0

Everything® **Resume Book**
$12.95, 1-58062-311-5

Everything® **Sailing Book**
$12.95, 1-58062-187-2

Everything® **Selling Book**
$12.95, 1-58062-319-0

Everything® **Study Book**
$12.95, 1-55850-615-2

Everything® **Tarot Book**
$12.95, 1-58062-191-0

Everything® **Toasts Book**
$12.95, 1-58062-189-9

Everything® **Total Fitness Book**
$12.95, 1-58062-318-2

Everything® **Trivia Book**
$12.95, 1-58062-143-0

Everything® **Tropical Fish Book**
$12.95, 1-58062-343-3

Everything® **Wedding Book, 2nd Edition**
$12.95, 1-58062-190-2

Everything® **Wedding Checklist**
$7.95, 1-55850-278-5

Everything® **Wedding Etiquette Book**
$7.95, 1-55850-550-4

Everything® **Wedding Organizer**
$15.00, 1-55850-828-7

Everything® **Wedding Shower Book**
$7.95, 1-58062-188-0

Everything® **Wedding Vows Book**
$7.95, 1-55850-364-1

Everything® **Wine Book**
$12.95, 1-55850-808-2

Everything® is a registered trademark
of Adams Media Corporation

$12.95, 304 pages, 8" x 9¼"

Your friends and family will be amazed with what you can do!

- Tutorials on the most popular programs
- Simple instructions to get your home page started
- Maintenance routines to keep your site fresh
- And much, much more!

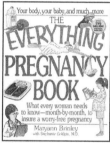

$12.95, 320 pages, 8" x 9¼"

A pregnancy book that really does have everything!

- Extensive medical evaluation of what's happening to your body
- Exercise and diet tips
- 40-week pregnancy calendar
- And much, much more!

EVERYTHING KIDS'®

Now Available!
Only $9.95 each